Leading Well

BUILDING SCHOOLWIDE EXCELLENCE IN READING AND WRITING

LUCY CALKINS

WITH MARY EHRENWORTH AND LAURIE PESSAH

PHOTOGRAPHY BY PETER CUNNINGHAM

Heinemann

DEDICATED TO TEACHERS™

*For the leaders of my life, Evan and Virginia Calkins,
with thanks for showing me the great joy of
working shoulder to shoulder with people you love
to make a difference in the world.*

Heinemann
361 Hanover Street
Portsmouth, NH 03801–3912
www.heinemann.com

Offices and agents throughout the world

© 2019 by Lucy Calkins with Mary Ehrenworth and Laurie Pessah

Cataloging-in-Publication data is on file with the Library of Congress.
ISBN-13: 978-0-325-10922-0

Editors: Karen Kawaguchi, Anna Gratz Cockerille, and Kate Montgomery
Production: Elizabeth Valway
Cover and interior designs: Jenny Jensen Greenleaf
Interior photography: Peter Cunningham and Nadine Baldasare
Cover photography: © Patrik Orcutt/Shutterstock
Composition: Publishers' Design and Production Services, Inc.
Manufacturing: Steve Bernier

Printed in the United States of America on acid-free paper

23 22 21 20 19 VP   2 3 4 5

CONTENTS

Registration instructions to access the digital resources that accompany this book may be found on page vii.

Welcome

Welcome. Come in. How glad I am to have a chance to work together. Simply because you are here, holding this book, I know something about you. I know your school is taking the high road to support state-of-the art reading and writing instruction. There are lots of paths you and your teachers could have taken that ask less of you and of them. My hat is off to you.

In this book, you'll receive some suggestions for how to help this work go well. But first, let me tell you a bit about the book, about myself, and about the organization I lead, and the reasons I think literacy reform merits your attention.

This books draws on the wisdom that my colleagues and I have gathered from decades partnering with principals. We've partnered with school leaders who lead schools of 3,000, as well as with those who lead tiny rural schools with just a handful of classrooms, with leaders of large urban schools that have become showcases for best literacy practices, as well as with leaders of schools under threat of imminent closure due to low attendance and test scores. *Leading Well* draws also on the wisdom of leaders of America's highest performing public and independent schools, of international schools in scores of countries, of some of the best charter networks. How fortunate we are to work shoulder-to-shoulder with educators who go to the ends of the earth to give children the richest possible education!

The good news is that *Leading Well* also stands on the shoulders of literacy experts from both within and from beyond our university. The book will bring you behind the scenes to learn from the leadership work that my colleagues and I do as we try to lead our organization well. Most of you will already know of the Teachers College Reading and Writing Project (TCRWP), our not-for-profit think tank at Teachers College, Columbia University. We presumably already partner with many of you and your districts, as TCRWP partners with thousands of, schools and districts from all corners of the world. Our partner schools usually implement the curriculum that we have developed, Units of Study in Reading, Writing, and Phonics. These districts invite Project staff developers to work on-site with their teachers and they send teachers and school leaders to the hundreds of workshops and institutes that TCRWP offers across the year.

You probably know my role as the Founding Director of the TCRWP, but you may not know that I was once an elementary and a middle school teacher. More than three decades ago, I worked with Don Graves and Don Murray to develop the approach that has come to be known as a reading/writing workshop approach, and since then, I have been at the helm of the TCRWP. I have special responsibility for TCRWP's grade 3–5 work and for leading the writing projects that the organization undertakes, including the Units of Study series and professional texts like the one you are holding. I co-lead the organization with Senior Deputy Directors Laurie Pessah and Deputy Director Mary Ehrenworth, who are both contributors to this book. Laurie was once a principal and a district leader, and has special responsibility for organizing our staff development in schools and our work with school leaders. Mary Ehrenworth has special responsibility for helping to extend our overall organizational knowledge base into new terrain and she joins me in leading the upper-grade work. The other leaders of our organization include Deputy Director for Primary Literacy, Amanda Hartman; Associate Director for Middle Schools, Audra Robb; Emily Butler Smith, who is Associate Director for Professional Development; and Colleen Cruz, Director of Innovation. I'd like to extend special thanks to Janet Steinberg, our Research and Data Manager, who contributed especially to several chapters in this book.

Like many of you, my colleagues and I grew up expecting to be educators, not CEOs. Every day, we continue to learn on the job about how to become the leaders that our people need us to be. Any advice that I give to you is advice that leaders at the Project have given to ourselves and to each other. Some of it has been forged in the fires of our own regrets, and much of what I've written for you is work we aim to do ourselves.

From the start, I know that each of you is reading this book from a different position. Some of you work with a leadership team to mobilize a school with thousands of children, others of you are all-things to a far smaller school. Some of you are weighing whether you want to undergo the reform effort involved in adopting Units of Study in writing or reading. Others of you have inherited a school that claims to be implementing this curriculum, but you wonder about the depth of that adoption. Yet others of you have a school in which this curriculum is the lifeforce of the school, and your concern is maintaining your teachers' growth curve.

One thing we know for sure. Being a leader involves making the minute-by-minute decisions about how our time is spent, how our community's learning lives are led. And even if we all had the same job, the truth is that each of us has made—and continues to remake—our own job description. We decide what to do and what not to do with our time; we decide which goals and values are priorities.

I know that as you live through your days, you also decide how much of your life will be invested in supporting this work. My hope is that this book will convince you that the work we share deserves to be high on your priority list. This is a cause that is worth working hard for.

I understand that the suggestions in this book may call for a higher level of involvement and innovation from you than may be usual. I understand that usually when a new curriculum is adopted, as occurs every few years in far too many places, the district or the state or the feds announce a new initiative, and schools gloss a new patina over the surface of their instructional core. This "business as usual" approach to school reform is part of the challenge. These norms explains why many of you and many veteran educators will approach this entire process of literacy innovation with a healthy dose of cynicism. As Dan Lortie, author of *Schoolteacher,* a study of American education, has said, "American schools are characterized by a constant flurry of change, and by an underlying sense that the more things change, the more they remain the same" (2002). He points out that the way kids are taught today in many schools is not all that different from the way they were taught in Colonial America. Lortie cites "new math," as an example of how most reform efforts go, pointing out that for many schools, what started out as "new math" was chopped and sliced, twisted and tweaked, so that it would fit into the underlying assumptions that characterize American education, so that in the end, "new math" ended up looking very much like "old math." So yes, you can be entirely forgiven for being hesitant to join the excitement over reading and writing workshop, for rolling your eyes a bit at my pleas to consider giving your life to this cause.

But having said all that, I still want to tell you that the kind of literacy-based school reform that I describe here, and that my colleagues and I have supported in so many schools, *is* different. I know you have a world of responsibilities on your plate. I know that literacy is but one topic among so many that demand your time. However, I want you to know from the start that when reform in literacy is your priority, this reform can be the driving force for school and community-wide changes that go far beyond reading and writing. Mark Pingitore, principal in Barcelona recently pointed out that in his school, reform in literacy has done nothing less than to create a culture of continuous improvement. Principal Jessie Miller from Katy Texas agrees. She says, "Reform in literacy has helped us become empowered to see endless potential in not only our young readers and writers, but also in each other, as we embrace the messiness that comes with growing." Mark Federman, principal at East Side Community High in New York City, puts it this way, "It is impossible to name just one secret ingredient that leads a school to success. However, the right focus on literacy provides the opportunity for deep and far-reaching change." Reform in literacy can shift the culture of a staff toward investment, growth, learning, and bravery in facing challenge.

And now, a request: as you talk about this series and the TCRWP in the world, we hope you will refer to it as *an approach*, not *a program*. And we'd like to ask of you that you give full credit for the work to the whole organization of 100+ staff members and authors by calling it the "TCRWP approach," or the "Units of Study approach" or as "reading and writing workshop," and not simply the "Lucy Calkins approach."

This book is roughly chronologically organized for leadership work, starting with our advice for launching and relaunching reform in literacy and for working to get essentials in place. The book then moves to a discussion of ways you and your teachers can raise the level of teaching. This process is a cyclical one, as you will always be involved in helping your school and district participate in that ongoing cycle of goal-setting, innovation, reflection, goal-setting, and revision. In the final part of the book, you'll find advice on putting structures into place to support school and community-wide change, including ways to identify instructional patterns in your building, and ways to recruit parents to partner with you to support literacy at home. Part Three also includes some thoughts on supporting your own professional learning. You'll find it easy to dip into chapters which are applicable to you.

I hope that this book inspires conversations and analysis, reflection and growth. I know change will not come overnight. I know the struggles might seem insurmountable at first. But I also know that it is in these moments of struggle that people have the opportunity to become new versions of themselves. I wish you all the best as you undertake the loftiest of goals: helping each staff member and each student in your school become their best selves.

—Lucy Calkins

Online Digital Resources

A variety of resources and links to accompany this book are available in the online resources. To access and download the online resources for *Leading Well: Building Schoolwide Excellence in Reading and Writing*:

1. Go to www.heinemann.com and click the link in the upper right to log in. (If you do not have an account yet, you will need to create one.)
2. Enter the following registration code in the box to register your product: PGTL_CHW9
3. Enter the security information requested.
4. Once you have registered your product it will appear in the list of My Online Resources.

(You may keep copies of these resources on up to six of your own computers or devices. By downloading the file you acknowledge that they are for your individual or classroom use and that neither the resources nor the product code will be distributed or shared.)

Planning for Literacy Reform

PART ONE contains practical advice to help you start—or restart—the exciting, energizing, messy, difficult, always exhilarating work of reforming reading and writing instruction in your school. On the pages that follow, you'll find support for making important early decisions that will determine how the work will go, for sharing leadership and fostering buy-in, and for honing your visions of literacy reform and communicating those visions to your people.

◆ ◆ ◆ ◆ ◆

1 Setting Up for a Strong Start (or Restart)

Most of you, my readers, will have already launched reading and writing workshops in your schools, so this chapter may come after the fact. I'm mindful, however, that you function as spokespeople and supports for other school leaders, and the truth is, it matters how this work is rolled out. For those of you who are just getting started, or who are mentoring colleagues in getting started, one of the first choices you'll make is whether to launch with writing workshop only, with reading workshop only, or with both. You'll probably support both of these eventually, as well as the Units of Study in Phonics, and you'll probably want this to eventually be a whole-school/district effort. However, that doesn't mean that you must start by launching your whole school into everything at once. There are advantages to launching with a subset of early adopters who are willing to serve as models, and there are also advantages to doing the opposite and starting with your whole school, en masse. There are many entrance ramps that can lead into literacy reform.

However you start the work, it is important to remember that at the start of a reform initiative, you need to be unflagging in your positive, trusting commitment to the work. As Goethe has said, "The task of a leader is to develop confidence in advance of victory, in order to attract the investment that makes victory possible—investment of talent, attention to resources, and effort." Anticipate that your teachers will have misgivings. They will encounter trouble. They will question this entire direction. Don't respond by fueling their doubts—even if secretly, you begin to wonder yourself. Peter Elbow calls this "playing the believing game." You need to demonstrate unflagging support and enthusiasm to have a chance to reap the benefits that this reform can bring.

IN THIS CHAPTER, YOU'LL FIND . . .

► Advice on whether to launch with both reading and writing or with writing only, if you are just beginning Units of Study

► Descriptions of alternate rollouts, including launching with a subset of teachers and launching with fewer units

► Tips for achieving a relaunch, if your first attempt at launching Units of Study did not meet your expectations

► Answers to getting started questions, including: choosing curricular pathways, ways to orient teachers to the curriculum, and conducting initial assessments

It will also be important for you to find ways to help your teachers achieve early wins. When you visit a classroom that has just started a reading workshop, ask children to wave the books they are reading above their heads and then celebrate the sheer beauty of their enthusiastic faces, their fabulous books. Invite children to lay their drafts out on their desks, turning the classroom into a Gallery of Writing, and then move among the desks, oohing and aahing, asking the class to do the same. You'll want to tell the class that you told all your relatives that there are kids all over your school who are avid readers! Read your kids' writing as if it is sheer gold and encourage your teachers to do the same. The writing needn't be great yet—you and your teachers can try reading *any* writing with an actor's voice, savoring every word.

You'll want to celebrate your teachers as well as your students. Tell one that you peeked into his classroom and saw him sitting at a child's side, listening raptly to the child. Say, "I wanted to take a photo, that moment was so beautiful." Join a study group, listen spellbound to the teachers' talk, and then interrupt for a second to tell the group that their conversation is what you dream of for the whole school.

Meanwhile, help your teachers capture evidence of improvement. Does one child actually make a character talk in his story, adding quotations? Does another take a stab at revision, adding a detail into her draft? Do you enter a classroom and see the whole class reading, lost in their books? Do you overhear one teacher sharing a child's Post-it® response to a book with another? Does a parent tell you that her child is reading at home for the first time? How beautiful! Recognize and reward these early wins.

For now, you absolutely need to look past the inevitable mess-ups so you can build momentum behind this initiative, helping your teachers be on fire with the joy that comes from experiencing their own growth as teachers and their students' growth in reading and writing.

Deciding Whether to Launch with Writing or Reading—or Both

The most common pathway into workshop instruction is to start with reform in writing and then progress to reform in reading. However, it needn't go that way. If you have fabulous classroom libraries brimming with high-interest books within your students' reading ranges and you also have duplicate copies of great books for partnerships, the reading workshop may be easier to launch than the writing workshop. That will be especially true if your teachers already know how to conduct running records and to channel students to books that are within their reach. The biggest problem with starting with reading rather than writing will be that if children are not working in writing workshops, their writing about reading will probably be dramatically less proficient and fluent than the examples we showcase in the Units of Study, and that problem may not get addressed

until you *do* adopt writing workshop. But yes, starting with reading is a good option if you have rich classroom libraries.

That said, it is more common for a district to first embrace the writing workshop. If you take that path, you'll find that your teachers' experiences with the writing workshop will have direct, instant, and tremendous payoff when they extend their focus to include the teaching of reading.

Of course, a fair percentage of schools just dive in by launching reading and writing simultaneously, fully aware that this will be a work in approximation, and that's okay. It really helps if those teachers already have a background in balanced literacy, just perhaps not in Units of Study. At the least, it helps if the teachers already know how to give running records and if they have classroom libraries—and if not, that is probably the place to start. But yes, it is possible for schools to just dive in. "This is our children's only chance at first grade or sixth grade," they say. "How can we *not* at least try to give them access to this while they are here with us?"

Will it be too much to tackle reading as well as writing?

Some schools adopt writing and then worry about taking on the additional step to bring in reading as well. Principals worry that taking on a reading workshop, as well as writing, might overwhelm teachers. If your teachers have spent a year or two working with the writing workshop, however, embracing reading won't be a big deal. In fact, it will probably even be a relief. Once teachers have done the hard work of learning how to lead effective writing workshops, they will find that it's relatively easy to build on that foundation by teaching reading in ways that align to their writing instruction. If the writing workshop has gone fairly well, the shift to reading will be seamless and will generate far more energy than it consumes. And as soon as the primary grades have gotten the reading workshop well off the ground, they'll presumably want to include Units of Study in Phonics as well.

The hard part, then, will revolve around helping teachers learn to lead effective writing workshops in the first place. You can expect that your teachers will unanimously say, "It's . . . *a lot,*" and "This is not for the weak of heart." But they will also say, "Holy moly, my kids' writing is definitely getting better." If things are going well, they'll add, "And they *love* it. They don't want to stop writing." Those responses have been so unanimous, so widespread, that if those *aren't* the responses you are getting from your teachers, try to figure out what's going on. They may not actually have taken up the work.

Make it as easy as possible for teachers to feel successful.

Given that undertaking reform in writing is, as your teachers will tell you, "a lot," you'll want to do everything possible to lessen that burden. What you don't want is for your teachers to adopt a diluted, fragmentary, hybrid version of the writing workshop. If your school adopted Units of Study without receiving professional support, that may have happened. You might also find that half your teachers embrace writing workshop and the other half resist it—again, not something you want. That will lead to a division in your school.

One of the most important payoffs of this reform is that once teachers across a school embrace a workshop approach to teaching writing, they will be able to participate in a shared professional conversation. They'll be able to consolidate and compound their knowledge and skills because they'll all be working within the same ground rules, abiding by a shared philosophy, experiencing similar challenges, and responding to them with shared methods.

Michael Fullan, author of dozens of books on school reform, has said that if professional study is going to make a difference in our schools, it can't just make the *individual* smarter; it needs to make the *school* smarter. In most schools, capacity is far too scattered. That is, Sarah knows A, Tom knows B—and if their individual knowledge is not aggregated, it's not particularly consequential. If your faculty ends up divided, with some teachers aboard this reform and others in lock-knee resistance to it, you lose out on the most important rewards.

How, then, can you make it easier for all your teachers to have a strong start teaching a workshop? The upcoming sections are written as if you opt to start with writing, but they are equally applicable if you start with reading.

One Launch Option: Launch with "Early Adopters," a Subset of Experienced Teachers

First, you will want to decide whether to stagger your school's adoption of a writing workshop approach, so that only your "early adopters" get started first. The advantage is that you can give those teachers extra time to plan and extra resources to support their work, because it will be a smaller number of teachers and therefore less costly and intrusive. Also, their effective implementation means they will be able to provide the school with on-site visiting sites. You'll note the challenges they face when implementing the reading or writing workshop, allowing you and other school leaders to anticipate and address predictable challenges that the entire staff will eventually encounter. Tony Bryk, the president of the Carnegie Foundation, suggests that "starting slowly and learning quickly" is a good choice if you don't have enough of "the public will" and enough strong internal capacity to support a large-scale adoption. By starting with early adopters, you can develop both the public will and the internal capacity to support the later full-scale adoption.

Enlist teachers from all your subgroups.

If your "early adopter" teachers get started on their writing workshops before others do, you'll want to be sure this group includes experienced teachers who have strong management skills, the trust of their colleagues, and ties to all the important subsets of your faculty. If none of the teachers from one subset sign on, I suggest you go to one or two of those teachers and personally ask for their participation. You might say, "I'm going to be learning alongside the teachers who get off to an early start on this. I'm hoping you'll be in that group, because I've been hankering to spend more time in your room. Would you consider being among those to get an early start on this work, so I can have the chance to learn with you?" And you might add, "It's important for our community that this work go well, and your skills will be tremendously useful in that endeavor." Chances are good that the teacher will be pleased to be asked.

There will probably be a teacher that you ask to be part of this group because you know that if she is not at the table with an initiative, she's apt to sabotage it, so her support is critical. If you think you can tap into her better self, ask her to join. Make sure the group includes teachers from your highest grade levels (fifth? eighth?) because typically, those teachers do not want to learn from teachers of younger children, whereas the reverse is rarely true.

The good thing is that if just 20% of your teachers form a group of early adopters, it won't be unduly expensive or difficult for you to shower this group with extra professional development, extra planning time, extra resources. You'll read more about ways to support this group as the book continues, but for now, suffice to say that everything we recommend will be especially important for this group.

Use terminology that points teachers in the direction you want them to go.

A small tip. You'll want to refer to this group as *early adopters*, not as a pilot group. When principals say, "We're going to pilot this approach," that brings out the naysayers with a vengeance. Even if the truth is that you *are* planning to watch the work unfold to make sure this is the path you want your whole school to take, it will serve you best to act as if this *is* the way your school will be going, so the question is not *whether* but *when* teachers will get started teaching writing workshops. Again, we'll discuss the pros and cons of "mandating" this (or any) approach later.

If early adopters get started in advance and if they welcome one and all to learn from their efforts, you will probably want the rest of your staff to launch their writing workshops in late spring of that year, after high-stakes testing, so they get a start teaching this way during the final month or two of the school year. Those months are a safe time to try new ways of teaching because teachers already have their classroom management well under control and know their children. If teachers teach their first unit to the children who will be leaving them in another month or two, those teachers and children will be more primed for their September workshops. Then, too, teachers will be much more able to engage in summer planning for the upcoming year if they have had a month of immersion under their belts. They'll read the curriculum with far greater knowledge because of that month or two of advance work.

Another Launch Option: Launch the Whole School, with Fewer Units, and without Much Assessment

You may decide instead to ask all your teachers to get started during the same year, in which case you might reduce the demands by asking that they all teach just two or three Units of Study during that first year and by reducing expectations for assessment. Schools that have taken this path have sometimes found that it is easiest for teachers to teach the first narrative and opinion/argument writing units from their grade-level kit, or, for teachers in grades 4–6, to teach those units from the Up the Ladder kit. Again, keep in mind that another possibility is to launch with just a single unit, taught at the tail end of a school year.

Keep an eye on pacing.

No matter how you launch—but especially if you support teachers in teaching just two or three units in the first year—help your teachers avoid stretching out the units to more than five weeks each. For teachers and students to get the full power of a unit of study, most sessions last just one day and one session immediately follows the next. If teachers divide every session across two or three days and add everything but the kitchen sink to the sequence of instruction, students do not experience the true power of the units. These units are not designed as a smorgasbord of minilessons to sprinkle across the year. Instead, they are a researched, coherent curriculum. A skill is taught, extended, incorporated into a larger set of skills. Then those skills are transferred, built upon. The sequence and pace of instruction are essential to the power of the units.

Stretching out a unit so that it lasts longer than five weeks also reduces the expectations for students' work. If a unit is written so that eighteen sessions support kids in writing two major pieces of writing, and if the teacher turns eighteen days of instruction into thirty-six days, the teacher has just diluted expectations for student work by 50%. Even if teachers are only teaching two units during their first year, each unit should last no more than five weeks, so that students work with intensity and zeal—an important aspect of this instruction. In the intervening weeks, teachers could then return to their old ways of teaching (or, more often than not, you'll find they opt to teach yet a third unit from the set).

I strongly recommend that you go a step further and expect all the teachers at a grade level to decide *together* when they will launch and when they will finish each of the two or three units they'll teach. It's best if the teachers across a grade level teach these units in sync because that will allow them to tap into the extraordinary power of being able to support each other's teaching.

Many principals ask teachers to share the dates of their end-of-unit celebrations in advance, so that you and students' parents can be sure to participate in those grand events. This has the double benefit of making it more likely the units will actually end when planned! It's important for a unit to have nice momentum, building toward an exciting end point. This gives teachers an early win. The Units of Study Facebook pages have lots of videos showing celebrations that schools have devised to mark the completion of a unit. The energy created with a good celebration will take your community far.

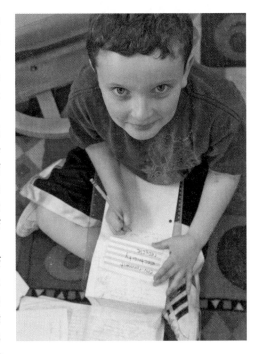

Provide extra planning time.

You may want to stagger the times when different grade levels are having a go with a unit, so that you can manipulate schedules to give those who are working with the new curriculum some extra planning time, extra opportunities to visit each other's classrooms, and extra support from coaches, specialists, and especially, from you.

Obviously, the question will remain, "What do teachers do in the remaining months?" There probably was a business-as-usual approach already underway in your school, so just this first year, you can have your teachers shift between that approach and the units of study.

If you go with this approach, of asking your teachers to teach two or three units in the first year, I recommend that you ask your teachers to teach these two units prior to February. That way, you create a buzz around the workshop early in your school year, and many of your teachers will end up teaching yet more units before the year is over.

Consider postponing performance assessments.

I also suggest that you lighten the load for your teachers by suggesting they postpone work with performance assessments and learning progressions (on-demands, performance assessments, rubrics, checklists, learning progressions—in general, the system that is described in *Writing Pathways* and *Reading Pathways*) until their second year. The exception is that you'll want teachers to conduct the first baseline on-demands in writing, even if they simply store those away so that years from now, they can retrieve students' baseline levels, in case you want that data. You'll also want teachers to conduct running records in reading so they'll be able to channel students toward books they can read with fluency and comprehension, and they can watch over their students' progress.

Achieving a Relaunch

If your school has been struggling with, or "dabbling" in, the Units of Study for years, and your instincts are that a relaunch is in order, my first suggestion is to spend time on a listening tour. You'll want to tell teachers that it is clear to you that the work isn't going as well as it typically does—and let them know that you look forward to understanding their perspectives, to tapping their insights.

Much of what I suggest in these early pages will still be relevant to you, although you'll need to speak of the work you suggest teachers do as a *relaunch*, not a launch. The special challenge you face, as a leader whose learning community is in some chaos, will be addressed in Chapter 13, "Leading Adults Can Be Tricky." To plan a relaunch, you'll need the knowledge from the first two parts of this book to be well under your belt.

The Getting Started Questions: Choosing Curricular Pathways, Provisioning Your Teachers with the Curriculum, Orienting Teachers to the Units of Study, Conducting Initial Assessments

I've talked about launching as if there isn't preliminary work required to get started. You may be uneasy over all the unaddressed questions, thinking, "Do we *really* just dive in?" I have two answers to that.

First, this curriculum is best learned in action, alongside kids. Your teachers are not going for perfection. Instruction can be—it inevitably *will* be—a work in progress. There are no lists of pointers that will save teachers from their insecurities and mistakes as they plunge into this. What I can promise, however, is that every day, at least for the first few years, their teaching will become stronger and clearer and more deliberate. They'll be very different teachers after *a month* working inside Units of Study, and their growth will be even more dramatic after *a year* working within this curriculum. The important thing about the Units of Study is that this curriculum has been written by an organization that provides professional development around the globe and that has done so for decades. These units have been researched and refined in many classrooms. Our mission is to teach and empower teachers and to support them as lifelong learners within shared communities of practice. The Units of Study are designed as professional-development-in-a-box, although we know that true professional development happens once this curriculum is taken *out of the box* and brought to life by teachers and kids.

But second, yes, there are a few getting started questions that I can answer here. Next, you'll find suggestions for choosing the sequence of units your teachers will teach, getting teachers set up with the Units of Study kits, and conducting initial assessments to gather baseline data as you launch.

Choosing Curricular Pathways in Writing and Reading

In kindergarten and first grade, your teachers can simply dive into the Units of Study books. As this book goes to publication, the Units of Study in Phonics are just out. We are encouraging schools to consider the option of aligning all their language arts instruction, but we also know that Units of Study in Writing and in Reading work alongside other approaches to phonics. To be candid, however, we fully expect that most schools will end up integrating the units in reading, writing, and phonics. Those units are designed to be launched at the start of the year, and they include the work that socializes a class of little ones into workshop routines. The units are also designed to support children who do not necessarily come to kindergarten with prior knowledge of reading, writing, or the alphabet. Encourage your teachers to dive right in.

If your teachers are just launching the Units of Study for the first time, your students in some of the upper grades may not be totally ready for the rigorous instruction of the units. The curriculum was written to work well for students who are growing up within a K–8 system that supports their growth in reading and in writing. Some teachers relish the challenge of bringing kids up to speed, and when they do, kids tend to rise to the occasion in ways that dazzle everyone. Still, even if yours is a high-achieving community, teachers in grades 2, 4, 5, 7, and 8 will rightly feel as if the curriculum assumes prior knowledge and skills their students may not yet have. (Note that students in grades 3 and 6 can simply dive into those units.) For their first year or two teaching this curriculum, upper-grade teachers who are working with kids who have no prior experience with this approach will need to ramp their students up. We have provided a number of resources to help you develop the curricular plans that are right for your students and your teachers, starting with this chart outlining suggestions to help your teachers develop the reading, writing, and phonics curricular plans for students who are new to workshop.

- **Up the Ladder kit:** We especially recommend that teachers in grades 4–6 use the three Up the Ladder units—to give students access to narrative, opinion, and information writing. Teachers will want to integrate these units into their regular Units of Study. Deciding on the first year's sequence of units will take some time (and this probably should not be your time), but it is important work for teachers to do before you order the Units of Study kits.

- **Video Orientations:** We have made orientation videos of forty to seventy minutes each that are on the TCRWP and Heinemann websites—one for each grade-level group of teachers, and one for writing and one for reading. These videos include suggestions for ways teachers can alter the sequence of units (usually by borrowing from prior years) to address some predictable challenges. You'll want to provide time for the teachers who will be teaching writing or reading Units of Study to watch the orientation video for their grade and for that subject together. Ideally, teachers have time to pause the video periodically to talk, and ideally, they watch the orientation videos with their kits in hand. It should be noted that we made these prior to releasing the Up the Ladder units for grades 4+ writing.

- _If . . . Then . . . Curriculum: Assessment-Based Instruction_ **book:** The opening chapters in the _If . . . Then . . . Curriculum: Assessment-Based Instruction_ book for any grade level also often address the possible sequences of units, although those recommendations do not take into account our newer additional units, such as _Word Detectives: Strategies for Using High-Frequency Words and for Decoding_ (Grade 1), _The How-To Guide for Nonfiction Writing_ (Grade 2), or _Literary Essay: Opening Texts and Seeing More_ (Grade 5). You can find up-to-date recommendations for sequences of units on the TCRWP website (www.readingandwritingproject.org) on the Resources page, as well as on www.UnitsofStudy.com. You'll find special recommendations for schools with students new to the work or below benchmark, schools using Units of Study who have on-site TCRWP staff developers, and schools using the Units of Study series without on-site staff developers. Here are a few hints you might provide to teachers whose students are new to workshop.

Suggested Curricular Plans for the Start of the Year for Students New to Workshop • Grades K–2

GRADE	READING	WRITING	PHONICS
K	Launch with Reading Unit 1, *We Are Readers*. Then we hope teachers can develop a unit based on the "Emergent Reading: Looking Closely at Familiar Texts" synopsis in the *If . . . Then . . . Curriculum: Assessment-Based Instruction* book. 🖐 Follow with *Super Powers*, Unit 2 (which becomes your third unit), aligned to the matching phonics unit.	Launch with Writing Unit 1, *Launching the Writing Workshop*. Move to *Show and Tell Writing* (an additional unit available outside the main grade-level box), which supports phonics. Follow with *Writing for Readers*, Unit 2 (which becomes your third unit).	Launch with Phonics Unit 1, *Making Friends with Letters*. Then move to Unit 2, *Word Scientists*. Follow up with Unit 3, *Word-Part Power*, which is designed to be taught alongside the reading unit *Super Powers*.
1	Launch with Reading Unit 1, *Building Good Reading Habits*. Follow with *Word Detectives: Strategies for Using High-Frequency Words and for Decoding* (an additional unit available outside the main grade-level box). Then proceed in sequence, adding in a few spring units.	Launch with Writing Unit 1, *Small Moments: Writing with Focus, Detail, and Dialogue*. Teachers could then tweak and reteach Unit 3 of kindergarten, *How-To Books: Writing to Teach Others*, using new mentor texts and lifting expectations. This lets kids experience the unit a second time, but it feels newish because of the changes teachers make to the unit. Then move to *Nonfiction Chapter Books*.	Launch with Phonics Unit 1, *Talking and Thinking about Letters*. Then move to Unit 2, *The Mystery of the Silent* e. Follow up with Unit 3, *From Tip to Tail: Reading across Words*, aligned to *Nonfiction Chapter Books*.
2	Launch with Reading Unit 1, *Second-Grade Reading Growth Spurt*. Teachers could then tweak and reteach Unit 3 of first grade, *Readers Have Big Jobs to Do*, using new read-alouds and lifting expectations. Then, add in a few spring units.	Launch with "Revving Up Writing Muscles," the mini-unit in the online resources for Unit 1, *Lessons from the Masters*. Then teach Writing Unit 1, *Lessons from the Masters* followed by *The How-to-Guide for Nonfiction Writing*, an additional unit published outside the kit. Next, teach Unit 4, *Poetry*.	These books will be published in 2019 They'll be aligned to the reading and writing units for Grade 2.

Suggested Curricular Plans for Students New to Workshop • Grades 3–8		
GRADE	**READING**	**WRITING**
3	Teach the units in order as they are, adding in *Mystery*, an additional unit outside the third-grade kit. This unit is really close reading in disguise! Unless students are reading well below benchmark levels, we suggest this be your second unit. Otherwise, teachers can adapt *Bigger Books Mean Amping Up Reading Power* (Grade 2, Unit 3) or *Series Book Clubs* (Grade 2, Unit 4) as their second unit. After a second fiction unit, shift to *Reading to Learn* (Grade 3, Unit 2), with other fiction units coming later. *Character Studies* (Grade 3, Unit 3) is essential prior to high-stakes tests.	Teach the units as they are. Be sure to add "The Literary Essay: Equipping Ourselves with the Tools to Write Expository Texts that Advance an Idea about Literature," probably in approximately January, a unit in the *If . . . Then . . . Curriculum: Assessment-Based Instruction* book.
4	The grade 4 reading units, as they are, will be fine. If students need ramps up to any nonfiction units, teachers can revisit and adapt *Research Clubs* (Grade 3, Unit 4) to prepare students for Unit 2, *Reading the Weather, Reading the World*. For those who teach *Reading the Weather, Reading the World*, and/or *Reading History*, we especially recommend the specific Classroom Library shelves that support these units. If teachers are teaching both writing and reading, the online resources to link the American Revolution Reading and Writing units (*Reading History* and *Bringing History to Life*) will be critical. The content (weather, the American Revolution) can be altered if your curriculum doesn't forward those topics. Tap the Facebook commentary for support substituting topics.	If students do not bring strong experience in personal narrative writing, use Bends I and II of the Up the Ladder narrative unit to provide a foundation before reading *The Arc of the Story*. Another option is to teach the entire Up the Ladder unit and follow with *The Arc of the Story* later in the year. For information writing, students without background will benefit from either the Up the Ladder information unit or *The Art of Information Writing* (Grade 3, Unit 2) prior to—or if necessary for a year—instead of, *Bringing History to Life* (Grade 4, Unit 3). For opinion writing, *Boxes and Bullets* will work without special support. If students need a ramp, teach the Up the Ladder opinion unit or *Changing the World* (Grade 3, Unit 3) prior to *Boxes and Bullets*.
5	Launch with the Reading unit *Character Studies* (Grade 3, Unit 3), which rapidly immerses students into character analysis, partner work, and clubs. Teachers will still want to teach Unit 1 of Grade 5, *Interpretation Book Clubs*, later in the year. Unit 3, *Argument and Advocacy*, will be especially helpful for high-stakes tests. We especially recommend the Classroom Library shelf of books supporting this unit.	Teachers can start right in with Writing Unit 1, *Narrative Craft*, perhaps borrowing a few start-of-the-year sessions from *Crafting True Stories* (Grade 3, Unit 1). Or they can begin with any of the bends of the Up the Ladder narrative unit. For information writing, teachers will need the Up the Ladder information writing unit or *The Art of Information Writing* (Grade 3, Unit 2) prior to teaching *The Lens of History* (Grade 5, Unit 2).
		The Up the Ladder opinion unit will be extremely helpful prior to teaching *Shaping Texts* (Grade 5, Unit 3) and *The Research-Based Argument Essay* (Grade 5, Unit 4). There is also a new not-to-miss additional unit of study, *Literary Essay* for fifth grade.

Suggested Curricular Plans for Students New to Workshop · Grades 3–8		
GRADE	READING	WRITING
6	Launch with the curriculum calendar, *Maintaining an Independent Reading Life*, available in the online resources for *A Guide to the Reading Workshop, Middle School Grades*. Then move into *A Deep Study of Character*, probably followed by *Tapping the Power of Nonfiction* and *Social Issues Book Clubs*.	We don't recommend starting with fifth-grade units, which assume students are in their sixth year of workshop. The sixth-grade units assume that students are coming from a variety of backgrounds, so they provide a kind of relaunch of workshop. Writing Unit 1, *Personal Narrative*, is a fine place to start. If teachers or students need extra support getting started on workshop teaching, the Up the Ladder units will be tremendously helpful. Teachers might teach selected bends and then shift into sixth-grade units, or they can teach the sixth-grade units later in the year.
7	Teachers may want to first teach the curriculum calendar, *Maintaining an Independent Reading Life*, available in the online resources for *A Guide to the Reading Workshop, Middle School Grades*, and then share *A Deep Study of Character* with sixth grade. The following year they can launch directly with *Investigating Characterization*. Seventh-grade teachers will also want to study *Dystopian Book Clubs*, *Historical Fiction Book Clubs*, and *Tapping the Power of Nonfiction* and decide if they will teach one or two of these, or if, in their first year, they want to stick with *Social Issues Book Clubs*.	Teachers may want to consider the sixth-grade writing units, which launch students into workshop as well as into narrative, information, and literary essay. The following year, seventh-graders can move into the seventh-grade units.
8	If this is students' first year, teachers may want to launch with *A Deep Study of Character*, or at least Bend I of that book, before moving into either *Investigating Characterization* or *Literary Nonfiction*. Later, they could teach any of the following: *Dystopian Book Clubs* and *Historical Fiction Book Clubs*. If students need more support, teachers could teach *Tapping the Power of Nonfiction* before *Literary Nonfiction*.	We suggest launching with either *Personal Narrative: Crafting Powerful Life Stories* (Grade 6, Unit 1) or *Writing Realistic Fiction* (Grade 7, Unit 1). Even in students' second year of workshop, we suggest teachers may want to launch with "Memoir: Writing to Reflect on Experience and Suggest Thematic Connections" from *If . . . Then . . . Curriculum: Assessment-Based Instruction*, and save Unit 1, *Investigative Journalism*, an exciting but challenging unit, for later in the year.

Provisioning Your Teachers with the Curriculum

You will not want to make the dire mistake of thinking you can get only one kit for each grade level, assuming teachers can share a kit of Units of Study books with each other. Teachers need to have their own copies of the unit they are teaching, even when they coteach (such as in an IEP classroom). We are all for cutting costs whenever possible, and you'll see lots of suggestions for doing so, but this is one corner you simply can't cut. Teachers will need to teach with their Units of Study book in hand, to be able to check in on parts of the lesson even as they teach. Teachers will need to mark up their books. It is conceivable that those marks are made on Post-its or in pencil, so the book can be passed along to other teachers in subsequent years, but we don't recommend that. The truth is that in relation to financing a school for success, this curriculum itself is inexpensive and teachers need access to the curriculum they are expected to teach.

The only way to share Units of Study books is to organize the sequence of units that a teacher is teaching so that the books that a teacher is *not* using at one time in the year can be lent to support another teacher. For example, if your first-grade teachers begin the year by borrowing *Becoming Avid Readers* (a kindergarten reading unit) to give their kids a ramp up to the first-grade curriculum, then the book that the first-grade teachers are *not* using could be lent to the second-grade teachers, who might want to start their year using that first-grade book. This only works if you strongly enforce start and stop dates for units, but that has other advantages. I am all for teachers in later grades borrowing books from earlier grades and tweaking those earlier units, so they are newish for the subsequent grade (when the unit is sometimes being retaught, with new texts and new tips). And I am all for teachers opening the Up the Ladder kit and distributing those books across grades, so this kit can actually help your teachers at grades 4, 5, and 6. But don't take the risk of suggesting teachers teach Units of Study, and then not give them the Unit of Study book they are being asked to teach. Teachers will always need a copy of the unit they are currently teaching.

Helping Teachers Who Complain that the Units of Study Require Too Much Reading

I'll respond to this question throughout this book, but for now, the important thing to say is that under no circumstances should one person on your staff (or in your district) make abbreviated versions of the Units of Study books and pass those versions along to teachers instead of the units themselves. That is absolutely *not* the way to go. Each session in each unit has been drafted and revised a dozen times or more by true experts, so I am adamantly against asking someone possessing none of that writing skill nor that expertise to "improve" on them. The results are far from being improvements! Typically, your assigned rewriter eliminates the inspiration, the heart and soul, the ambitiousness, the choice, and the lessons on agency and growth mindset, while also eliminating the high-level professional development that is woven throughout the units.

Yes, teachers will need to make some choices, cutting some parts, revising others. But those choices need to be made by the teacher who knows her students and knows herself, himself. And everything that is cut from a minilesson, a mid-workshop, or a share could become support for conferring and small-group work.

As problematic as it is for one teacher to rewrite the Units of Study for colleagues, it is even more concerning if the teacher does so by turning these into PowerPoints. More on that later—but please don't support that.

Setting Teachers Up to Use the Kits

You will want to encourage teachers to read a few key chapters of *A Guide to the Writing Workshop* (or *A Guide to the Reading Workshop*) as soon as possible, including the chapters on minilessons, small-group work, and management (these are usually Chapters 6, 7, and 8). These *Guides* provide direct, fast-paced, practical help with the methods of instruction that are essential to every day across every K–8 year. It will be a crucially important resource before teachers get started and for their first few years.

The *Guides* deserve to be read, discussed, and reread, and studied alongside the extensive video collection on TCRWP's Vimeo site (vimeo.com/tcrwp). Channel teachers to read a chapter on minilessons, then to watch videos of effective minilessons, then to study their upcoming unit of study, discussing how those minilessons illustrate the principles they've just read about.

You will also want to point teachers toward the online resources that accompany each Units of Study set. There are directions for how to access these in the "Welcome to the Unit" or "An Orientation to the Unit" section for each unit. If your teachers have yet to tap into these resources, you'll be their hero for life if you point the way! The online resources include a wealth of information and reproducibles, including orientation videos, teaching charts, student work, read-aloud guides, homework ideas, pages of pointers, and so much more. Help teachers log on and peruse these resources, perhaps at a grade-level meeting early in the year. These resources do get updated, so be sure to remind teachers to check them often.

Of course, there are other essential materials, and those will be discussed in Chapter 4, "First Things First." It will be important to address the issue of provisioning chapters early on, since some materials—starting with rich class-room libraries—are game changers for kids, and since we have found that when teachers do not have what they perceive to be essential materials for a successful reading/writing workshop, this can become a gigantic obstacle for those who are reluctant to embrace the innovation in the first place.

Orienting Teachers to Their Unit of Study Kits and to the Organization and Principles of Every Unit

Each of the Units of Study kits is organized similarly, so be sure that someone helps your teachers to get the broad landscape of how each of the kits go. Here are the key pointers that your teachers will need to know—and that you need to know as well.

Each unit begins with an overview at the front of the book. It is important for teachers to read the overview before launching a unit since that will help them grasp the work that kids do throughout and be ready to bring students along the larger storyline of the entire unit. Each book supports a four- to five-week unit—and no longer—and contains three (or occasionally four) "bends in the road." Each bend contains four to seven sessions, lasts a bit more than a week, and supports a coherent chunk of work. Sometimes a grade-level group of teach-

ers decides to teach only two of the three bends in a unit, saving the third bend for a later time—or in middle school, for use in social studies or science classes. Bends often end with a minor celebration, and there is always a major celebration at the ends of the units.

Each session contains a minilesson that has been written out in the words the author says to children when teaching that minilesson. As written, each minilesson can be taught in ten minutes (although looking back now, I agree some need to be abbreviated, even for our New York City speed-talk!). Occasionally, if the minilesson includes extra time for kids to read or write, or if the minilesson launches the entire unit, teachers may need to allot a few extra minutes to it, but the goal is to limit minilessons to ten minutes—to protect kids' time to work on their own important reading and writing.

The minilessons each have the same predictable architecture. The minilesson starts with a connection, including the teaching point, which is often added to an anchor chart at the end of the minilesson. Next, the teacher has a few minutes to teach something, then kids have a few minutes to have a small "go" with whatever has been taught. The minilesson wraps up with a link in which the teacher reminds kids of all the options they have to work on that day. The link usually references the anchor chart that brings together the instruction from across the unit to remind kids to draw on the full repertoire as their work requires.

The conferring and small-group write-ups in each session contain the most important advice teachers will need to work in assessment-based ways with their students, although on any given day, teachers will draw also on this portion of preceding sessions. Give teachers time to preview the small-group work and conferring and to plan for these. If teachers make "toolkits"—more on that later—it helps to channel them to especially mine these sections, as well as the rubrics, checklists, exemplars, and progressions in the *Pathways* books. (You'll find more information about toolkits in Chapter 6, "From Good to Great: Supporting Teachers' Continued Growth.")

Teachers will find the student work shown early in the Units of Study books to be incredibly important, because that work will give them a vision for the sort of work that the unit aims to teach. Often, the best way to get to know a unit is to study the examples of student work. Then scan the anchor charts that appear at the ends of the bends, and then go back and read the orientation section at the start of the book, which lays out the pathway the instruction will take.

The units are designed so that once your teachers have become oriented to a unit, they can open a unit book and begin to teach on Day One. The one exception is when kids are brand-new to reading or writing workshops. In that case, teachers in a few grades may want to add a couple of days that orient students to the whole idea of a reading/writing workshop. The Unit 1 books in grades K, 1, 3, and 6 do this work already, but in the other grades, if kids are just entering their first ever writing or reading workshop, teachers might draw on a few launching sessions from the first units in grades K, 1, 3, or 6. The "Suggested Curricular Plans for Students New to Workshop" chart shown earlier in this chapter will help provide guidance for that.

Conducting Initial Assessments

For now, this section can only focus on assessment in writing. If you begin with reading, our thoughts on assessment are more complicated (see Chapter 15, "Advice on Using the TCRWP Assessment System").

Baseline data is precious. It can help you communicate with stakeholders and help you secure funding. It can also help teachers and kids see their own progress. Getting baseline data is easy—these first assessments aren't viewed as windows into teachers' current teaching, so they don't make people defensive, but instead act as a way to mark the starting point before that teaching begins. Once teachers have launched writing workshops or reading workshops, you can never go back and get that baseline data. So be sure that every student who will participate in a writing workshop provides a "before" sample of on-demand writing in the first few days of school (see Chapter 2, "The First Step: Conducting On-Demand Performance Assessments" of *Writing Pathways, Grades K–8* for directions). You'll want to get this even from your youngest writers, because their growth will be particularly spectacular.

You may decide that while it's important for teachers to look at students' on-demand pieces, it isn't important to *score* their kids' writing just now. Scoring can be a complicated and demanding process, and your priority for now is to help teachers get started teaching this curriculum. If teachers are just getting started, they can save the scoring for another year, and for now, just copy or scan the pieces so you have the data, and then give the pieces back to kids. Teachers can then ask kids to study their on-demands, perhaps with a checklist for goal-setting, and to put the on-demands into an early and earmarked spot in their collections. Later—even just a week later—teachers can remind kids that their writing should already be way better than that start-of-the-year writing. At parent-teacher conferences, teachers can show the before and after pieces to illustrate students' growth.

> *Baseline data is precious. It can help you communicate with stakeholders and help you secure funding.*

2

You Can't Be the Only Leader—But the Job of Delegating Leadership Is Yours

Y ou are the single most important factor in determining the success of your school's implementation of Units of Study in reading and writing and in raising the level of literacy instruction across your whole school. This book will help you learn from other school leaders who've shown what strong, near-magical school leadership can be. This chapter and the ones that immediately follow will lay out the work that needs to be done at the start of this implementation. If you've already gotten started, but without a lot of TCRWP guidance, you'll probably find that this chapter helps you get the work off to a second start, this time with renewed energy and clarity.

Determine the leadership responsibilities needed to support literacy reform.

First, you need to compose your own job description. What will be your responsibility? What can you outsource to others? The answers will depend on the composition of your team and the ways you use that team. It will also depend on your knowledge of reading and writing instruction and your eagerness to be a curricular leader. Keep in mind that teachers can be important players on a school's leadership team. They can form a kind of literacy cabinet, implementing, innovating, and supporting the work. Inviting some teachers into the inner circle of this work can provide the effort with far more horsepower. It can also bring your potential naysayers away from the margins and into the heart of this work.

IN THIS CHAPTER, YOU'LL FIND . . .

▶ An overview of the leadership responsibilities needed to support schoolwide literacy reform

▶ Important advice on delegating and enabling others who can then play leadership roles

▶ Tips for tapping into your teachers' talents, helping them coauthor this work

Below is a list of responsibilities that either you or another leader needs to do. I've noted the jobs that I think absolutely must be on your shoulders, and those that you can outsource. You'll see that it is not necessarily essential that every school principal devote himself or herself to being the most important curricular leader in a school. Michael Fullan recently suggested at a TCRWP event that too much emphasis has been put on the principal as curricular leader. "Your school absolutely needs curricular leadership," he said. "But your first and most important job is *not* to provide that leadership yourself, firsthand. It's to make sure that *someone* has the time and the skillset and the support to provide that curricular leadership." Over time, you'll want to become as capable as possible as a curricular leader, but first and foremost, heed Fullan's advice. Remember the adage from Gandhi, "A sign of a leader is not how many followers you have, but how many leaders you create."

Leadership Responsibilities for You to Take On

▨ Make a plan—and staff it—for leadership of this work, drawing on the talents of your people and setting co-leaders up for success.

▨ Communicate a vision for your school's next steps with enthusiasm. Convey that this is enough of a priority that time needs to be allotted.

▨ Help teachers become a learning community, taking risks together, feeling comfortable with being learners. Dignify on-the-job learning. (See Chapter 7, "Build a Culture of Ongoing Learning).”

- Celebrate early successes in ways that energize teachers and students and bring more teachers into the work.

- Find and address trouble, especially resistance (as in, teachers whose instruction hasn't changed). Address this in ways that achieve results. (See Chapter 13, "Leading Adults Can Be Tricky: Responding to Trouble").

- Bring parents and the larger community into this work, communicating the rationale, conveying great enthusiasm, pointing out early results, inspiring trust. (See Chapter 17, "Engaging Parents as Partners.")

Leadership Responsibilities that You Might Outsource

- Provision classrooms with essential materials. Prior to this, decide which classrooms will participate, and be sure those classrooms choose a curricular path for which the necessary resources can be provided. You'll find options for curricular pathways in Chapter 1, "Setting Up for a Strong Start (or Restart)."

- Orient teachers to the curriculum; help them access the online resources, the upcoming overview the upcoming unit, plan lessons, and make a schedule.

- Help teachers conduct early and essential assessments of their students and anticipate adaptations based on their students' strengths and needs. For reading, this will require helping teachers give running records to their K–6 students.

- Help teachers lead lively, brief minilessons. Use study groups, demonstrations, and videos to help teachers gain an image for how to conduct ten-minute minilessons. Coach into this. Steer teachers away from making PowerPoints and from overreliance on technology for minilessons.

- Help teachers manage their classroom, keeping kids engaged in sustained writing and/or reading.

There are chapters in this book that can help you support the people who are leading the curricular leadership parts of the list above—and yes, we hope in the end that *you* play a big role as a curricular leader. But there are even more important priorities for you.

A big part of your job will involve communicating the vision for this work to teachers and eventually to parents. In addition, you'll create a culture of collaborative professional learning in the school, making your school into a place where teachers are willing to take the giant risk of being public learners. You'll need to help create and celebrate early, short-term successes, doing so in ways that fuel the energy that this reform requires. Each of those priorities will be addressed in an upcoming chapter.

Make a plan—and staff it—for leadership of this work, drawing on the talents of your people.

Identify and recruit leaders.

Your first job involves delegating responsibilities. As leadership expert and author Jim Collins (2001) famously said, "You first need to get the right people on the bus," and that is true for this reform effort. You will want to rally particular teachers and leaders to play central roles in this work. If you have a literacy coach, he or she will presumably assume many responsibilities. If you don't have this luxury, you and your assistant principal (if you have one) will need to do more curricular leadership. You will probably also recruit teachers to take on leadership roles. Select your leaders with care—their interpersonal skills will make or break the reform effort. You'll need to channel, coach, and supervise those who'll play central roles, so that the effort goes well.

Your best potential leaders are those who, when tapped, ask with humility, "Me? You think I can be of help?" This is not a great job for people who long to have power to lord over others. In fact, the most important way you can help those you tap as leaders is to emphasize that their job is to cheerlead and to support their colleagues. It is amazing how often people who are given leadership roles regard that as an invitation to become bossy.

Set the stage for leaders to be successful.

You also need to help your potential leaders to have the time, professional training, and power that they require to do their jobs well. For example, if you want your reading specialist, Ryan, to function as a part-time supporter of the teachers who are implementing the Units of Study for Teaching Reading, you'd be wise to send him to TCRWP for an institute or at least for a daylong conference. If that isn't possible, consider paying for a few days of intensive study of the units. If you can help Ryan partner with other teacher-leaders or site-based coaches, that alliance will be worth its weight in gold. Hopefully, he will end up becoming engaged in his own intellectual development and will pour hundreds more hours into his study, but priming the pump helps make it more likely to happen.

Then keep that momentum going by helping your in-house leader schedule and plan ways he'll support others. Talk together about his schedule, so that he can work shoulder-to-shoulder with teachers in ways that they can plan for and anticipate, making the help more potent. (You'll find more about this in Chapter 8, "Provide Teachers with Professional Development.") For that to happen, you will probably need to outsource some of his prior responsibilities.

When the moment is right, let the rest of your staff know what you have entrusted this person to do. If you say something like, "I've asked Ryan to come in to our second-grade classrooms twice a week to be an extra pair of hands, helping you reach all your kids and get them all reading up a storm right away," then those teachers won't wonder why Ryan is suddenly stopping by more often. They'll also know how to make best use of him—as an extra pair of hands, teaching alongside them in parallel ways.

Position your leaders as coaches, not assistants.

You will probably decide that you want your in-house leader to function as a coach to the teacher, rather than provide extra hands, extra reach, in the classroom. That is vastly more powerful, but it runs against the norms of many schools, so if you envision Ryan functioning that way, you need to put some weight behind that and plan to provide follow-up support. You'll want to be explicit, saying, "I've asked Ryan to work with each of you, during both your prep sessions and in your classrooms, to demonstrate and to coach you so that he can help you keep your minilessons and small groups lively and brief." You may need to add some rationale for why you believe Ryan has superior skills at doing that work. If you have sent him off for deeper study, you can say, "I'm hoping that Ryan will be able to draw on what he learned last week when he was at the Toolkit Institute at Teachers College. It'd be good for us all to learn from that."

Because teachers may be reluctant to learn from their peers, it may be especially important for you to demonstrate that you are dying to learn from whomever it is that you are hoping to elevate. Come to the professional development with a notepad in hand, and plan to nod a lot and scribble notes to yourself. Best yet, ask your in-house expert to coach you. What a difference fifteen minutes of your time can make if you spend it that way!

More on this later, but for now, our point is that your literacy coaches and lead teachers often need your invitation, your clarity, and your public direction to step up to teaching their colleagues. Ryan can't just stop into classrooms and ask to teach that day's minilesson, so he can show the teacher how to do a better job at it. You need to set up the structure in which this happens. We are continually amazed at how often a talented, knowledgeable coach or lead teacher longs to be of help to other teachers but isn't given the invitation and the position that allows him or her to do that work. You can, and you need to, finesse that bit of social engineering.

Consider recruiting grade leaders.

In many schools doing this work, one teacher from each grade team becomes the point person to support others in the implementation and organization of the work. Often, teacher-leaders emerge organically, because of their passions, their knowledge, and their desire to learn. It's likely that for each grade level, you can think of one teacher who seems a natural fit to lead the team's literacy work. This teacher isn't necessarily the most senior person on the team. She is the one who seems to be doing the job of a teacher-leader already: inviting team members into the classroom, seeking out professional development, doing research, being a humble source of suggestions.

Dear Literacy Cabinet,

I'm writing to invite you to our first meeting of the year. Let's meet at 7:30 A.M. on Wednesday, September 8th, in my office. I'll have breakfast and coffee ready for you! We'll end at 8:30.

The school is so lucky to have this leadership team, and I am, as well. At this first meeting, let's talk about:

- How we want to adjust our schedules so that you and your grade-level colleagues have more time to plan together, and more ways to teach together.

- Your ideas for how grade-level planning meetings can become all we dream of. What can your role be, what can my role be, in getting these off to a new start?

- How we can build energy in us around the teaching of writing and reading this year. What can I do, what can you do, to celebrate successes? Bulletin boards? PTA? the local paper?

We have a lot to do. If you need support in making sure your kids are picked up in the yard, so that you can stay until 8:30, let me know.

All the best,

Principal Y

Draw on the talents of your people in ways that make them co-leaders of this initiative.

Listen and observe to identify teachers' unique gifts.

As you make your way through this reform process, you'll discover other jobs that give you a way to tap the talents of your people. To figure out ways for people to contribute, listen to them. I've come to believe in the deep, lasting value of half-hour, one-to-one conversations. The conversations go better if they are scheduled, so people can prepare for them. You could write to your teachers and say, "We'll be continuing our reform effort in ELA this year, and I want to take stock of where we are in this work and where we could go next—and ways you could help us move forward. Could we chat next Wednesday so I can hear your thoughts on this? I'd love to know ways you could help the schoolwide aspects of the effort and also, ways I could be of more help to you."

Just as a great teacher figures out what her students care about and inspires them to do big important work that stems from those priorities, a skilled leader does the same. You may never have imagined that one teacher might take on the job of filming book buzzes schoolwide, but if you have someone who is eager to do that—why not? You may not have conceived of a teacher leading kids to contribute to the local newspaper—but if you have someone on staff who is hankering to do that, it'll surely help create a buzz!

Shortly after I arrived as a new faculty member at Teachers College, Arthur Levine came aboard as president of the college, and the first thing he did was to embark on a listening campaign. He held one-to-one conversations with each and every faculty member. Arthur began his conversation with me by asking about my childhood on a farm in western New York, then asked about my early teaching, and then asked how I drew on all that now. He also asked about my dreams as a faculty member, as a leader of TCRWP, as a citizen of the College, the nation, the world. The conversation took half an hour—and created a foundation for a lasting partnership.

The lesson: listen to your people. If you want this work to be well loved by them, remember that they will care most deeply about this initiative if they feel as if they've been at the table. Listen—and use what you hear to help bring your people with their energy and enthusiasm into leadership roles.

You might suggest teachers bring artifacts to the conversation. For example, ask teachers to bring one student's writing, so the two of you can talk off that work. In the discussion, you could ask things like, "Can you take me to the part of this child's work that shows some of the teaching you feel especially good about?" You might ask, more generally, "Walk me through what the child is doing, and fill me in on what you think about that work." As you listen, be attuned especially to that teacher's particular strengths and passions. What might this person be able to teach others, or to contribute to the schoolwide effort?

For example, you may hear that one teacher is especially excited about ways that mentor texts lift the level of her kids' writing. In that case, you might ask that teacher if she'd be willing to co-lead a schoolwide study group on that topic or to help you reorganize the school's book room to highlight potential mentor texts. You might ask if she'd be willing to be part of a committee to advise you on ways to spend book money.

If your speech pathologist is able to help with phonics instruction around the school, by all means champion that work and build a structure so it happens. In hundreds of TCRWP schools, paraprofessionals are taught to work one-to-one with first- and second-grade readers who lag behind. Go for it! You will find that your teachers and other staff members have surprising gifts to bring to the community—and when you showcase and cherish those gifts, the energy for this work will rise.

The bigger point is this: your people want to be seen, to be listened to. We often tell teachers that at the start of the year, *kids* seem to be hiding. Their writing is bland, general, safe. Their scrawl is often so teeny-tiny it is hard to read. In the writing workshop, teachers issue that call that is so reminiscent of some of our childhood hide-and-seek games. "Olly olly in free! Come out, come out, wherever you are!" They encourage students to take risks, dive in, and get started on this important work. Great leaders need to issue that same call to their people, "Come out, come out, wherever you are!"

Ask experienced teachers to mentor new teachers.

What a difference it can make if you give teachers a mentor, especially if that mentor teaches the same units at the same time. The mentor teacher need not necessarily be one of the most experienced teachers on a grade, although it can be delicate if you ask a relatively new teacher to mentor a newer one. You could try sending out an email, asking one and all to volunteer to mentor new teachers. If that email goes out on the Friday before a long holiday weekend, chances are good it will fly under everyone's radar. Few will show interest—then you can recruit the specific people you want, quietly. Meanwhile, if a teacher wonders why she wasn't asked, you can remind her that the invitation went out to everyone.

If at all possible, I encourage you to pay the mentor to spend a full day planning with the new teacher. Sometimes the payoff needs to come in release time later in the year or in the opportunity to do some additional study. If the mentor and mentee can spend a day at the start of the year, planning to align their teaching, we have found they often end up spending untold hours together—far beyond anything you could finance. It matters, however, that you create the official setup for that work to begin.

Champion your teachers.

It's impossible to overemphasize the good you can do if you suggest that a grade-level team of teachers apply to present their work at an upcoming professional conference. "The world should hear about this work you are doing with fluency," you might say. "You should apply to present this at the next meeting of the National Council of Teachers of English." Alternatively, you could channel a teacher to build upon her work by seeking a DonorsChoose grant or by turning to any one of many other sources for funding. We've included a list of conferences, funding sources, and other resources in the online resources for this book, but know that if you simply distribute this list to all your teachers, you miss out on its potential power. What will matter is that you have gone to one specific person and shown that you recognize that person's talents. What matters is the message you send when you recognize that person's gifts, and say, "You should teach this to the world!" or "You should make this into a crowning project for your grade level!" and then channel that teacher or that group of teachers to a possible funding source. Whether the funding comes through, whether their application is accepted, is less important than your message: "Come out, come out, wherever you are!"

If you champion the work of teachers who have not, until now, been recognized as stars, your support for those individuals can send consequential messages to your organization because other teachers will see that colleague of theirs suddenly emerge in glory. Remember when Susan Boyle went out on stage on the television show *Britain's Got Talent* several years ago? She looked so dowdy, so ordinary, so like us, like our moms, like our sisters. Then she belted out "I Dream a Dream" from *Les Misérables*. Did your heart soar? Did you find yourself practically on your feet with the thrill of it all? That is the same response that your teachers will have when you locate your own Susan Boyle and bring her front and center, glorying in her star quality.

Long ago, Don Murray described the teaching of writing, saying, "We see more in our students than they see in themselves." That is our mission.

3

Communicate the Vision, Build the Energy

Whether or not you played a key role in deciding that your school will implement a writing or a reading workshop, you absolutely need to be the person to communicate this vision to your people. For almost thirty years, the TCRWP has convened the school leaders from the 300 schools that are geographically closest to us for a State of the Union year-end conference, and at every single one of those conferences, my keynote speech has included this quotation from the Foreword of that classic book on promising American companies, *In Search of*

Excellence. Tom Peters and Robert H. Waterman Jr. (2015) summarize all their findings on their deep research into promising companies by saying this:

> Let us suppose that we were asked for one all-purpose bit of advice for management, one truth that we were able to distill from all the excellent companies research. We might be tempted to reply, "Figure out your value system. Decide what your company *stands for*. What does your enterprise do that gives everyone the most pride?" . . .
>
> I believe the real difference between success and failure of your work lies in the question of how well you bring out the great energies and talents of its people. What does it do to help these people find common cause with each other?

There may be no more important job than that of being the Keeper of the Vision. You must be the one to raise the flag high and say to your people, "Come one, come all. We have important work to do!"

Provide a "drumroll" for the work to signal its importance.

You needn't tackle the all-important job of providing a drumroll for this work on your own. Consider tapping into the resources at TCRWP for help. Your teachers' first impressions of this work will be super-important. For example, you may want to consider sending your teachers to a conference day conducted by one of the leaders of the TCRWP. Scheduled periodically throughout the year, such days dot the country, and bringing your people can make a giant difference. Of course, it will be absolutely vital that you attend the day as well and sit front and center as a public and enthusiastic learner.

You might also consider joining with a team of teachers to attend one of the twenty or so institutes that TCRWP leads each year. Every October and March/April, TCRWP also leads free "Saturday Reunions," open to all, and many districts send busloads of teachers. It can also be helpful to visit a school that has reading and writing workshops well underway. You'll want to check with the school first, perhaps sending a knowledgeable scout ahead to make sure that the visit will work for you. You might also ask TCRWP for suggestions.

Many schools have asked for a teacher-leader from another district to come to their school and talk about the work, showing some student work and helping teachers imagine what involvement in Units of Study is like. If you call on the right person, that can be magical. Alternatively, you can figure out another way to immerse yourself in a bit of the work—attending a conference, watching a few hours of video tapes, reading the *Guide*—and then talk about your own experience with what you see.

No matter which methods you use to bring your people closer to this work, you will need to be unapologetically passionate about the mission inherent in reading and writing workshop. Tell your teachers that yes, this will ask a lot of them. Yes, this is *not* the easy path. But the kids need the opportunity to become powerful readers and writers. And your teachers deserve the chance to be a learning community together.

Frankly, what we are saying is that the rollout for this work can't be business as usual. Business as usual has been for school leaders to mandate a program, leading implementation by being compliance managers and checking on whether those involved are doing their assigned task. Lyle Kirtman, in his 2013 book *Leadership and Teams: The Missing Piece of the Educational Reform Puzzle*, tells about a study that involved giving Myers-Briggs personality tests to leaders from education and other fields, including not-for-profits, businesses, and politics. This data showed that when looking at four attributes—dominance, influence, compliance, and steadiness—leaders in most fields outside of education lead by relying on influence and sometimes dominance. Leaders in the field of education, on the other hand, tend to lead through compliance. It's a "gotta find out who's naughty or nice" form of leadership. It doesn't work well.

Although most educational leaders lead through compliance, the *most effective* leaders lead through influence. In TCRWP classrooms, these are the leaders who are on fire with a moral mandate to turn all kids into passionate skilled readers and writers. These leaders say things like, "The kids have no union rep, so my job is to advocate for them. And I can't sleep at night thinking that some kids don't have access to the best, most rigorous reading and writing instruction available."

A decade or so ago, Joel Klein, Chancellor of the New York City school system at the time, mandated that teachers in every school across NYC teach a reading/writing workshop. Klein didn't ask our advice about whether this approach could be mandated and whether it could work for all teachers, without them necessarily receiving professional development or curriculum support. Concerned, I phoned my friend Jack Gillette, then a professor at Yale School of Education and later Dean at Lesley University School of Education, and I asked for his advice. He said something I have remembered since. "When an approach is mandated, it is tempting to think that inspiration becomes *less* important. After all, the approach has been mandated—teachers have no choice. Although the temptation is to bypass inspiration and focus on the practical details of implementation, in fact, when something is mandated, inspiration becomes *more*, not less, important."

Don't fall into the trap of thinking that your teachers only need inspiration at the very start of an implementation. The reason that I have, for thirty years, returned to the Peters and Waterman quote about the need for visionary leadership is that in fact, the harder and more important work of rallying teachers around a vision comes in subsequent years, when teachers may be prone to settle for a low level of implementation, or for a "rinse and repeat" form of teaching. If a teacher isn't getting *better* as a teacher of reading and writing, she'll be getting worse. The job

of improving literacy education is a lifelong job, and one of the hard parts will be helping teachers to avoid the plateaus that are so common, several years into the implementation.

Donald Murray, the man who is often heralded as "Father of Writing Process," once said, "My greatest fear is the teacher who says, 'I know how to make reading/writing connections. I know how to confer in ways that help writers. I know the qualities of good writing.'" He added, "My greatest fear is that we will suffer hardening of the ideologies, that we will lose the pioneer spirit that made this field a great one."

In later years, you will be rallying teachers around specific missions. One year, your school may take on the mission of making sure that *kids* are the ones working the hardest, that struggle is welcomed. Another year, your school may work toward classrooms that brim with cross-curricular transfer. You may rally teachers to reach toward teaching in ways that ring with greater depth and authenticity. The specific goal that you identify in those subsequent years will be less important than the fact that you continue to rally your teachers to reflect, assess, and work deliberately toward ambitious ways to improve their teaching.

You may be wondering less about the goal that you will rally your teachers around and more about how you can be the one to do that. You may be thinking, "I'm not the charismatic type." You may be worrying, "Public speaking isn't my thing." There aren't easy answers to these concerns. Everything you read in this book and in our other materials will help, as will the experiences you have working with your teachers and children. It matters that you make sure to create opportunities in your own life for you to be inspired, remembering, as Howard Gardner has said: "Leaders need to retreat to the mountains." I hope that Teachers College is a metaphoric mountain for you!

Tips to Help Leaders Communicate Their Vision and Create Enthusiasm

Build urgency.

In a 2007 article for *Harvard Business Review*, John Kotter outlined eight key steps for transforming an organization—advice that is relevant not only to businesses, but also to school organizations. Kotter suggested that you need to create a sense of urgency that compels your reform. You may need to identify a crisis that makes maintaining the status quo riskier than embracing change. When Joel Klein sought to push New York City toward balanced literacy, he described what he saw as a crisis in the city. "Right now," he said, "we have a tale of two cities. We have a thinking curriculum in half the city, and a non-thinking curriculum in the other half the city. And the city is divided by race and income. We need to bring a thinking curriculum to the entire city." That message rallied all of us behind his mission.

To stir up urgency for reform, you may want to survey kids about their attitudes toward reading or writing, or gather data on the volume of reading or writing that students are currently doing, or ask teachers how much help they have received thus far in teaching writing. Then again, the adoption of new standards or new observational frameworks can help you create urgency that can sometimes work for the good. When there are no dragons, there are no heroes.

Create a mantra.

Choose ways to describe this work, even going so far as deciding on a mantra. There are reasons why presidential candidates hang onto phrases such as "Stronger Together." Alliteration, strong verbs, and rhythmic phrases can be useful. Here are some examples of mantras used in schools:

- Our goal is to help kids live joyfully literate lives.

- Our school is becoming an oasis for reading and writing.

- Real reading and real writing are at the heart of our day.

- We're a community of practice. Everyone's learning curve is sky high.

- We move mountains to support independence—and interdependence.

- We embrace struggle. It's how we all outgrow ourselves.

- We're all aboard authentic literacy.

Use stories.

Tap the power of Small Moment stories. What is it about a reading or a writing workshop that resonates for you personally? Think about specific, detailed images and stories that capture the grandeur of this work, and think about the images and stories that resonate for you. Did you watch first-graders pass a brand-new book among them, smelling it, rubbing their hands over the glossy cover? If so, tell everyone how that moment gave you goosebumps. Did you overhear a child asking to bring *two* books home, one for her and one for her little brother? Did you watch a young writer reread her essay, muttering to herself, "Wait, I gotta say *'why?'* I gotta add evidence," and did you think to yourself, "I only learned to do that in college—she's ten and she's doing that!"? The way you talk about your teachers' and your children's work will inspire others. Trust in the power of details. Remember Roy Peter Clark's advice in his book *Writing Tools*: "Get the name of the dog" (2006).

Find glory.

Make sure that you see glory and beauty in the work teachers are doing—and that you help them see it as well. Remember this story. When President John F. Kennedy visited the NASA Space Center, legend holds that he saw a janitor carrying a broom and asked him what he was doing. The man responded, "Mr. President, I'm helping to put a man on the moon." People need to know they are part of something significant. Make sure that everyone knows the work he or she is doing is miraculous.

Focus on the big picture.

It is easy to get caught in the weeds, to focus on the minutiae. Try to guard against that. It doesn't matter that minilessons are *exactly* ten minutes long—although yes, protecting kids' time to read and write does matter and yes, that means abbreviating our minilessons. But the point is, if you do want to comment on a minilesson being too long, talk about it in ways that remind teachers of the deep, important, beautiful rationale for things, instead of harping on and obsessing over "shoulds" and "rules."

Remember William Ury's advice. In his book on negotiations, *Getting Past No* (1993), he says that when you find yourself in a difficult negotiation, what you need to do—the all-important internal action—is to stop. To pause. To get to the balcony. He goes on to explain that looking over the broad landscape allows you to say, "What are my core convictions? Where is my yes?" Ury adds, "Reach down to your core values, your deeper purpose, to what is right and true for you and find your yes."

Work toward the positive.

There is a bumper sticker that says, "Give up. It hurts less." But giving up actually hurts; despair hurts. Work toward the positive. Hold onto hope. What do you *support*? Remember that when Nelson Mandela wrote about his forty-year fight against racism and apartheid in South Africa, he didn't call his autobiography *Long Walk from Apartheid*. Instead, he called it *Long Walk to Freedom* (1995). It wasn't, for him, a battle *against* something so much as a battle *for* something.

> Work toward the positive. Hold onto hope. What do you support?

Look beyond test scores toward more enduring goals.

Test scores matter in a lot of complicated ways, and you can trust that this work, when well implemented, almost always leads to high achievement on state tests. We discuss that in Chapter 16, "A Few Words about Test Prep for High-Stakes Tests," and yes, we understand that results matter. But if you try to rally teachers to teach in these ways *because* that'll produce results on high-stakes tests, you make a mistake. Even if this year you do get those results, no matter how well your teachers teach, your school won't have an unbroken record of ever-increasing test scores. And ultimately, teachers need to teach toward goals to which they can hold themselves accountable. In the end, test scores are out of their control. And it just plain *is* the case that sometimes, wonderful teaching does not produce the wonderful results that we all expect. You are far better off to rally teachers toward goals they can reach with zeal and wisdom. So even when test scores are good, don't cite them as the reason to do this work. What goes up will come down. Plus, no one wants to live for the goal of higher test scores. Aim for goals that your people will embrace, and the scores will be an extra byproduct.

Remember the advice of Howard Gardner who said some years ago at Teachers College, "We have to attend to the development of truth, beauty, and goodness."

Use your voice to draw people in.

I recently attended a wedding in which both the bride and the groom had written their own vows—a lovely way to sanctify that important moment of the ceremony. The groom had decided that after saying his original and heartfelt promises, he would end the vows by returning to the beautiful, age-old words, "for better or worse, in sickness and in health, for richer or poorer, to love and to cherish, till death do us part." But at that very moment, he lost confidence in his decision to end with those traditional words, and so he raced through them, one line tumbling onto the next—and the powerful impact of those traditional words was lost.

That was a reminder. The way you speak matters. Your attentiveness to what you are saying, your belief that your words matter makes a difference. We once had a friend who had such a beautiful voice that we jokingly said he could say the alphabet in a way that was moving to listeners—and he could. Remember that when you are preaching, as any good leader sometimes needs to do, your tone and aura and presence matters.

Share your dreams.

Talk about this work in ways that will tap into your people's better angels. Yes, you want to give kids the skills to be proficient readers and writers—but why? Share the *why's* that ignite this work. Do you dream of a day when all your kids are lost in books, because you believe that books can teach us to walk in the shoes of someone different than ourselves, to see through the eyes of someone whose life is different than our own, and increasingly, in today's world, you believe that is work worth living toward? Do you want kids to be able to write in ways that make the world a better place? Say so. Find your *why* and share that. Remember that Martin Luther King didn't say, "I have a ten-point plan." He said, "I have a dream" (1963).

Of course, as important as it is that you articulate a vision for your school, in the end this imposed vision needs to be replaced by teachers' own personal visions. Fullan has an all-important reminder for us, as leaders. He writes, "As any innovation unfolds, leaders must pay close attention to whether they are generating passion, purpose and energy—intrinsic motivation. Failure to do so is a surefire indicator that the innovation will fail."

We are reminded of Donald Murray's very simple advice to teachers of writing—and this is equally pertinent to teachers of reading. "The ultimate mark of a successful conference is that the writer leaves, wanting to write." The mark of successful school leaders is that your teachers come to school every day, eager to teach—and to learn.

Lifting the Level of Teaching

PART TWO builds on the vision set in Part One with in-depth descriptions of ways to lift the level of literacy instruction in your school. You'll find supports for helping your teachers to build an instructional foundation buttressed by shared planning and curricular resources. Next, you'll find ideas to help your teachers get the most out of professional development, followed by tips on how to set up a culture of ongoing learning in your school.

❖ ❖ ❖ ❖

4

First Things First: Build an Instructional Foundation

Almost 35,000 people participate in each of three Facebook pages for Units of Study—one devoted to writing, another to reading, and a third specific to reading and writing in middle school. These people form a supportive community for teachers who are working with Units of Study. Often, I'll see a teacher write a post that says, "I am so overwhelmed. I'm just starting Units of Study and there is so much to learn. I don't know where to start."

Time and again, I then see fifty, sixty, seventy people respond, and the overwhelming message is always the same: "Forget about mastery. Just dive in. For now, focus on understanding the flow of a unit and on giving lively, brief, effective minilessons."

I think that is the right answer. That is, early on in their work with Units of Study, your teachers needn't worry about small groups, or about the quality of their conferences, or about providing students who struggle with reading or writing with extra support. Those topics are important, but before a basketball coach can coach a youngster to do a better job dribbling the basketball, the entire team generally needs to be able to carry on, playing the game. The team needs to know the rules of the game and which basket is theirs. It's the same with a reading or a writing workshop. First things first: before teachers can do anything else, they need to get most of the class generally engaged in the main work of the unit. In this chapter, I'll overview the most important work in reading and writing, then I'll offer some unit planning tips to help your teachers support this work right from the start. If your school has been using Units of Study for a while, read this chapter as a reminder of the all-important things you need to continue to be sure are in place, and if your school is just launching Units of Study, this chapter can provide you with a North Star.

IN THIS CHAPTER, YOU'LL FIND . . .

▶ Suggested first goals for your teachers to arm your reform efforts, in reading and writing

▶ Recommended steps you can take to support these goals, such as providing resources and ensuring reading and writing time are protected

▶ Tips to support your teachers' unit planning so that the goals described in this chapter are prioritized

▶ Suggestions for observing teachers and giving feedback in ways that support first goals

If your school is taking on reform in both reading and writing, the first goals for your teachers are as follows.

Reading Goals

▪ Provision students with a wide variety of high-interest books.

▪ Channel students to books within their grasp.

▪ Support students in reading a lot, carrying books between home and school, and meeting with partners to talk about parts of the books.

▪ Establish the structures and culture that support students in reading with engagement.

Writing Goals

▪ Support students in writing often, with fluency, about topics they care about, for an audience of other kids, working on kinds of writing that they've seen other writers attempt.

- Protect time for sustained writing.

- Establish a safe, listening culture in which students will want to write.

- Channel students to admire examples of the sort of writing you then invite them to do.

The curriculum embedded in the Units of Study can help teachers reach these goals and can also help students progress, step by step, toward more proficiency as readers and as writers.

Reading

Provision students with a wide variety of high-interest books.

Stephen Covey (2004) is famous for the advice: "First things first." If one of your priorities is that your youngsters grow up loving to read, there is nothing more important than provisioning them with high-interest books that are accessible to them. This is not an easy challenge to meet, and you'll absolutely need to issue an "all hands on deck" call for help.

In most classrooms, libraries are in dire need. All too often, schools purchased classroom libraries a decade ago for imaginary classes of kids who all read roughly on grade level. Given that most classrooms contain students whose reading levels are distributed along a bell curve, with as many students reading below grade as those reading above grade level (and many more reading below grade level at the start of the year), such libraries are not apt to match the readers in a classroom. This is especially true when one keeps in mind that students who are reading below grade level will need to read shorter, more accessible books. They'll proceed through books at a much faster clip and will therefore need more books than their classmates who are more proficient readers. Of course, in schools where most students read well below grade level, chances are especially good that the libraries do not come close to matching the actual reading abilities of the students. For these and other reasons, we urge you to create an all-hands-on-deck task force to investigate your classroom libraries.

One of the first things you'll want to do is to go on a search through your building, looking for books that have been shelved away and can be brought out. Perhaps your science teachers once taught a unit on forces and motion and that unit was long since abandoned. Chances are good there were some reasonably good books that were abandoned along with the curriculum, and they could be retrieved and given a spot in a teacher's nonfiction library. Perhaps you have class sets of some books that your kids are no longer trudging through en masse. Those sets of books can now be distributed so that every classroom gets a few of them.

Then, too, you'll want to rally your teachers and your parents to write grants and persuasive letters and to conduct bake sales to generate funding for more books. See the online resources for suggested sources of funding for books—but know that you have local sources as well that are just waiting to be tapped. ✳

Even if your first thought is, "We've got tons of books," you may still want to investigate your classroom libraries. We've been helping schools take stock of their libraries and found, for example, that even in one of New York City's showcase schools, the first classroom we visited had only three books that had been published in the last five years. In another showcase school, we randomly selected one classroom to study—it was an inclusion fifth-grade classroom. Although many children in that class were reading levels M/N/O, the very well-stocked library had almost no books for those students. A third school found that although they'd prioritized including books with diverse characters, almost none of their books were written by #ownvoices authors who shared the identity of their characters.

Upkeep of Libraries

A great classroom library looks a bit like a great bookstore. Such a library is organized to help students find and develop favorite authors, series, and genres, making it easy for kids to make thoughtful book choices. It lures kids into reading and sustains them once they are reading.

If your teachers seem overwhelmed with the upkeep and organization of their libraries, suggest they recruit students (and perhaps parents) as librarians. We've seen first-graders sort favorite read-alouds by theme or topic. We've seen third-graders reorganize a classroom library, making enticing labels for baskets, breathing new life into the library, and inspiring kids' reading lives. We've seen eighth-graders make it clear that the dystopian section should be a big part of the library.

You will probably want to learn about the TCRWP Classroom Libraries Project. A few years ago, Shana Frazin and I rallied our entire organization to search the world to locate 800 people with deep expertise on children's literature: professors, authors, librarians, bloggers, critics, reviewers, and teachers who are experts on children's literature. TCRWP worked for a year, with help from these 800 experts, to design classroom libraries and library shelves containing the books that we knew would make reading irresistible to kids. We curated libraries of 400 high-interest fiction and nonfiction books for below-benchmark readers, as well as equally large libraries for readers roughly at benchmark, and we designed shelves to support historical fiction, mystery, fantasy, and so much more. If your teachers are desperate for well-curated collections, these libraries—or some of the individual shelves within them—may be a gift.

When examining your libraries, pay special attention to the nonfiction sections. In schools that are teaching Units of Study, students read nonfiction for significant parts of the year. Yet we find that classrooms often have few high-interest, accessible books. As a result, for half the year, kids read articles that have been printed off from the computer. That's not going to lead to reading achievement or to engagement.

When we curated the classroom libraries, we considered issues of representation and diversity. We strove to provide texts that celebrate multiple perspectives, cultures, histories, and identities, as well as to include texts with diverse authorship. This isn't easy—only 7% of new children's books published in 2017 were written by Black, Latin/o, or Native authors. When children meet characters who look and feel like they do, and who have experiences similar to their own, they see themselves in the pages of those books. Another way to ensure classroom libraries meet the needs of all children is to provide books in children's first languages in classrooms with English language learners.

When you are choosing books for classroom libraries and the school library, we encourage you, too, to think about cultural relevancy. It's a never-ending, but extremely valuable task to continually build libraries that reflect the cultures and identities of your students. As you do this work, there are some important questions to ask, including:

- How can we deepen the representation of our students and families in the books children will encounter in our school?

- How can we be careful about issues of stereotypes in the stories and nonfiction we read with children?

- How can we particularly seek stories and nonfiction texts that will support underrepresented or disempowered voices?

- How can we pay attention to the authors of books as well as their subjects, so that we seek authentic representation?

- How can our libraries offer windows and mirrors for our children, so that reading strengthens their identities and voices, and fosters sympathetic imaginations?

There are researchers and book publishers at the forefront of the work in this area. We encourage you to turn to WeNeedDiverseBooks.org, #ourownvoices, and publishers such as Lee and Low Books, as well as to the profound work of researchers such as Gloria Ladson Billings, Geneva Gay, or Sonia Nieto. For additional suggestions on books that feature diverse characters and reflect the lives of the wide range of students in your classrooms, we've put some links in the online resources. ✋

Books to Support Content Areas

You'll also want to be sure that when teachers teach social studies and science, they have collections of accessible trade books to support the curriculum. On topics that are new to youngsters, it is especially important that they can literally "read up" on the topic, starting with books that might, at first glance, seem too easy, and then progressing into denser content texts. Richard Allington, in his article "You Can't Learn Much from Books You Can't Read," reminds us that most kids read nonfiction well below the level they read fiction, and that for them to learn content, they need lots of texts they can comprehend. Take a look at your social studies and science collections, and make sure that you have easier books on the topics that your children will be learning about through their reading (2002).

Channel students to books within their grasp.

Provisioning classrooms with adequate libraries is a start, but if kids are slogging through books that are way too hard or whipping through books with an inadequate level of challenge, their reading growth will be stunted. Allington suggests a way for you to conduct a quick assessment. Go into a classroom and ask kids to put all the texts that they have in their desks or in their book baggies in a pile on top of their desks. Then go among the kids, perhaps recruiting another member of your administrative team to join you, asking a sampling of the youngsters to open one book after another to a random page and begin reading aloud. Listen for fluency—does the student read in a way that it sounds like talk? Also listen for accuracy—is the student reading with at least 95% accuracy? What percentage of these texts are ones the student can read with both fluency and accuracy? You won't do this quick assessment for all your students, but in a fifteen-minute visit to a classroom, you can ascertain the extent to which kids are spending their school days reading books they can actually read. For kids to progress, they need the opportunity to read, read, read.

To match kids with high-interest, accessible reading, teachers in grades K–6 also need to conduct some kind of reading assessment (we recommend running records). This can be used to guide each student to the kinds of books that he or she can read with a high percentage of accuracy. That process can consume literally weeks of time—or not. We strongly encourage you to move heaven and earth to make this happen as expeditiously as possible. Here are a few suggestions for helping your teachers match kids to books as quickly as possible at the start of the year.

- If a teacher assessed children's reading levels during the prior year, he or she must pass the results of those end-of-year reading assessments on to students' new teachers. Then the new teachers can channel kids to read books that are one level below those they were reading at the end of the previous school year. You'll need to establish open communication and transparency among teachers at different grade levels, so that if the teacher in the higher grade can't fathom how the teacher in the earlier grade assessed a child as reading at a particular level, those discussions can take place. The encouragement to speak up when this happens is a way to norm assessments across your school.

- If teachers did not assess kids for their reading levels during the previous year and if you have students' standardized test scores, you might examine those test scores and suggest that the kids who excelled on that test make their own book choices. Later on, teachers can investigate whether those choices are appropriate, but at the start of the year, especially in schools that are just beginning this work, matching *those* kids to books won't be their priority. Instead, encourage your teachers to focus first on assessing kids who scored well below grade level on the high-stakes test. Teachers can use that test score to give them a ballpark estimation, thereby making their running records more efficient. This is true for grades 6–8 as well. If students scored level 1 on your state test, they don't read at grade level. You need to find out what level they can handle with ease to see if you have books for them.

- Issue an all-hands-on-deck call for assistance conducting running records. If specialists haven't yet begun their special assignments, ask them to push into classrooms to help teachers with these time-consuming assessments. Require that all student teachers receive training in conducting running records and focus their first days on pitching in to the effort to get kids matched to books.

- Channel teachers to read *A Guide to the Reading Workshop* and *Reading Pathways*, for help conducting these assessments as efficiently as possible. Refer to the *Guide for Primary Grades*, Chapter 6, pages 59–62; *Reading Pathways* (grades 3–5), Chapter 3, pages 33–46; and *Guide for Middle School Grades*, Chapter 4, pages 38–39.

- If possible, send your reading specialists into classrooms to use their superior skills assessing children. If those specialists match, say, a low/middle/and high child to appropriate books, those assessments will help teachers who may have never received formal professional development in reading assessment to gauge whether their assessments of other children are accurate. This will help teachers think, "If Jack is reading N, then that must mean that Liza should probably be reading M."

- Readers who are reading below M will need a more complete battery of assessments, including high-frequency words and a developmental spelling inventory that will illuminate their grasp of phonics. Primary teachers can help upper-grade teachers learn to do these assessments.

It won't help teachers to know the levels of text complexity that their students can read if they don't know the levels of text complexity for the books in their classroom libraries. If classroom libraries have not yet been leveled, buy pizzas and hold leveling parties on Saturday mornings, Sunday evenings, or after school. Bring classroom libraries into the faculty room and ask teachers to each invest a little time during any free moment to assess a few of the books that will be right there, before them. Channel your paraprofessionals and your security guards and your school secretary and your parent volunteers to help, and be sure you join in as well, visibly. This work is not rocket science. Mostly the process involves looking the book up. Your teachers can visit Fountas & Pinnell's website and subscribe to the Fountas & Pinnell Leveled Books website. Many book levels are available on Google. You and your teachers can decide whether the levels of text complexity should be signaled with colored dots on the book's jacket or with a letter, written prominently on the cover of a book—or whether they should be only in a teacher's notes. But one way or another, teachers will need to know the levels of text complexity for many of the books in their libraries. This is especially important for lower grades; few believe that six-year-olds should be expected to weigh whether a book is just right, agreeing instead that it helps to be able to channel youngsters to bins of books that will be right for them.

Support students reading a lot, carrying books between home and school, meeting with partners to talk about parts of the books.

Even after you have moved heaven and earth to help teachers have the books they need for their kids to read up a storm, that storm sometimes doesn't happen. You will need to keep an eye on the volume of reading that actually occurs in your classrooms.

Another assessment suggested by Allington is this: Walk the hallway of your school, glancing into classrooms as you proceed down the corridor. In what percentage of the classrooms are almost all the kids engaged in reading or in writing?

If interested, most kids are passively listening, and you first need to help your teachers recognize the problem and confront it. Our Units of Study channel students, starting in second grade, to keep logs in which they record the number of minutes spent reading in school and at home and the number of pages they read during that time—or in middle school, the number of pages they read overall, from bed to bed. Kindergartners and first-graders can track their reading volume in simpler ways. For example, kindergarteners can stick a Post-it to the back of every book in their baggie, tallying each time they read it. By the start of first grade, students learn to tally on a small Post-it in the corner of a reading mat, as they move through their stack of books, using that number to set goals for the next day. Those logs are only useful if students regard them as valuable data and use them to track progress as they work toward increasing stamina and engagement as readers. Once the focus shifts to the quality of students' thoughts about texts (an appropriate shift, once the year is well underway), then the logs slip into the background and that's a good time for teachers to suggest that most students record their thoughts rather than their volume of reading. Some students will still need to record minutes and pages of reading—and will need someone to help them watch over this data as carefully as a runner watches over his running data.

You'll want to remind teachers to be sure that students in grades 2–3 are eyes-on-print reading for twenty-five to thirty minutes a day in school and some amount of added time at home. You'll want to talk up the importance of students in grades 4–5 reading even more than that in school and at least half an hour most nights at home. By middle school, we suggest that students try to fit as much reading as possible into their lives, which usually means in school for about thirty minutes and outside of school for forty-five minutes or more, as many days a week as they can. Of course, teachers will have to help some students build their stamina over time.

When readers talk with someone about their reading or read favorite parts aloud to each other, there is an authentic accountability to comprehension that is far more powerful than any set of text-based questions could ever be. For that reason, we urge you to encourage classrooms to set up reading partnerships as soon as possible. In the youngest classrooms, children can sit knee-to-knee, taking turns reading pages in a shared text, chatting about what they notice. Older students can talk together about books in partnerships and clubs in ways that extend their thinking from plot summaries to deep analysis and introspection. Teachers shouldn't expect partner conversations to be perfect at the start, but you'll want to encourage them to get partnerships up and running early on, dedicating some instructional time to helping kids talk well about books.

Sometimes you'll visit a classroom and get the feeling that the reading logs and the emphasis on volume are all about compliance. If this is happening, you might convene teachers and suggest it might be time for a relaunch. (In the online resources for *A Guide to the Reading Workshop, Middle School Grades*, there is a mini-unit "Maintaining an Independent Reading Life" under the Chapter 4 Curriculum Calendar link that can help with this work. We've put that mini-unit and sample logs here in the online resources as well, in case you want to provide it for your teachers.)

You can also check to see if your teachers modeled how they use a log or statistics to reflect on how reading is going, and how to give a partner advice after studying his or her reading life. Check in with students and ask, "Why does it matter to keep track of how reading is going for you? How might that help your partner, if you can see how much he or she has been reading? How might you help your partner, or other readers?"

Establish the structures and culture that support students in reading with engagement.

Although asking students to log how much they read will help teachers track their reading volume, it will be the work of creating a culture of reading that actually ignites their love of reading. The Units of Study themselves will go a long way toward helping teachers learn ways to rally kids to love reading, but you'll want to gather teachers together and ask for their ideas as well. This needs to become a moral imperative, a schoolwide mission. You'll want to approach this mission with enormous fervor—to help your teachers to do likewise.

Start by thinking about ways in which you, personally, can demonstrate a love of reading. That will be easier to do if you actually do get started reading some fiction books. Find someone on your staff or in your family who knows you well and can help keep you "in books." At TCRWP, Shana Frazin selects books for the whole staff to read, and the Project finances a giant Project-wide book club. This summer, we were all given copies of *Manhattan Beach, Us Against You* (the sequel to *Beartown*), and *Educated*.

Look around your office. Does your office send a message that you are some-one who loves books? Once you have begun to wear your love of reading on your sleeve, look around at the people near you to see if they have books on display.

Of course, you'll want to be very public about your love of reading. At New York City's East Side Community High School (6–12), the principal, Mark Federman, says he and the kids talk about "coming out as readers." They salute people who have the courage to be public about their love of books—and Mark is the most public of all. When a new book comes out that Mark knows his teenagers will love, he convinces the publisher to give him hundreds of copies of the book at an unbelievable price, and then he goes door to door, classroom to classroom, talking up the new book and letting kids know that if any of them want to read it, they can have a copy, as long as they promise to come to a pizza book club to talk about it.

Meanwhile you can help teachers to be equally public about their love of reading. If a child says, "I didn't read last night," help your teachers to say some-thing like, "Awwww. Rough night, huh? I hate it when I'm so crazy-busy that I can't read." How entirely different the message would be if the teacher had instead said, "You need to read every night so you pass the test."

Ask your teachers to carry books around, and you do the same. Tell kids, "You have to read this! I know you'll love it." Suggest that your teachers keep stacks of new books on their desks. Ask your school librarian to talk up new books and to help teachers know the new titles well enough to do the same. Be sure that across the school, there are waiting lists for popular books.

There is no question but that book buzzes make a difference—times when teachers or kids give little trailers on books that they believe kids will love, reading just one juicy part aloud. It's especially powerful if the books promoted are on the easier side and are part of a series, since that way, promotion of one book ends up being a promotion for a whole line of books.

This book can't do justice to the topic of how teachers can promote a love of reading, but that will absolutely be high on the priority list for your school.

Writing

We introduced these writing goals at the beginning of this chapter, and now we'll delve into them.

- Support students in writing often, with fluency, about topics they care about, for an audience of other kids, working on kinds of writing they've seen other writers attempt.

- Protect time for sustained writing.

- Establish a safe, listening culture in which students will want to write.

- Channel students to admire examples of the sort of writing you then invite them to do.

Support students in writing often, with fluency, about topics they care about, for an audience of other kids, working on kinds of writing they've seen other writers attempt.

Writing is so concrete and visible that it is particularly easy to see ways in which the curricular reforms that you and others advocate do and do not have traction. Every minute of kids' writing time leaves a record. This means that the teaching of writing provides you with amazing opportunities to actually see the extent to which your curricular leadership—and the curricular leadership done by others—actually effects concrete changes in what kids do, day in and day out.

When you have just initiated or revved up writing reform, chances are good that you will see many teachers merely dabbling in the new curriculum, adding bits and pieces of it to their old stuff. This is how many teachers respond to any reform effort. This presents giant problems because the instruction kids receive ends up a mish-mash of conflicting messages, with almost zero continuity, resulting in compromised opportunities for real development. The power of the Units of Study in reading and in writing is that they offer kids a coherent curriculum, in which one day stands on the shoulders of and builds off another. That power is lost when the curriculum is a hodgepodge.

> *Because effective writing instruction yields almost instant, meaningful results, you'll be able to look for concrete evidence that your teachers have changed and are actually teaching writing every day.*

Because writing is so visible and concrete, you will have many opportunities to monitor teachers' teaching practices. You can hold teachers accountable for actually engaging in the reform—and the good news is that when they *do* embrace a writing workshop with intensity, they'll experience huge rewards in the form of student growth. Because effective writing instruction yields almost instant, meaningful results, you'll be able to look for concrete evidence that your teachers have changed and are actually teaching writing every day—and you can then teach teachers that when they take on new practices, there can be dramatic results. The payoff for reform in writing will be amazing. Your leadership in writing can teach your people that growing professionally can be thrilling.

The concreteness of writing, however, also poses a risk. The risk is that because kids' writing is so visible and in-your-face, it becomes almost too easy for your leadership to follow the compliance model. Recall that most educational leaders over the decades have led with a sort of "got my list, checking it twice, gotta find out who's naughty or nice" mentality. Although you want to be aware of whether your teachers are actually teaching writing every day or not, that doesn't mean that whenever you see that a teacher has *not* made time for writing, that becomes an occasion for scolding. You might, instead, see that as an opportunity for you to work harder toward inspiring that teacher to give this a go.

Listen through kids' writing to the kids themselves.

So vow to study student work and—above all—respond to work in ways that build up teachers' and kids' energy for writing. Laugh at the funny parts of student work, cry at the sad parts. One of the hardest parts of teaching is that it can be lonely, so it will be precious if you and other administrators function as company for classroom teachers, sharing their heartfelt responses to the kids' writing—and through their writing, to the kids themselves.

When you visit a classroom and look at student work, you might think about ways in which your presence can make kids more eager to write and teachers more eager to teach writing. When you see a notebook or folder that has only a little writing in it, you might say to that child, "I'm so interested in your stories, and I know others are, as well. Tell me one!" When that child is done, say, "You have to write that!" The child will be glad you came.

You'll want to find things to compliment in the classroom, so the teacher will be glad as well. "Some of your writers have such quirky stories. You must be doing some great modeling." Or, "Your kids are beginning to talk like writers. They know where they are in the writing process, and they can talk about what they're working on." Remember what David Rock says about minimizing threat perception. When people are anxious, their processing shuts down. When they feel safe, they can listen. Bring your most generous self into the classroom, so that when you do want to talk about hard parts, your teachers are more willing to listen.

Note signs that student work is aligned to the writing workshop philosophy.

As you visit classrooms to observe students writing and study their work, you may want to keep these thoughts in mind:

- Students in a class will each be writing on a different topic. If they are all writing under a shared umbrella topic, they will have chosen different subtopics.

- Each student's text will be different in structure and craft. The pieces, for instance, may all include something—say, dialogue—but that will be in different places in the text and done differently. They won't, for example, all have the same transitions, or all begin or end all in similar ways (as in, all starting with a question).

- The published writing looks less like compositions of yesteryear and more like publications. Instead of the text starting with the date, the school, and the class, it starts with a title. The format suggests it is written for an audience, not just to get a grade.

- There are earlier drafts and notebook entries or research notes for any published writing in grades 3–8. Studying the sequence of work one child did prior to publication, you can see evidence of the stages of collecting, drafting, revising, and editing.

- The folders don't contain prefabricated, teacher-made graphic organizers or worksheets of any kind. Students may map or sketch or jot to plan their organizational structure, but if they do that, they'll each do that differently. In K–2 classes, the folders include lots of booklets where students have drafted and quickly revised different pieces.

- Kids aren't writing genreless "compositions" or "papers," but are instead writing book reviews, editorials, arguments, lab reports, and how-to texts. You can sense that the writer thought, "How does this kind of writing go?" and looked at mentor texts, trying to write like those texts.

- The finished published writing probably doesn't have marginal corrections from the teacher's red pen. Teachers may have written tips onto rough drafts (although these are often given orally), but usually out of respect, the final draft doesn't have red pen marks all over it. If there is a response, it is usually on a Post-it, and in a note at the end.

Talk back when student work isn't aligned to a workshop approach.

If you get accustomed to checking in on the writing work kids are doing in your school, and you look at the work they do throughout the whole day, you'll probably see that some of your teachers will still be assigning kids topics, asking for one-shot, genreless writing, and shepherding kids to all write in a format that the teacher provides. You will absolutely want to address this. Here are some tips for ways you can do so:

- Suggest that the writing workshop approach actually represents beliefs about how people learn—including the belief that even young people can be invited into the heart of a discipline, given the chance to do work that resembles that which the pros do. Professional writers don't write with graphic organizer worksheets. Even when a group of writers are all writing about the same topic—say, the Electoral College—each writer still chooses his or her subtopic/angle. If kids across a school are writing like professional writers, the showcase in the school's front foyer won't celebrate a class set of compositions on the same subtopic.

- When you see instances in one classroom of ELA writing that doesn't seem aligned to the Units of Study, you might explain to the teacher that you are trying to get your mental arms around the curriculum she is teaching and ask her to show you the unit and the session that provides you with the context you need to understand that day's instruction. If the instruction that sparked your inquiry represented something from the teacher's former curriculum—perhaps a worksheet, for example—and the teacher might say that she has added something she thought the kids needed, then ask her to also show you writing that *does* reflect the unit. Try, as you look at it, to notice that classroom's progress through the unit, checking that the unit will be done in five weeks. Don't hesitate to look inside kids' folders and notebooks, since that is where you can see the goods.

Protect time for sustained writing.

The challenges of teaching writing are entirely different than those of teaching reading. Whereas you need loads of books to support reading, a writing workshop just requires paper, pens, notebooks, folders—and *time*. Time becomes the hard part when the topic is supporting the teaching of writing.

Teachers don't need to be cajoled, encouraged, and mandated to teach reading or math, but somehow, writing has been knocked off the list of basic skills in our schools. For decades, lots of schools have regarded writing as a frill. Some teachers teach writing, others don't. And many of those who do teach writing marginalize it by jettisoning writing when the schedule gets crowded.

If you can tackle this one challenge, you will make a giant difference for your students. If teachers aren't teaching a writing workshop at least four days a week, your students' growth as writers will take a hit, as will the success of your school's work with Units of Study. Take this challenge very seriously. Think about ways you can move heaven and earth to encourage your teachers to treat writing with the same respect they give to math and reading. The payoff will astonish you, because kids' growth will be dramatic and highly visible, and their growth in writing will lift the level of their thinking across every subject.

It can help to have in mind a general guide for the volume of writing you'd expect in a week. For kindergartners, expect that by early winter they'll be writing a few three-page booklets a week, with several sentences on each page. Their spellings will still be incomplete approximations, but that won't hold them back from writing a lot. By the same point in second grade, expect children to be writing several five-page booklets a week, with a paragraph on each page. By third grade, children will spend a lot of time writing on notebook paper, sometimes contained within a notebook. By December, they'll probably write about a page a day in school and hopefully more at home. By fifth or sixth grade, that volume will have doubled, although often the handwriting gets smaller or the kids will be typing, so it may appear that they're writing just about a page and a half a day in school, and similar amounts some evenings at home.

That volume will depend on kids' writing experience. At the start of the school year, older students who haven't grown up writing will look as if they are inscribing in marble. They can take half an hour to write three or four lines. After a few months, they should become fluent as writers—and this development is critical. Volume, fluency, and stamina are not *everything* in writing, but without them, it is very hard for a student to write well.

Discover and support classrooms in which kids are not writing.

Early on, set up ways to discover classrooms in which kids are not writing regularly and with fluency and stamina. You will not want weeks or months to go by before you begin tackling this. Writing, like reading, is a skill that is learned in practice. And alas, all too often, kids end up just having ten or fifteen minutes of time in school each day to actually write. This is a crisis and you need to be on the alert for it.

It is easier to detect a lack of writing than it is to detect a lack of reading. To systematically check in on the volume of writing occurring in your school, ask teachers to bring all the writing that one or two representative children have done so far in the year to a grade-level meeting that you (or one of your representatives) attends. Ideally, it works well if you can ask teachers to bring a mid-level writer's work as well as the work that a strong writer has done. You'll probably focus more on the mid-level writer, but asking for the work from a strong writer as well makes it more likely that the mid-level child is actually representative of the bulk of the class.

Then you'll want teachers to work in pairs, studying first all the writing that one of their mid-level children has done. Ask them to leaf through a chronological collection of the writing, noting specifically how the volume of writing that the child typically does in a day has evolved over time, and noting the number of days in which the child has been writing. You'll want teachers to start at the beginning of the collection and to leaf through it, saying, "Here is Monday's writing, Tuesday's, where's Wednesday? Thursday? Here is Friday's work again." You can watch this process and quickly see that there will be some teachers whose kids are rarely writing, and some whose kids write very little on any given day. That is bound to surface.

If the issue is widely shared, address it with the whole group. "What can I do to help you actually get writing time every day? What's getting in the way?" If there are one or two teachers whose kids aren't writing, you will instead hold that conversation with those individual teachers.

There will be several contributing factors to the problem, but the most obvious will be that teachers are not actually teaching writing. Half your teachers might *say* they teach writing every day, but if that is true, you'd see the results in the students' collections of writing. And if the writing workshop is on-again, off-again, with kids starting a piece on Monday and getting back to it on Thursday, you can give up on this instruction ever working.

Roland Barth, the founder of the Principals' Center at Harvard Graduate School of Education, once told a group of TCRWP principals that the health of a building relates to how many elephants are in the room. The elephants in the room are the issues that everyone is talking about in the bathroom and the parking lot, but no one is talking about in the light of day. "Get those issues into the public square," Barth has said.

Tackle the inflated curriculum and make time for writing.

The issue that all your teachers will be talking about is time. They have a point. You can't ask them to add fifty minutes a day for writing without helping them know what they can subtract. And the answer to that question needs to be site-specific. One place to begin is by subtracting time spent on skills out of context. Yes, K–2 teachers will need twenty to thirty minutes a day for phonics. Teachers in grades 3–5 will need ten minutes a day, several times a week for spelling and vocabulary. Middle school teachers may need to alternate at the end of every month, shifting between units in reading and units in writing. But your teachers do not need to teach capitalization and punctuation outside of the writing workshop. You can help them save time by deleting time spent on worksheets. It may be that elementary science needs to replace art as one of the specials, or that elementary teachers need to alternate between social studies and science units, or that middle school humanities teachers need to plan for shorter units.

An investigation will also yield tremendous amounts of wasted time in the school day. Perhaps in your school, the morning announcements start twenty minutes after students arrive and last ten minutes, inadvertently signaling that the actual beginning of school occurs almost half an hour after the official start time. Why not jump-start the day at the minute school is said to begin? Then, too, time may be wasted with interschool phone calls as teachers attend to phone calls from the office, the guidance counselor, or another teacher. Eliminate those wasted minutes, and you can help teachers carve out more time for teaching writing—and for everything else.

In tens of thousands of schools, teachers see that once kids begin to soar as writers, everything else changes, and so they prioritize providing regular time for writing. Kids' writing skill allows them to think and talk more probingly about reading, to organize new information and construct theories about social studies and science, and most importantly, to *think*. The payoff to strong writing is dramatic and beautiful to see. But you will never see that payoff if writing isn't treated as a priority subject.

Establish a safe, listening culture in which students will want to write.

Think for a moment about times when you have talked to someone who truly *listens* to you—something magical happens. You find yourself talking in such detail, regaling your audience with gritty specifics that you'd entirely forgotten until now. You find yourself reliving the event, rethinking the idea, swept up in the passion of it all. One thing you say makes you think of another, and ideas snowball. As William Stafford describes writing, "You are off and running, exploring territory that is new for you."

That is the central drama of any good writing workshop. Donald Murray (1992), father of writing process, describes it this way:

> I hear voices from my students they have never heard from themselves. I find they are authorities on subjects they think ordinary. I find that even my remedial students write like writers, putting down writing that doesn't quite make sense, reading it to see what sense there might be in it, trying to make sense of it, and–draft after draft–making sense of it. They follow language to see where it will lead them, and I follow them following language. It is a matter of faith, faith that my students have something to say and a language in which to say it.

In classrooms where teachers listen keenly to young people and teach them to listen with equal attentiveness to each other, students will have no dearth of ideas to write about. You can help to create that listening culture. Go into a classroom when kids are writing, pull your chair alongside a youngster, and ask, "What are you writing about?"

The child will give you the headlines, the abbreviated summary. If this is narrative writing, you're going to want to help the child relive the small moment. It can help to ask something like this: "Wait. Where were you at the beginning?" If the child answers with a generalization, press for details. "You were home, but where, exactly?"

Once you get details enough to re-create the scene for yourself, do so. "Okay, so you were sitting on the stool in your kitchen, and your dad was making pancakes. Then what happened?"

Again, if the child produces generalizations, press for details. "You say your mom came into the room and yelled at you. What exactly did she say?" Once you get a detailed, specific start to the story, tell it back to the writer and let the writer just go-go-go, telling you the whole rest of the story while you listen raptly, or perhaps shifting already to pouring that story onto the page.

That interaction is a way to prime children's pumps when they are writing narratives, and there are different ways to do that when they are working on other genres. Our point is simple, however. *Listen!* And help teachers to listen. Intent, rapt listening, and respectful "saying back" of what children have said thus far can go a long way toward helping kids know their lives and their ideas are worth writing about.

Channel students to admire examples of the sort of writing you then invite them to do.

As the saying has it, "A picture's worth a thousand words." That is so very true. When teaching people how to make something, it is infinitely powerful to show examples of that kind of thing—and to help the maker develop language for annotating what they see. Skilled teachers select examples that represent a horizon—that are a stretch, but are within grasp.

You'll want to check in with your teachers and students to make sure that students are studying mentor texts as a way to become familiar with a genre and as a way to raise the level of their own writing. Your goal is that kids learn that whenever they want to write a new kind of thing, they'll think, "I'd love to see an example of that kind of writing" and then they'll study the example to steer their own work.

Know that in our Units of Study, kids will regularly study mentor texts. As a school leader, you might give teachers time to preview mentor texts, or to mark them up together, annotating the places in the text that they might highlight with their students. You might ask for suggestions for a schoolwide mentor text or ones that might become gifts for each grade-level teacher. The student samples in *Writing Pathways* are a gold mine for writing exemplars, and you'll find it is endlessly fascinating to study them with a group of teachers, developing your abilities to notice and name what works in those pieces. If a child's writing is similar to the exemplar pieces for grade 2, help your teachers see that the exemplars for grade 3 are marvelous mentor texts for that child—and that is true even if the child is in middle school. That is, adult published mentor texts are precious and worth studying, but it is especially helpful for kids to apprentice themselves to writers who are just a bit stronger than they are today.

Help teachers reimagine lesson planning.

The outcomes described above are necessary but not sufficient. Students also need all the specific skill development that will take them to and beyond global standards and that will help them become lifelong readers and writers. The Units of Study have been carefully designed and written in ways that enable even teachers who have not received state-of-the-art professional development to rise to these monumental challenges. They provide a curriculum for students *and* for teachers, and they are rich enough to support years of continual study.

The books, themselves, however, are just black marks on paper. Like the score of a symphony, they need to be brought to life. In education, we lump all the work that goes into preparing to teach into the term "lesson planning." And the interesting thing is that we act as if everyone has something similar in mind when that term is used; yet the truth is, there is a world of difference in what teachers do in the name of lesson planning.

Rethink your policies around lesson planning.

You might begin with a little inquiry of your own. Go to an especially effective teacher (ideally one who is effective with this curriculum) and ask that teacher what he or she does in the name of lesson planning. Do the same for a less effective teacher. Chances are, they both think that what they do in the name of lesson planning is the norm—and chances are, their interpretations of lesson planning will be worlds apart. And frankly, you might find that you too have a very different image of what you hope your teachers are doing in the name of lesson planning.

My first suggestion is that you make space in your own mind and in your teachers' lives for a new interpretation of lesson planning. Make sure that everything you are asking your teachers to do is actually lifting their knowledge and skills and their readiness to teach well. I don't recommend asking teachers to recopy Units of Study sessions onto a new kind of paper or rewrite them in the teachers' "own words." That's busy work and frankly, when a teacher is teaching a minilesson that she has reread several times and understands deeply to a group of kids sitting in front of her, she *will* put it into her own words. Hopefully she stays close to the written text when that language is especially apt or particularly beautiful and departs from it to draw on an example from her own life or her own class.

Worse yet, don't think that it is a good use of a teacher's time to turn the published session into a PowerPoint presentation for kids! There is almost nothing that can make a minilesson worse than teaching it via a PowerPoint. Minilessons are meant to be "I-thou" conversations, with the teacher sitting before the class as when doing a read-aloud, talking directly and intimately to the students who huddle close. PowerPoints, on the other hand, introduce a distance and a cold formality that is the exact opposite of the warm, collaborative learning environment that the minilessons are intended to create.

You may be asking, "What does lesson planning entail, then, if it's not making a concise rewrite of a minilesson?" In brief, it involves getting to know the unit and the lesson so deeply that you are at home with it, thinking about small adaptations that allow you to teach it with voice and traction, planning ways to keep the lesson brief and lively, studying student work, and preparing for small-group work and conferences. That's a lot!

Rally your teachers to reinvest in a new sort of lesson planning.

You will probably want to begin by conveying to teachers that lesson planning is absolutely essential to the work of going from theory to practice. When teachers plan their teaching, they stand on the shoulders and walk in the shoes of other experts to develop more expertise on whatever they are teaching. Lesson planning is a high-level intensive course of study. Lesson planning also provides teachers with the invitation to think about ways to make sure they can bring that knowledge to their kids in ways that build off of the quirky specificity of their kids, and link to the work their kids have been doing.

Some lesson planning is collaborative, allowing teachers from across a grade level to discuss and digest and practice what they are learning from the distant mentors (the coauthors of the unit) and to cumulate their thinking about how to bring that knowledge base to life. When a cohort of teachers plan together, they work collaboratively to co-invent ways to teach. You will absolutely want to champion the importance of co-lesson planning, and to do everything you can to raise the level of this heady intellectual work. In Chapter 7, "Build a Culture of Ongoing Learning," I delve further into the power of collaborative planning and offer tips on how you can move heaven and earth to give teachers time for this to happen.

Help teachers become familiar with the broad plan, goals, schedule, and materials for a unit—and learn how to do this for any unit.

Emphasize that unit planning is actually more foundational than lesson planning. A teacher needs to be able to see the broad landscape of where he or she is attempting to take kids instructionally. That's why backward planning is so very important. It's important to be guided by a North Star.

Of course, once a teacher has taught Units of Study for a year, that prior experience allows the teacher to have a broad view of the pathways along which the students will travel. The challenge is for teachers to be able to gain this perspective even in their first year working within this curriculum. The easiest way to do this is to start by providing them with at least a full day and ideally a week of professional development in either the writing or the reading curriculum. When that sort of overview isn't possible, it becomes especially essential that the teachers across a grade level are given at least an hour or two to overview and plan for an upcoming unit of study—ideally about a week before the start of the unit.

In many schools, teachers sometimes use a process that we refer to as jigsawing to acquaint themselves with the upcoming unit. Before the group meets, a facilitator looks over the Orientation (or Welcome) to the unit, dividing up roles. That person may decide that the members of that planning group should all read the overview of the unit, which is typically two pages long. Those two pages usually provide a concise understanding of the "why" behind the unit. Then the facilitator will divide up the remaining sections of the unit's front matter. Typically, one person is designated to read the overview of Bend I that is part of the front matter, the first session in Bend I, and the anchor chart and student work at the end of that bend, and others do similar work for the other bends. Each person reads his or her allotted pages while sitting alongside each other in the meeting, and then after a few minutes for quiet reading, each person teaches the group about his or her section.

Another even better way to become acquainted with an upcoming unit is for someone who knows that unit well to select half a dozen especially key sessions from the first two bends of the unit, and then to give micro-versions of those minilessons to the grade-level cohort of teachers as if they were the kids. Those micro-versions of the minilessons can contain just the teaching point and a bit of the teaching, and each can last about two minutes. The teachers, then, do the work of each day for three or four minutes, pretending to be the kids, and then the facilitator calls, "It's tomorrow" and proceeds to give the next micro-lesson.

Here are a few tips you might give teachers to help maximize their planning time and guide them quickly to understand the heart of a unit. If you follow these recommendations, you'll encourage teachers to first immerse themselves in a unit by trying some of the work they'll ask kids to do. Then, you'll recommend a specific sequence for reading a minilesson, not in order, but starting with the link at the end of the minilesson. Then teachers will familiarize themselves with the expectations for kids' work. Reading in this way supports teachers in doing some backward planning and helps them to keep an appropriate focus on the work that kids will be doing, because this is where the learning happens.

Tips for Lesson Planning within a Unit of Study: For Teachers

- Prior to launching the unit, you and your colleagues will want to begin by getting to know the arc of the unit. Be sure that you read the front matter to the unit. You might divide up responsibilities for overviewing the unit, so that one person is given one bend to study and teach others about, another, another bend. Skim the first sessions of each bend. Study the anchor charts and the examples of student work at the end of bends, looking at how the student work matches the bullets on the anchor charts. Discuss how you will access the materials you need to teach the unit. Decide on whether you will do all the recommended assessments or abbreviate some of them. (See the chapters on assessment in the *Guides* for reading and writing.)

- Ideally, try your hand at some of the work you are asking kids to do. There is nothing that can breathe more life into a unit than you and your colleagues giving abbreviated versions of key minilessons to yourselves and trying your hand at the work those key minilessons ask kids to do. Do the work of Day One for four minutes, then announce, "It's tomorrow" and hear an abbreviated version of Day Two's minilesson, try that work for four minutes, then perhaps bypass a session or two to get to an important upcoming one. To do this, dole out minilessons

to each other and spend no more than five minutes to prepare to teach a micro-version of that minilesson. There is lovely energy when time is limited, and people need to prepare with great urgency and then wing it, approximating it.

- On the evening before you teach a session, you might read over it this way: First, read the link at the end of the minilesson and glance at the small-group work and conferring and at any examples of student work. Aim to get clear on what you hope your kids will be doing that day. If this is an Up the Ladder unit, read the "In This Session" box to help you get an idea on what to expect that day. Next, read the teaching point. Read it several times, saying it aloud to yourself until you feel at home with the song of it. Next, check out the teaching, noticing which method you'll use to teach and what materials you'll need. Minilessons draw upon only four methods, and these are described in the *Guides* for the reading and writing units. The active engagement section requires a similar glance. Finally, read the connection at the beginning of each session and begin tweaking the lesson so it'll work for you.

- To tweak a minilesson, you might make your notes in the Unit of Study book, probably in pencil. You might make marginal X's to signal some examples or points that you think are excessive and that can be deleted, or make notes on how to rewrite an anecdote or to alter a reference so it fits your class. If you are altering a piece of writing or an anecdote, you might do this on a Post-it that replaces a bit of the published minilesson. You will probably star parts of a minilesson to deliver almost verbatim and note parts that you can improvise. This process of reading over a minilesson should take no longer than it takes to deliver the minilesson—about ten minutes. The preparation is usually done with the assumption that you will be holding the book as you teach, but not reading directly from it, save for perhaps reading the teaching point to make sure you hold to those words, and probably reading some quotations, perhaps some lists.

■ Then lesson planning involves thinking about the remaining forty minutes of the workshop. You might read over the small-group and conferring write-ups from that day, reviewing earlier and later write-ups as well. You'll find precious additional help in charts within the *If . . . Then . . . Curriculum: Assessment-Based Instruction* books for your grade level's writing units. You might study whatever student work you have access to so as to group kids that have similar needs, then you could develop tools to use in those small groups and conferences.

Some Words of Caution as You Help Teachers to Plan Units

Teachers will sometimes suggest alterations. "My kids are different," they'll say, "and I'd like to tailor instruction in ways that support them." That sounds perfect, marvelous, but a word of caution. More often than not, we find that such a message is actually code for "I'd like to keep teaching the way I used to teach," or "I'd like to throw in a lot of worksheets." I strongly advise against that, especially in the first year. Doug Reeves has done research on innovations and he suggests that innovations that are done to low or average levels of implementation have very little chance of accelerating achievement. Innovations that are done to high degrees of implementation have high likelihood that they'll accelerate achievement.

Yes, we hope teachers take the eighteen to twenty sessions in a unit of study and teach the unit for five weeks, which means adding in sessions that essentially give kids more time to do the work they've been taught. Teachers may also delete a session or two that seem too challenging for all their kids and turn those sessions into small-group work. Deleting a few sessions gives teachers another opportunity for adding in some teacher-authored sessions that are responsive to the needs a teacher sees before her. When teachers author their own sessions, they may decide that the content of a share session or a small-group write-up is so important that it merits more time, and they write that content into a minilesson. Teachers may also prepare an additional session that helps kids get ready for the celebration.

Before turning from this topic, we need to address the challenge that teachers face if their kids are operating at proficiency levels that are well below the levels for which a unit is intended. If these are students in grades 4–6 writing workshop, we encourage teachers to rely on the Up the Ladder series to accelerate kids' progress. Those units do not replace the regular units, but they function as ramps, helping students become prepared for the grade-specific units. For other subjects and grade levels, teachers may want to borrow Units of Study from earlier grades to help prepare their students for grade-level work. Teachers can't teach the entire year from an earlier grade and still be in compliance, but if your sixth-graders are reading L–O levels of books, for example, teachers may profit from borrowing Unit 3 or 4 from third grade as a quick launch into reading. If your second-graders don't yet know that they can write a sentence, teachers might borrow the kindergarten opinion-writing unit and teach that to their second-graders, adapting it somewhat. Most units are written in such a way that (with some adaptations) they would even be challenging and fun for you and me, so certainly they'd be applicable to children a year or two ahead. Just be sure that within the scope of a child's year, that child also has access to grade-specific curriculum. That is, use this as a ramp.

Finally, a word about how lesson planning changes as teachers become more familiar with the units and more proficient with workshop teaching. You will find that your teachers are engaged in a continual process of revision and improvement of their teaching. For example, a cohort of teachers will decide to make their read-aloud work more aligned to their curriculum. To do that, they will select a book that they will read to their kids across all classrooms, but first they will read that book together, spying on their own reading of the book, noticing the intellectual work they are doing as they read. They will probably think about ways they could invite kids to do similar work as they participate in the read-aloud. They'll place Post-its where they'll pause in the read-aloud to think aloud. They might then pull back and ask, "What is the theory that is informing this plan? Is that actually the theory we want to live by?" They'll get input from others and then revise their plans. This is lesson planning—and professional development—at its best.

The time is here for a revolution in lesson planning, and the urgency to turn schools into places where kids and teachers are on fire with learning makes this the work we all need to be doing today. The conversations that we have around our teaching, reading, writing, and leading make us into the thinkers and people we are—and lesson planning is just one more forum for those conversations.

Observing Teachers and Giving Feedback in Ways that Support First Goals

When observing teachers who are teaching Units of Study, it will help you if you have guidelines for the priorities that you should see in the classroom that will indicate successful implementation of each particular unit. TCRWP has developed such "Look Fors" for the schools with which we partner. For example, here is a snippet of the list of "Look Fors" for fourth-grade reading unit one, Interpreting Characters.

When you enter a classroom and students are engaged in this unit, you might look for:

■ Students are matched to texts. If teachers have the assessment data from the year before, then they could decide to just get students into books at those levels and hold off on doing the more formal assessments until the middle of the unit. If teachers do not have levels from last year or you are concerned about if those last year levels truly match your readers, then you will want to be sure that teachers are assessing students to get them matched to books. Either way, you want to be sure that assessment does not take over reading workshop. You want to see the unit starting in the first days of school and moving along.

■ As part of this, you'll want to make sure that teachers assess their classroom libraries relative to the projected reading levels of their students to ensure that they have enough books to keep students reading a high volume in this and future units.

■ Look to see how teachers have organized their classroom libraries. Many teachers put out some sections of their libraries at the start of the year and hold other sections back until later units. In general, you will want to look to see that they have organized their libraries in ways that are engaging and accessible to students.

We've included the full version of this list, and similar "Look Fors" for every grade's first unit of the year in the online resources that accompany this book, and encourage you to either partner with TCRWP or to develop your own guidelines for other units.

5

Help Teachers Lift the Level of Their Methods of Teaching

When teaching a reading or writing workshop, your teachers will draw on only a few methods of teaching. Those methods will be used repeatedly—and the methods are mostly the same whether one is teaching five-year-olds or fifteen-year-olds reading or writing. And when a teacher becomes more skilled at any of these methods, those skills will pay off in every day's instruction, across every unit of study. If you want to rally your entire faculty to work together to become more skilled at a method of instruction, this work can involve everyone and will have benefits for everyone. This also means that if a few teachers become particularly strong at one method or another, you can use those teachers' skills to lift the level of everyone's skills, schoolwide.

Interestingly enough, methods of teaching reading and writing have great transference to other curriculum areas, starting with math. But that is another topic, for another book!

There are five particularly important methods of instruction, and each of these has been written about very clearly in the *Guides* that are part of every Unit of Study kit and are also sold separately. The key methods are these:

- Giving effective minilessons

- Conferring

- Leading small groups

- Reading aloud and supporting a whole-class book talk

- Managing workshop instruction

IN THIS CHAPTER, YOU'LL FIND . . .

► Descriptions of key teaching methods used in workshop instruction and ways you can support teachers at getting better at these, including:

  ► minilessons
  ► conferring
  ► small-group instruction
  ► reading aloud

► Ways to help teachers to develop the classroom management techniques needed for effective workshop instruction

As the school leader, you do not need to be an expert on these methods—your most skilled teachers will probably be better at these than you will be—but it is helpful for you to have a bird's-eye synopsis of what matters most in each of these methods, some tips about the sorts of hints that teachers especially benefit from, and guidance about resources you can draw upon when attempting to help your teachers.

One Key Method: Giving Effective Minilessons

The first method that your teachers will need to learn, the one that will have the most immediate payoff, involves giving effective minilessons. When teachers lead effective minilessons, those short bursts of instruction will mobilize the whole community to be on fire as readers and writers and will immerse the kids in an understanding of the important work they are doing. Although small-group instruction and conferring are critically important, when teachers are skilled at giving minilessons, that teaching can drive a huge amount of progress. Those minilessons can also create the context in which conferring and small-group work is feasible—because kids are engaged in their work.

To help teachers become skilled at giving minilessons, you and they need an image of what an effective minilesson feels and sounds like. If you go to the video orientations that are on both TCRWP's website and in the online resources for each reading and writing unit of study, you can watch a TCRWP staff developer giving a minilesson and follow along on the written minilesson as you watch, noticing ways in which the person does and does not stay close to the text or refer to it as she teaches. Know also that we recently videotaped eighty minilessons—all of the ones we wrote for the Up the Ladder: Accessing Grades 3–6 Units of Study writing series—and you and your teachers could also watch these.

A minilesson should feel like a huddle at a football game—or like read-aloud time. The kids pull close, and the teacher leans forward in her chair and talks directly, simply, briskly to them, then shows them how to do something, demonstrating. At certain points in the minilesson, kids talk with a partner for a minute or two, or jot an idea, then the teacher reconvenes the class. The minilesson is brisk. It usually lasts about ten minutes.

You need to be clear about what does *not* happen during a minilesson. The kids are not all facing the screen with the teacher off to the side. Neither the kids nor the teacher are reading from a PowerPoint. The teacher also does not elicit the content of the minilesson through a question-and-answer format that goes on forever! Children usually talk in pairs and sometimes jot during a mini-lesson—that interval lasts a minute or two, and is not followed with one or two children (only) reporting back and the whole group listening.

During the minilesson, you should be able to follow what the teacher is teaching the kids, to learn with them. And the minilesson should feel highly engaging to both you and to the kids.

Teachers will tell you that they cannot give the minilessons in the Units of Study books in ten minutes. They'll say the minilessons are too wordy. They may even ask for someone to abbreviate the contents. They are right that

some sessions may need to be weeded. My colleagues and I look at some of the middle school and upper-grade writing units and itch to do a bit of pruning. But here's the thing: different parts *should* be pruned for different classes of kids. And even the parts that might get pruned are important for teachers to know—think of those parts as staff development. The units we've written more recently—the reading units, the Up the Ladder units, and the primary units—do not seem too long to us. We can easily teach those minilessons within ten minutes, and your teachers will learn to be able to do so too.

So how do you help your teachers learn to give quick, lively minilessons—and to do so easily?

In graduate classrooms and summer institutes at Teachers College, when we want to help people become more effective at leading minilessons, we start by locating two fairly straightforward minilessons, usually ones that are taught in sequence. Most minilessons in K–2 and in the Up the Ladder series are fairly accessible, so we direct people to one or two of those minilessons. We try to choose minilessons that have been videotaped. (As I mentioned previously, all the Up the Ladder minilessons have been recorded on video.) 👏

After distributing one minilesson or another to the teachers, we ask them to read and talk through their minilesson. Usually in a group of four people, two work on one minilesson, two on another. Each partnership talks through what the end goal of their minilesson seems to be, gleaning this goal from the link section of the minilesson and by reading the section that describes the conferring and small group that follow the minilesson. Then we ask each partnership to spend a few minutes with their minilesson's teaching point, saying it over and over until it feels almost like a mantra. The teaching point is the heart of the minilesson and crystallizes what is being taught in that day's minilesson. Occasionally, a few small tweaks might make the teaching point easier to say aloud, but mostly the challenge is to internalize it, to hold it close. When we are writing the minilessons, it often takes a few hours to craft a single teaching point, and many minilessons harken back to teaching points from previous days.

We then ask folks to look over the teaching portion of their minilesson, analyzing the method used in the teaching. Is the teacher teaching by demonstration, in which case the teaching will be a how-to text, showing kids steps 1, 2, 3 for doing something? There are a few alternate methods that could be used instead. We also ask teachers to think about how they'll pull off that part of the minilesson in just a few minutes.

People also look over the active engagement, the "now you try it" part of a minilesson. Often that part channels kids to work with an entirely different text—perhaps with a book the class read earlier, a picture book, another student's writing or the teacher's (pretend) writing. Sometimes teachers alter this, channeling kids to use this time to plan how they'll apply the teaching to their own writing.

After setting each partnership up to talk over their minilesson, we suggest that the partners break their minilessons into parts and prepare to jigsaw deliver it to the other partnership. The two who deliver a minilesson can mark it up, noting places where they may actually almost read the text and places where they can totally improvise it. They think about gestures they can add, times they might stand up, lean close, hold the book, put the book down. After reading and talking about the minilesson, each person takes three minutes to get his or her part ready to deliver. Then, each partnership delivers its minilesson to the other partnership. The partners give each other feedback, and if there is time, they redo the minilesson. The second time, they time the minilesson, making sure it lasts no more than ten minutes.

TCRWP once brought in a public speaking coach to work with us. At his direction, one after another of us jumped to our feet at the front of the room to give an off-the-cuff speech, addressing a topic on which the person had no advance notice. After each person spoke, the coach would give him or her (and in so doing, the rest of us) some feedback. Then, that person would try his or her little talk over again, incorporating the feedback. The coach suggested that we use bigger gestures, remembering that the air between one's arms and one's body conveys an air of confidence. Instead of pausing mid-sentence and adding an "ummmm" to hold that pause, we could pause at the punctuation and remain silent as we thought of what to say next. If we were standing, we could plant our feet solidly on the floor and stand still, without twisting and turning.

That day was full of whoops and hollers, and we had an absolute blast! If opportunities to learn to deliver more effective minilessons felt a bit like that day, then across the world, reading and writing workshops would be transformed.

Another Key Method: Conferring

When I help teachers understand conferring, I do so by asking them to think about a time when their principal observed them to give them feedback. I say, "Think about a time when that interaction not only felt good but also lifted the level of your teaching in lasting ways." I ask them to contrast that memory with the memory of a time that was just the opposite. "What was the difference?" I ask.

You could do this same exercise, and chances are your answers would match your teachers' answers. If you think of a time when someone watched you and gave you feedback in ways that lifted the level of your work, it's probably the case that the observer saw more in you than you saw in yourself. Your coach probably saw potential in you that you hadn't even recognized and rallied you to work with new zeal to actualize that potential.

Remember that insight when you watch your teachers confer with young writers and readers. As Don Murray always used to say, "In a good conference, the writer leaves, wanting to write. The writer's energy for writing should go up, not down."

Help teachers internalize the architecture of a conference.

It is worth helping teachers internalize the architecture of a conference, because a conference illustrates principles of good teaching that will always be important—and will be important in any discipline. In the hurry of classroom teaching, we all give conferences that are less than the complete, perfect conference—but still, knowing how to confer well matters.

A reading or writing conference, like a teaching observation, begins with the teacher listening, researching. Often the teacher will ask open-ended questions such as, "What are you working on lately as a reader? What new work have you been trying to do?" That question can be asked in a flippant voice and will result in a curt answer, or it can be asked as if this is the biggest and most important question of all. Tone matters.

The important thing is that to help someone, the teacher needs to know what the learner is trying to do, planning to do next, and what the learner thinks about the work. So this research phase of a conference is the time when the teacher listens, trying to figure out what the youngster usually does as she reads or writes, what the youngster is about to do next, how the child assesses what she has done. The listener asks questions such as, "Is this one of the best pieces of writing you have ever done, or is it more in the middle? What would you do to make this even better, if you were going to work more on it?"

After researching to understand the learner's intentions, strategies, and next steps, the teacher then makes a compliment. Ideally the teacher compliments something that the learner has just started to do, something on the learner's growing edge. "Do you realize how huge it is that you linger at the ends of chapters like that? Most kids don't—I'd love for you to teach the class that someday."

Then the conference turns to the teaching. Usually this part of a conference begins with the teacher asking if it is okay for her to give a quick tip, and then the teacher teaches in a way that resembles the teaching point of a minilesson. That is, instead of saying, "What do you think of the father in this story?" the teacher teaches more explicitly. "You are growing ideas about the main character, which is great. You'll find that any book becomes even more interesting if you can think in equally deep ways about some of the minor characters. It can help to ask, 'Why might the author have included this person in this story?' For example, what are your thoughts about the father?" A good teaching point is relevant not only to the current text but to future texts as well.

In a conference, once the teacher has set a learner up to do some work, she might take a minute to show the learner how she would do that sort of work, and/or she might ask the learner to get started doing that work while she watches, coaching into what the learner is doing. In a sense, those portions of a conference are like the teaching and active engagement sections of a minilesson. Sometimes in a conference, the teacher senses that the youngster doesn't need more support, that he or she is ready to dive in and try whatever it is the teacher has taught.

Help your teachers get better at conferring.

When teachers are new to workshop teaching, they sometimes watch experienced teachers confer and marvel at how spontaneous and yet how on-point the teaching seems, as if the experienced teacher had pulled the perfect teaching point out of thin air. The truth is, the best conferences are not really spontaneous, but are based on a great deal of study and planning. To support your teachers in getting better at small-group instruction and conferring, a good starting point is to refer them to the conferring chapters in their *Guides,* and then channel them to watch some of the conferring videos on the TCRWP site, talking between those videos and the chapters that discuss conferring. The *If . . . Then . . . Curriculum: Assessment-Based Instruction* books within the writing Units of Study kits also contain an if/then chart that helps teachers anticipate the most common conferences they are likely to give.

Above all, however, every session in the units sets teachers up for the conferring that he or she will be apt to do that day. The challenge is that teachers often don't take the time to read those sections, focusing all their planning time instead on the minilesson. Help them to realize that when teaching with the support of a unit of study, the fact that the book exists should hopefully free teachers up to be able to spend more time studying student work and thinking about ways to lift the level of that work.

Another Key Method: Small Groups

Help teachers understand the value of small-group instruction.

Small groups are key to helping students practice and improve their reading and writing skills. They allow teachers to efficiently help students lift the level of their work, while providing students with more of the teacher's focused attention. But small groups can sometimes be a source of anxiety for teachers. The units of study provide support for small groups in each individual unit, and the *Guide* that accompanies each grade-level set provides a full chapter to support teachers' work with small groups. But teachers will also need your support and encouragement as they gain experience with workshop teaching.

The most important thing to say about small groups is that you should see them happening! One of the reasons it is so critical to establish a well-managed workshop early on, where readers and writers know how to carry on independently, is that this allows teachers to focus their attention on conferences and flexible small groups. While kids are immersed in their writing or reading, teachers can pull together not just one but several small groups each day. There needs to be a clear message that leading small groups is totally important—and also totally doable.

All children deserve some small-group instruction. Some will benefit from help with reading comprehension, or with ways to elaborate to support opinions they are writing about, or with using short vowels to spell new words, or with using academic vocabulary to talk about a character's personality. No matter the focus, small groups are meant as assessment-based instruction designed to take kids further. The teacher gathers some information on what students need and are ready to learn, either prior to workshop or on-the-run during work time, and gathers a group of students who share a similar need. The teacher might get a small group going, then leave that group working while she launches another small group or checks in with or confers with other students. The teacher then returns to work again with the members of that first small group.

Help teachers get better at small-group instruction.

When you watch small groups, you'll want to be looking for children to be as active as possible. Small-group work serves a different purpose from minilessons. Whereas in minilessons, you'd expect to see the teacher doing a fair amount of talking, in small groups you'd expect to see students actively engaged in individual or collaborative work, while the teacher coaches in, offering lean prompts to raise the level of that work. The idea is for the teacher to support students in work that is just beyond what they are doing independently, while the teacher shifts between observing, coaching, and scaffolding that higher-level work.

To coach and support each learner, the teacher needs to get students working independently or in pairs, so they do one thing and then the next thing and then the next, without needing to wait for the teacher to give them the next set of instructions. If a teacher is teaching a group on raising the level of writing a summary, for example, instead of saying, "First look at these samples of summaries and read each one," which would lead students to follow one step and then wait for the teacher again, the teacher is more apt to say, "Will you look at these samples of summaries and assess which one is most like yours? Then set a goal for yourself." As the students get started doing that work, soon the teacher can follow up with, "Once you have your goal, start revising your summary." Students can then carry on with their work, freeing the teacher to coach and support each student in the way that student most needs.

As you're watching, you also might look to see who does the majority of the work. The cognitive load should always be on the students. If you see the teacher talking almost the whole time, the students probably aren't getting enough practice time. Remember that they are getting pulled from their reading or writing to be in this small group, so the group needs to help raise the level of their work and afford them the opportunity to practice.

In general, small-group work is more effective when teachers lead fast and frequent sessions on a topic across time instead of leading one heavyweight small-group lesson every few weeks. It helps to work with a particular small group for no more than ten minutes a day, spread out over three days, rather than for a half hour stretch of time. The added advantage of more frequent, shorter sessions is that teachers can release scaffolds, increasing the complexity of the work as they can turn more of the work over to the students in each subsequent session. When you observe a small group, then, you won't necessarily expect that the students will all master the skill being taught by the end of the group. When the group ends, you might ask the teacher his plans for next steps to get a sense of how (and if) he plans to support students toward independence with the skill.

Reading Aloud and Leading a Whole-Class Book Talk

Help teachers understand the power of read-aloud.

Although the read-aloud happens outside of reading workshop at a separate time, when done well, the read-aloud becomes the engine and the bedrock of reading workshop. Read-aloud helps to create a community of readers and builds a culture of valuing and savoring reading. During read-aloud, the class gathers close as the teacher reads aloud to them. Students laugh and gasp and perhaps cry over the books their teacher reads. The characters become as well known to them as friends, and nonfiction topics become every child's new fascination. And so, read-aloud time helps to build a community of people who know the same stories and bond over books.

During read-aloud, students see a model of proficient, engaged reading. They'll see all of the strategies they learn in reading workshop come together and work in conjunction with one another, and they'll have a chance to practice those strategies. In these ways, read-aloud becomes interactive and almost like a scrimmage to prepare for the game of independent reading. Then too, read-aloud powers the reading workshop because during minilessons, when teachers demonstrate a strategy, they will want to demonstrate on a text that is familiar to the class—and what better text than the read-aloud? In addition, teachers can refer to the read-aloud in their small-group work and conferences to support students in practicing comprehension strategies. A read-aloud can also be used as a mentor text for writing, and so read-aloud can power not just reading, but also writing workshop.

Help teachers get better at conducting read-alouds.

To help teachers get a vision for what interactive read-aloud looks like, you might encourage them to watch the videos of interactive read-aloud and whole-class conversation on the TCRWP website (www.readingandwritingproject.org) and Vimeo page (vimeo.com/tcrwp). You (or your literacy coach or other support staff) might help teachers notice that read-aloud should feel intimate, with students gathered close. The entire read-aloud feels interactive, with prompts, gestures, and pauses that aim to keep students listening and thinking actively, alongside the teacher. The teacher makes these moments feel like she is truly thinking and mulling over parts. Her tone is ruminative: "Hmm, . . . I'm pausing here because I'm starting to notice . . . I'm beginning to wonder . . ." At other points in the read-aloud, the teacher channels the students to turn and talk, stop and jot, or act out a scene. All of these bits of interactions have the goals of bolstering engagement and helping students practice the thinking work the text seems to be calling readers to do.

Occasionally, in the middle or at the end of a read-aloud, the teacher might channel the class to have a longer book talk about the text. This conversation is also referred to as a whole-class or grand conversation, because the intention is for the whole class to take part in it and ideally, for the class to take responsibility for running the conversation. In this sort of conversation, the teacher often begins by asking students to talk in partnerships to get ready, and then invites one student to start off the whole-class conversation. This conversation should sound like a journey of thought, with students contributing organically, disagreeing with each other at times, and growing new thinking through the conversation.

Though the teacher is not a major voice in the conversation, the teacher can still do a great deal to support the goal of the conversation as a journey of thought. Much of this work happens on the outskirts of the conversation. Expect to see the teacher dipping in and out among students, whispering quietly to one student, then leaving that student to whisper to another. The teacher is working to prompt the students to help them enter the conversation, to support them in building onto what others have said, to get them to hold others accountable for referring to the text, to raise a new perspective on what is being discussed.

The teacher can display (and nonverbally remind students to use) talk charts, providing students with sentence prompts that support them in building on each other's ideas ("I also think . . ." "Can you say more?" "So what you're saying is . . ." "What you just said makes me wonder . . ." "Can you give an example?") The goal is to hear students question each other and build a conversation about the book, referencing the text.

In middle school classrooms, where there is often not enough time for a separate read-aloud time, the Units of Study suggest teachers begin each new bend of reading workshop with a read-aloud. This read-aloud then threads through the rest of the bend in the minilessons, anchoring the unit.

Managing Workshop Instruction

Classroom management is a very big deal—but sometimes, the message has gone out that only novice teachers struggle with classroom management. Teachers can end up feeling ashamed if they need help with management, as if that is a sure sign of a deficiency. You'll want to alter that message, right away.

To do so, think for a moment about your own version of "classroom management." For us, as leaders of TCRWP, managing our wonderful team of people is not easy. Often, creative, inspired, overworked people cut short procedural details. This is understandable, but the consequence is that some people spend endless hours chasing after and cleaning up after their colleagues, learning time is sacrificed, and in general, efficiency is lost. So yes, the leaders of TCRWP have trouble managing our workers. We ask for them to file receipts, to answer surveys, to sign up for groups, and when some of them need constant reminders, we have trouble figuring out how to institute structures and systems that actually work, so that no one needs to spend their life hounding people. You no doubt have your own parallel management challenges—the adult version of classroom management is a challenge for any organizational leader. Keeping our people working to the maximum, with the greatest possible levels of efficiency, will inevitably be a challenge. It helps to realize this is a challenge for most leaders.

Chances are good that classroom management could be strengthened in many, if not most, of your classrooms, if you and your teachers really pause to think about it. Many former teachers from KIPP (Knowledge Is Power Program) schools gravitate to TCRWP, and whenever they participate in our graduate programs, intern at our best schools, or join the staffs of those schools, they help us look at our classroom management through new lenses, noticing the number of wasted minutes in a day. From this indirect source, we've deduced that the culture at KIPP schools seems to be one in which the message is crystal clear: learners need their eyes, their ears, their whole selves to be on-task, engaged, deep in the work. Every minute matters. If the tape dispenser needs to be passed among the kids in the meeting area, this needs to be a "fast-pass" that takes two minutes flat. Coming to the meeting area takes less than that. We could all learn from this mindset!

Experienced teachers can also think about whether their classroom management is teaching kids independence and interdependence. If the expectation is that at the end of every reading workshop, kids chart the number of pages they read that day, why would a teacher need to remind kids to do that on the tenth day of the school year, let alone the seventy-fifth? Don't we want to teach kids to assume more responsibility for self-monitoring?

When you address classroom management in a helpful, respectful, and collaborative way, you remind teachers that it's not just the students who are constantly learning and striving toward improvement, but that you are all part of a community of learners.

Our point is that you need to elevate the topic so that there is no stigma to teachers who are working on classroom management. Tell your staff that you are going to work on your version of classroom management, and then start addressing teachers who need constant reminders of due dates for paperwork, who come late to meetings, or who are on their cell phones inappropriately, acknowledging for teachers that you, like them, need to build systems that support efficiency and focus.

When you address classroom management in a helpful, respectful, and collaborative way, you send a clear message that improving classroom management isn't a task just for the novice teacher, but that even many experienced teachers can find ways to do things a little better, a little more efficiently, a little more effectively. When you create a culture of trust and support, you remind teachers that it's not just the students who are constantly learning and striving toward improvement, but that you are all part of a community of learners—students, teachers, and even you yourself.

For teachers who do need help on classroom management, here are some ideas:

Suggestions for Helping Teachers with Classroom Management

■ It can be valuable for an outsider to help a teacher get the year off to a good start. Sometimes classrooms become train wrecks and small incremental changes aren't enough. The teachers need an intervention. After a three-day weekend, kids can then come back to a new room arrangement, new seating chart, a new focus on how everyday structures will go. Perhaps someone coteaches in order to help the room get off to a second start. The "new start" should feel celebratory and fun, not punitive and micro-controlled.

■ Encourage teachers to think through each of the repetitive everyday structures in their reading and writing workshops with as much care as they'd think about hosting a wedding. Just as you think, "Where will the guests put their coats?" you need to think, "How will we get the kids to the meeting area?" Then, just as you think, "How do the guests get their coats at the end of the evening?" you think, "How will we keep the kids who arrive later into the meeting area to keep from stepping on the hands of the others?"

■ Help teachers think about the things that will be done every day, and figure out the smoothest, most efficient way to do those things—then literally train kids in how to do those things. Instead of the teacher in the meeting area distributing one paper to each of the thirty-two kids, distributing a second paper to those kids, then the same for a purple Post-it for each child, the teacher might decide to stack the materials that will get distributed into row-sized piles on the right edge of the meeting area, with each child's two papers secured together with a paper clip. Then the teacher asks, "Row leaders, will you distribute your materials?" There is

nothing especially important about that way of distributing papers, but the point is that everything a teacher does every day can be thought through in a once-and-for-all way.

■ Certainly the teacher will want to avoid chaos when possible, so if management is a problem, teachers might want kids to keep their books (today's and tomorrow's, plus their reading log and their Post-its) in a book bag strapped to their chairs. Partners may sit beside each other during reading time. Kids will have assigned seats in the meeting area, with the more disruptive kids front and center, intermixed with some of the more diligent students.

■ You might also make time for teachers to visit classrooms of those teachers who have especially good classroom management, and to get one-to-one coaching from one of those teachers.

■ When management is a problem, often the pace is too slow. Think about times you have hosted a birthday party for a young child. If the kids are acting crazy, one of the easiest ways to manage them is to keep things hopping. A new game! Time to play on the swings! Here's some cake! Children become disruptive because they are bored. Picking up the pace can help with engagement.

■ It helps to think, "When there are high levels of engagement, what do kids do?" Do they listen raptly to the read-aloud? If this is a class that needs to learn what that nice productive buzz feels like and if read-aloud supports engagement, then for gosh sake, read aloud three times a day!

- Be sure that any teacher who struggles with classroom management is extra-prepared for the content he or she is teaching. It can help to give that teacher (or those teachers) release time to practice upcoming minilessons with a colleague or a coach or to prepare for a few high-impact small groups. This preparation will give that teacher increased confidence, and that confidence is contagious.

- In classrooms in which children get wildly off task, often pacing is off in two ways–the teacher is taking too much time to teach and explain, so that teacher talk is long, and he or she is giving kids too much time for what was meant to be quick interactions such as partner talk. When teachers move briskly from instruction to independent practice, kids literally don't have time to get off task.

6 From Good to Great: Supporting Teachers' Continued Growth

esearchers are clear that when we take on a new learning project, our growth curve accelerates for a few years—and then it plateaus. Because most of my time and the time of other members of the Teachers College Reading and Writing Project is spent supporting schools that partner with us for years, even for decades, we have a lot of experience helping school leaders take good schools and make them great. Our primary focus, in fact, is on helping teachers to outgrow that predictable plateau that occurs when their teaching begins to feel like "been there, done that." We laughingly refer to that sort of perfunctory, almost rote teaching as "rinse and repeat."

Nurture your own and your teachers' sense of possibilities.

If you have visited one of the TCRWP's mentor schools, you'll understand the value of supporting good schools to become great schools. It is hard to find the words that do justice to the beauty one feels in those schools. Every time we return to one of the two or three dozen or so mentor schools in and around New York City, we literally pinch ourselves because the learning community in those schools feels so intensely alive. Over the past few years, we've seen schools throughout the world become equally amazing, and those schools, like our best local schools, provide horizons for everyone. The question is—how does a good school become a great school?

IN THIS CHAPTER, YOU'LL FIND . . .

▶ Ways to lift the level of instruction in your school from good to great, including:

  ▶ Visiting strong schools to set a vision for what is possible

  ▶ Supporting teachers' unit planning, including tips for revising existing units and for authoring new ones

  ▶ Making the study of student work a priority

  ▶ Offering workshops to ignite professional study, using toolkit making as a case in point

First, it will help if you, your school leaders, and your teachers nurture your own image of possibilities by visiting a school that is even farther along than your school. When you visit such a school, you'll see possible next steps for your own school. If you study the roster of institutes that TCRWP offers during the calendar year, you'll note that almost half of those institutes include a day of visiting schools together—know that those days are the favorite part of every institute. Visits like this make a big difference.

When Jamie, a principal you'll hear more about in an upcoming chapter, traveled with his teachers to visit a school that had been with TCRWP longer than his school had, he later told me that what he noticed was an intellectual depth to the teachers' and the kids' thinking. "In lots of ways, our school was similar to theirs," he said. "We could check off the things we already have in place. But what I noticed and I helped my teachers to notice was that there was a quality to the teachers' responses to kids, to the whole-class conversations, to the conferences, to our discussion with the teachers afterward, which made me think that our school needs to work toward more depth, more thoughtfulness, more intellectual engagement—on everyone's part." It is the mark of a great principal that he celebrates the realization that he and his teachers have a distance still to go, and helps his teachers embrace that idea as well.

At most of TCRWP's strongest schools, the principal works really hard to figure out next steps. At PS 158, the principal always asks one of the Project's leaders to join her and her grade-level leaders on a day in mid-May that is

devoted to next steps. The teacher-leaders, assistant principals, principal, building-based coach, and TCRWP leaders devote an entire day to studying student work, visiting classrooms, voicing bits of disequilibrium—all in the service of homing in on a horizon that will capture the imagination of the school's educators and make a significant difference. You need to have a horizon that you can reach toward—and your people need that as well. Award-winning poet Lucille Clifton once said, "Nurture your image of possibilities. You cannot create what you cannot imagine."

To support true excellence in a school or a district, the leaders need to understand the value of creating mentor classrooms and mentor schools. The tendency in education is to focus professional development dollars and time on the work of supporting new or less effective teachers and schools, and there is no question that that work needs to be done. But the Teachers College Reading and Writing Project has illustrated for the world that there are important reasons also to help teachers and schools make the journey from good to great, and that is especially important if those teachers and those schools embrace the role of helping others. Of course, the work of helping others is work that makes all of us wiser and more full of zeal, so once a teacher or a school becomes engaged in mentoring others, that teacher and that school's learning curve become sky-high.

TCRWP works with a number of huge counties that are implementing this work countywide, and more often than not, they bring us in to do two kinds of work. First, we do very large-scale days, such as a day with all fifth-grade teachers countywide, or with all reading specialists/literacy coaches countywide. And second, we work intensely in a handful of selected schools that dot the county. I recently asked a county leader from Georgia how the schools in which we are doing on-the-ground professional development are selected. She explained, "Some of them are among our best schools. We're taking fabulous schools and trying to create our own local lab sites that illustrate what's possible—rather like the schools you have in New York City that do that for us." Other focal schools are chosen because when those schools improve, the message will go out that this approach works for all kids.

Just as it helps a district to develop lab site schools, it helps a school to create classrooms that embody the best possible reading and writing workshop instruction. You might consider sending your most knowledgeable teachers to institutes and devising professional development opportunities that allow those great teachers to continue learning together. Meanwhile, perhaps your novice teachers can receive their professional development from that teacher who has just been sent to New York City! That is, when you think about which teachers can be supported from within the school and which will need help from outside, you may decide to bring TCRWP staff members or other national experts in to help your especially strong teachers become even stronger.

Help teachers reflect upon and revise units.

Another way to help teachers go from good to great, once you've helped them set a vision for what is possible, is to support them in developing a more sophisticated, nuanced approach to unit planning. When teachers are first learning to use Units of Study, they'll often stay very close to each session and to the trajectory of the unit as these are written. That is just fine, and it's a valuable way for teachers to learn about this kind of instruction. As teachers become more experienced, you'll find that they develop a different relationship with the units. Teachers within a grade level will begin to talk among themselves about adaptations they want to make, as a group, to the units. These are examples of the sorts of revisions that you'll see experienced teachers mulling over:

- Might we find a way, early on, to give kids a better sense of the unit's goal? Could we show them a video or a mentor text or provide more examples of good work?

- Might we decide to insert two or three days of work, highlighting a skill that isn't presently highlighted (as in supporting more narrative nonfiction)? If so, what will be cut to keep the unit the current length?

- Might we tighten some of the minilessons and increase the likelihood that they have traction by removing the practice text that threads through the active engagement section of many minilessons? Instead, we might channel kids to get started on that day's work during that part of the minilesson.

- Might we alter the topic that is studied throughout the unit, perhaps adjusting to new standards or to local emphases (e.g., the American Revolution isn't critical to schools in Japan, or forces and motion don't align with some states' science curriculum)?

- Might we substitute another read-aloud text or another mentor text, perhaps choosing one that is more culturally relevant to the school's population?

- Might we draw on our experience teaching particular sessions to improve those sessions?

- Might we bring our own writing front and center, instead of relying on the existing writing examples?

These are all wise revisions for teachers to make after they have taught the units for a year or two, and we hope that you dive into similar sorts of revisions. When a teacher says, "Most of my students are from Southeast Asia, so I want to include a picture book that will increase those students' sense of belonging," you'll absolutely want to embrace that instinct. Cultural relevance matters. When authoring units, we talk to teachers and librarians, comb through book lists, read and read and read, trying to find fresh texts written by a wide variety of authors, representing many different kinds of families, cultures, and individuals. We try to choose books that will engage kids, as well as reward the strategic thinking highlighted in the unit. And teachers who know their students are even better poised to do that work, if they have tons of time in which to do it.

In most cases, these revisions are best done after teachers have taught the existing units with fidelity for a few years (with the exception of a change in content focus, which may need to be altered right away). You will probably want to put some constraints on the process of revising the units, because you presumably do not want every teacher at a grade level to do this work in isolation, without discussing their intentions with each other. The risk of supporting an "anything goes," individualistic approach to the units is this: the units would no longer function as a common curriculum that binds teachers together across the grade level in ways that channel the more experienced teachers to support the less experienced teachers.

A great way for teachers to share their experience with this curriculum is to talk through proposed adjustments to a unit, deciding together whether those adjustments become long-term adjustments, shared by all teachers across the grade. If a teacher invents a minilesson that supports more work on a particular skill, encourage that teacher to bring a draft of that minilesson to her colleagues, to get their suggestions for improving it and to eventually put a draft into the file or binder that represents the cumulative, best thinking about that unit. Those files or binders need to be available to all teachers, so they can draw upon each other's collective experiences.

You also will probably want to be sure that teachers don't get themselves into a position in which every night they are committed to rewriting the existing minilessons. This often happens when teachers substitute another book for the current one in a unit, but don't comb all the revisions throughout the unit beforehand. The work involved in weaving a new book into a unit takes a great deal of time and considerable thought—threading carefully chosen parts of the new book into each minilesson in ways that support it, and that allow the text to be read aloud concurrently with the flow of that unit.

If your sixth-grade teachers, for example, decide to substitute one short story that now weaves through a unit for another, making that substitution will probably require at least forty hours of preparation time. It will be similarly ambitious to do that work with a third- or fourth-grade unit. This requires some full days of collaborative unit development and shouldn't be shoehorned into weekday nights.

If your teachers are doing the work of threading a new content focus into units, such as the information reading/writing units that address historical eras, they can find support in the Units of Study Facebook pages. Countless teachers have done similar work, and many are happy to share.

Given the size of the task at hand, when teachers want to substitute a new text or text set, be sure to give them some release time, perhaps over the summer, to weave these texts across the lessons of the unit.

Help teachers create new Units of Study.

The Units of Study are written in such a way that they help teachers author their own units on topics the units do not take up. The fully fleshed-out units in each unit set will not extend across an entire school year. Teachers will need to supplement these units with one or two of their own. It is far more challenging to develop a unit than people might expect, so we encourage teachers who are game to do this to give themselves lots of supports. The most obvious supports are the synopses of units that are contained in the *If . . . Then . . . Curriculum: Assessment-Based Instruction* books that accompany most grade levels' Units of Study. For example, those books contain summaries of how an upper-grade poetry unit might go, and teachers who'd be game for a gigantic challenge could begin with that synopsis and work together to flesh out minilessons, select mentor texts, plan small-group work, design an assessment, and so forth. We encourage any teacher who tries this to write a post in our Facebook group. That teacher would probably hear from others who have attempted the same project, and they can form a support group.

In some districts, individual schools each take on a different unit. It is ideal if those schools also provide teachers with a consultant who can help with that work for a day—with help from Georgia Heard or Audra Robb on a unit on poetry or with Colleen Cruz's help on independent writing projects, for example. Often district leaders then organize a Saturday where colleagues from these schools share their unit plans.

Prioritize studying student work.

When TCRWP hires new staff developers, one big thing we do is to watch potential hires confer with readers and writers. We do this because in the end, this work is at the heart of being a skilled teacher of reading and writing. Learning to confer well is ultimately the real difference between a good teacher and a great one. In a great school, teachers study students' reading development and their writing development with rapt attentiveness. And the quality of that attentiveness is markedly different from the norm. My first book was titled *Lessons from a Child*. In a sense, a skilled teacher of reading and writing is always someone who can take lessons from a child. We pull in to listen, we study student work, and we think, "What is this youngster on the brink of doing? What next step might make the world of difference? How can I help this learner take that next step?"

Learning to confer well is ultimately the real difference between a good teacher and a great one.

When teachers engage in an effective child study, you'll often notice:

- Observations lead to questions. If a teacher notices something in one part of a draft, the obvious question is, "Is that in other parts of that draft? Was that true before now? How has this changed over time? How is this the case for other students as well?" In this way, a small observation snowballs, often becoming a more theoretical question about kids in general, or a skill in general.

- Teachers are excited to study a problem that occurs in the work of many of their students, and they welcome the idea that this problem is a reflection of their teaching. One senses that these teachers feel that pinpointing the problem is a big step toward not only helping their students, but also improving their own teaching.

- Teachers tend to talk with colleagues about what they notice. When they talk about a problem they see in their children's work, that isn't a way of putting down students, but of mulling over next steps.

- There is a lot of fluidity between talking about how children do something and talking about how adults do it. It's natural for a teacher to notice that a few children are struggling with writing good endings, say, and for the teacher to then think, "How would *I* go about writing endings?"

Studying student work and observing learners at work—and helping teachers see that work as a mirror to their teaching—is the epitome of professionalism and deserves your absolute and total support. You can encourage teachers to do more of this work by giving them release time to do it and by showcasing any instances when teachers do this work.

When teachers—and you—study student work, it will immediately be clear that kids struggle with some things. There are things they do not yet know how to do. It is important to embrace those areas for growth and to resist making them invitations to blame. Remember that people grow by embracing struggle, by tackling things that are hard for them. Your fondest hope should be that when talking about kids' development, your teachers' language shows tentativeness and accountability. "I wonder why . . ." "Maybe I haven't . . ." You should worry, though, if your teachers' talk about kids sounds like this: "Our kids should *all* master . . ." "They will *all* accomplish . . ." "In third grade, they *all* . . ."

Your hope instead is that when asked about their kids' progress toward standards, your teachers might say, "We aren't sure how . . ." "It seems like one step toward that might be . . ." "We are noticing that many kids struggle with . . . and so we're going to try . . ." "We think for now we need to first get these kids to excel at . . . and only then can we channel them to . . ." "We're aiming to start next week doing . . . and then see how . . ."

To lure your teachers to be rapt students of their own students, consider inviting them to take a representative student and work in teams to study that one student's development. You might try channeling them to look especially at one of their strongest students, just because that opens a horizon that few spotlight. Strong students, like every other student, deserve the education of a lifetime, and sometimes teachers ignore those students. We find that giving these kids horizons and invitations can go a long way. Teachers might, after studying one strong student's growth over time, brainstorm ways to nurture the growth of all their strongest students.

Offer workshops to build expertise and ignite professional study.

In an upcoming chapter, I write specifically about professional development. Certainly, creating a culture of professional study across your whole school is one of the most important ways to achieve greatness. One way to help develop that culture will be to use faculty meetings and release days in ways that tap teachers' energy for continued study of a topic that can extend across grades, subject areas, and school years. We have found that when you ask teachers to come together in a shared study, they will be especially on fire about this if their shared work produces resources they can use immediately. If yours is a school that embraces Units of Study in Reading and in Writing, one especially popular and enduring topic for such a shared study is *toolkit making*.

Before saying more—let's be clear. Teachers who are just launching Units of Study in reading or writing absolutely do not need to concern themselves with making these toolkits. This is something for teachers who have been doing this work for years and are ready to take their teaching to another level.

What is a toolkit?

The easiest way for your teachers to think about a toolkit is to hold a Unit of Study book and leaf through it, thinking, "In an ideal world, what might I need to help bring this unit to life?" Those items might include teacher-written exemplar texts, exemplars from previous students, charts from the previous grade level that support more rudimentary versions of the same skills, charts, and mentor texts. The work of making a toolkit involves imagining the individualized help students are likely to need over the course of the unit. As teachers make toolkits, they preview, select, and rehearse their small-group plans. Teachers who have a plan and resources for small groups are more likely to convene and instruct small groups!

Toolkits can be begun in a one-day study group, but they are really a compilation of materials that one makes over many years. There is no advantage to a toolkit that is thrown together quickly or made by copying someone else's resources. The goal for a workshop on toolkit making, then, is not for teachers to leave with all of the materials they'll ever need to teach the unit. The goal is to provide teachers with the setup and know-how to develop their own toolkits over time. The toolkits are a way for teachers to personalize, plan for, and collaborate around an upcoming unit. The teacher toolkits can become models for kids who may want to collect and personalize their own tools, collecting them in their writer's and reader's notebooks.

As with any workshop, it helps to have a clear agenda and to stick to it. To organize this workshop, you (or your literacy coach, or a staff developer) might use possible components of a toolkit as agenda items. Plan the amount of time you'll spend on each component, so that you get to all of them. Don't worry if teachers don't finish making each thing on the list; in fact, they won't. Just get them going and then move on to the next component.

A Plan for a Toolkit Workshop

Following is a plan for a workshop on toolkit making, organized by possible components of a toolkit. For each component, I include plans for how that part of the workshop might go.

1. Exemplar Texts Written By Teachers: We have included teacher-written exemplar texts in many of the writing units, but your teachers may wish to write their own to substitute for the ones we have provided. To begin that work, encourage teachers to become students of the curriculum, doing the work that the minilessons and small-group write-ups suggest kids do. As they develop their own pieces of writing to replace those in the published unit, it helps to hold the published examples close at hand and to almost echo-write their own pieces, so that they make similar craft moves.

For instance, teachers might study the published exemplar and decide, "I need to begin with dialogue, like the one in the unit does. It should be just two lines or so. Then, I tell about the small action I am doing . . ." The reason to do that sort of echo-writing is that every move in the published text is there for a reason, and across the unit, kids will often study those writerly moves. So it will be important for teachers to have done similar work in their own exemplar.

Of course, teachers will often decide to deliberately write their drafts so that they are briefer and simpler than the examples in the books. Some teachers will actually write two exemplar pieces—each representing very different levels of elaboration. If a teacher has those two pieces, written in similar ways but at very different levels, she'll be ready to provide all kids with model texts that are within their reach.

When teachers substitute their own writing for the writing that threads through a unit, they will need to take their writing through all the same revision steps illustrated throughout the unit. The goal is not to quickly produce a final perfect text—instead, it is to use one's own writing to teach kids the steps they can take, the strategies that will pay off.

For a reading unit, you or the person leading this workshop might ask teachers to bring a text or two to the workshop, ideally one that they will read aloud or use as a shared text. Teachers will love having some time to read parts of the text, and to try the work of the unit as they do that reading, including doing a bit of writing about reading on Post-its at a level close to what they hope their students will be able to do. They might even make multiple Post-its at different levels to make a continuum of sorts. This work will be even richer if teachers have time to share their thinking and their jotting with each other.

2. Charts and Exemplars from Earlier Grade Levels: Any skill being taught at one grade level has also been taught in a more rudimentary way at preceding grade levels, so teachers may want to select charts and exemplars from earlier grade levels to help support their students' skill development. So, for example, in fifth grade, students learn to figure out several main ideas in nonfiction text, and they learn that those main ideas may be implicit. But some fifth-graders are reading nonfiction texts written at second- or third-grade levels, and in those texts, the main idea is usually very explicit—often even stated in topic sentences.

This means that fifth-grade teachers will want to mine second- and third-grade nonfiction reading units for charts, teaching points, and exemplar texts that teach kids to look for "pop-out sentences" when they read nonfiction. Fifth-grade teachers can also look to earlier grades for strategies to help teach the skill. In a third-grade unit, for example, kids are taught that they can use their hands as graphic organizers. The palm of their hand holds their main idea and each finger, a supporting point. They learn to read, searching to find the main idea that they hold in their palm and to list support points across their fingers. That graphic, and that strategy, will be enormously helpful for a small group of fifth-graders—and so fifth-grade teachers will want to duplicate that page of the third-grade unit, probably making tiny colorful copies of the chart on heavy card stock. An envelope holding a dozen tiny cards, each with that graphic, can become part of a teacher's toolkit.

That example, of course, is one among a zillion. Think about anything your teachers will want to teach, and remember that a more concrete, more explicit, more simplified version of that has been taught in an earlier grade level. Now imagine the crosswalks that your teachers will make if they devote a day to mining the units that their colleagues know and love!

3. Tools from *Writing Pathways* or *Reading Pathways*: Both *Writing Pathways* and *Reading Pathways* include a wide range of tools to support students' learning in writing and reading workshop, and teachers may want to include some of these in their toolkits. If teachers are making toolkits to support a writing unit, for example, you might ask your coach or a willing teacher to print out small versions of the student exemplars, checklists, and teacher demonstration pieces and provide each teacher with these supplies, printed out, ready to include in their toolkits. Have on hand glue sticks, small Post-its, and colored pens or markers. Invite teachers to mark up the student exemplars using small Post-its containing items from the checklists. Doing this has the added bonus of helping teachers become more familiar with these tools. "I've been thinking about you as a writer, and it occurs to me that you might be interested in ways writers create powerful endings to their stories," your teachers might say. "I've got a few exemplars that you and your partner may want to study." When teachers have had a chance to study and make tools, they are most likely to help students use them.

If your workshop is in service of a reading unit, you can draw on *Reading Pathways* for this portion (for grades 3–6). In this case, ask the coach or teacher to print out parts of the reading learning progression that goes with the unit, along with the matching student-facing checklists. Encourage your teachers to study these and mark them up. One thing they might do is highlight descriptions that represent work that is new to a level. This new work helps teachers remember what to look for and reinforce as they confer to help readers move to the next level.

Toolkits can become more inventive and deepen ideas—and help teachers go from good to great.

As teachers become more skilled in creating toolkits, they will continually find ways to improve them. As they see year after year how useful their toolkits are, extending across grades and subject areas, they will be inspired to study new shared topics and create toolkits based on their own ideas. They'll also want to share their toolkits with teachers across content areas or perhaps with teachers in other schools or districts. The skill of toolkit making in and of itself becomes a valuable, often-used resource for all teachers.

7 Build a Culture of Ongoing Learning

*M*y colleagues and I have helped tens of thousands of schools launch and sustain reading and writing workshops. In most of those schools, people tell us that the power of this work goes beyond what happens in particular classrooms. When schools undergo a schoolwide adoption of either a reading or a writing workshop, more often than not, this leads to powerful changes in the school culture. Above all, there is renewed energy for learning on the job and for shared professional study. This is both the result of adopting Units of Study *and* the means for achieving success with this curriculum.

No single chapter can teach all you need to know about the importance of establishing a learning culture, or about ways principals have nurtured that culture, but first things first. You personally need to dignify professional learning.

As a grown-up, it is not easy to learn on the job. It can be embarrassing to mess up. It's hard to go from being an accomplished teacher within a traditional classroom environment to a novice workshop teacher.

The thing you need to realize is that teachers are now being asked to teach kids skills that we didn't learn until college, if then. When I taught fifth-graders, I was regarded as a fancy, state-of-the-art teacher because I had my students go to the *Encyclopedia Britannica* and to one trade book, copy down facts onto notecards, then cobble those facts together, add some clip art, and make a report with chapters and a construction paper cover and yarn binding. Now, fifth-graders are asked to take a provocative topic—"Is bottled water good for the environment?"—and to research it from several perspectives, studying the angle from which each source is written and the bias that informs that source, noticing the arguments and counterarguments, and then they are expected to determine their own position and to bring forward and even analyze the evidence that supports their opinion. This sort of expectation requires altogether new methods of teaching both reading and writing. So yes, teachers need to learn on the job.

> **IN THIS CHAPTER, YOU'LL FIND . . .**
>
> ► Ways to make time for teachers to plan together
>
> ► Tips to ensure collaborative groups go well
>
> ► Suggestions for dignifying on-the-job learning by being a learner yourself
>
> ► Ways to anticipate and dissipate resistance
>
> ► Ways to energize your staff with celebrations of success

Learning on the job is becoming even more essential, because at least in the United States, graduate schools of education are under siege. Increasingly, states are allowing preservice teachers to get their certification through online courses, or through newly minted so-called universities that induct teachers into a particular charter school's marching orders. Student teaching often amounts to watching a few videos. In some states, as many as 40% of the newly hired teachers have gotten their entire teaching certification online. You see the results: you cannot count on new hires knowing how to conduct running records, or to match students to books, or to teach kids to read for the main idea, or to structure their writing. And meanwhile, remember, expectations have become sky-high.

So yes, schools need to become places where everyone's learning curve is high. And that is not business as usual. That requires a sea change.

Create collaborative communities of practice.

Roland Barth (2006), founder of the Principals' Center at Harvard Graduate School of Education, has said that usually relationships among teachers are like relationships among toddlers in the sandbox. One has a shovel, another has a pail. At no point do they share toys. They talk all the time but never to each other. Barth goes on to say that the single most important characteristic of an effective school is that teachers work collaboratively. He suggests there are levels of collaboration, with the lowest being parallel play or even competitiveness. Then there is the level that he describes with the term *congenial*. Teachers talk about a film they've seen, about the weather, their families, but never about their teaching. The highest level is what he refers to as *collegial* teaching, and this level is marked by teachers thinking of students as "ours," not "mine." They plan together. They share their materials and their ideas. They are in and out of each other's classrooms all the time, as are their kids. They wish each other well as teachers. Your goal is to help teachers achieve that highest level.

What a difference it makes when teachers' knowledge of good practice is shared! As Tom Sergiovanni says, "Intelligence needs to be socialized" (2004). Years ago, the annual conference for the National Conference of Teachers of English was held in New York City. TCRWP decided to work out the details so that hundreds of attendees at that conference would have the chance to visit NYC schools in which reading and writing workshops were well underway. At one school, visitors watched a teacher, Maria, convene her twenty-eight third-graders in the meeting area by saying simply, "Writers," and then scanning the room, waiting for each child to pause in what he or she was doing and to look at her. "Let's gather." Then Maria gestured for one table of children after another to stand, push in chairs, and walk to the meeting area where they sat in assigned rug spots, opening their writer's notebooks and starting to reread the previous day's writing.

Claiming her seat at the front of the meeting area, Maria began, "Writers, you have already learned strategies for supporting the claims you make in your essays." She referenced a chart, listing three such strategies, and said, "Will you show your partner places in your draft where you have done one of these strategies?" The children talked in pairs. Then Maria intervened to say, "Today I am going to teach you that essayists also angle their anecdotes to support their ideas. They pop out the part of an anecdote that especially supports their point. Let me show you." Maria demonstrated that strategy using her own writing, and then she supported her youngsters as they practiced that new strategy.

As Maria sent her writers off to work on their essays, one of the visitors whispered in awe, "How long has she been teaching?"

"Three months," I answered.

Shaking her head in disbelief, the visitor marveled, "How did she get to be so good?"

The answer, of course, lies in Maria's community of practice. Although she is a new teacher, Maria's methods of teaching are not new. They have, instead, gone through hundreds of drafts and benefited from the brilliance of scores of teachers. And Maria is not alone. If you establish a schoolwide approach to teaching writing, all your teachers—not just your first-year teachers like Maria—will benefit from standing on each other's shoulders. As Tom Sergiovanni reminds us, "The greatest asset a school has is its collective IQ" (2004).

A shared curriculum, taught at roughly the same pace, invites collaboration.

Linda Darling Hammond has pointed out that you can have far more effective PLCs (professional learning communities) if your teachers are teaching within a shared curriculum. When teachers are all working through the same unit of study, there is so much to talk about, so much to help each other with. But you won't tap into the power of that collaboration if teachers are only very loosely aligned. Instead, you need teachers to be teaching the same unit at roughly the same time. That way, they all approach this or that challenging session together, and they can ask, "How are you handling this?" Or, if they're all turning to the same mentor text at the same time, they can help each other annotate it.

I think that one of the life-giving mandates you can say to your teachers is this one: "In this school, we don't teach alone. We collaborate. The work is too challenging for any one of us to be an expert in everything, and we all get smarter and stronger when we can borrow on each other's expertise." That speech can provide you with the drumroll you need to ask (actually, to insist) that teachers at any one grade level agree on a calendar of units, setting shared dates for the end-of-unit celebration, five weeks after the unit begins. Make the celebration dates public so they function as all deadlines do—as lifelines that create urgency, intensity.

Teachers will need some time prior to a unit (and ideally in the midst of the unit as well) to plan together. I discussed the details of that planning in Chapter 4, "First Things First: Build an Instructional Foundation." To support a collaborative culture around shared professional learning, it is especially important to move heaven and earth at the start of this work and at the start of this year to make time for that planning to happen.

How do you provide teachers with the planning time they need? The answer is different if you are thinking about how to do this once or twice, early in the year, or if you are thinking about how to rethink your school's schedule so

there is more time for collaborative professional study in general, which we strongly advise. The first and easiest challenge is to simply make time for teachers to get this work off to a good start. The important thing for you to know is that if you personally and visibly go out of your way to provide teachers with time to study the new curriculum, they'll see this for what it is: a critically important signal that this work is important to you.

But making more time for teachers to plan together—and alone—is important not just at the start of the year, but always. Keep in mind that in Finland, often touted as having the best education system in the world, teachers teach around 600 hours annually—in America, that number is closer to 1,000 hours. In Finland, teachers have time every day to plan, learn, reflect, assess students' progress and prepare their own teaching. They have time not only to collaborate but also to participate in health and human wellness activities. And in America, we are so set on making sure our children "get ahead" and "achieve" that we entirely neglect to develop our teaching force.

Our American schedules might not have the same built-in time for collaborative planning, but you can still find ways to communicate to your teachers that collaborative planning is a mandatory, invaluable expectation that is part of your school's culture. And, you can help teachers structure the time they do have so that their planning is as effective and useful as possible.

Ways to Make More Time for Teachers to Plan Together

- Volunteer to take all the kids at a particular grade level into the auditorium where you, perhaps with help from the music teacher or from some other teacher, can work with the kids. You might read aloud selections from books that celebrate writing or reading, such as *Writing Radar* by Jack Gantos (a very funny book for grades 3–8 about the power of writer's notebooks) or *Ralph Tells a Story* (a picture book for grades K–2 about a young writer). Read your own writing as well. Talk about your reading. Perhaps give book buzzes, talking up great books that the kids could read. Highlight especially accessible books, go for humor. Ask others to help you do this.

- Ask a specialist to do some version of the above, and then volunteer to be that person's teaching assistant (TA), or channel someone else to be that person's TA. Ask the librarian or the art teacher to work with several classes of kids at once (pipe cleaner animals?) or organize Social Studies Movie Day.

Move mountains so the teachers see you are personally involved in helping them have the precious time they need to talk together at the start of a unit.

■ Before the school year even begins, with support from your district, you can schedule a half-day for professional study.

■ Host a barbeque at your house or a brunch at the local diner, inviting interested teachers perhaps from this or that grade level (or early adapters from a particular grade level). Some school leaders do this on one of those last days of summer. Point out that the time is voluntary, but pay for the food, be part of the work, and perhaps even bake brownies yourself (or follow my model and buy them from the bakery and hide all evidence of the bakery box)!

■ As early in the year as possible, consider whether upcoming pupil-free days can be devoted to literacy professional development and grade-level planning.

■ Look for opportunities within your own school calendar to bring teachers together to plan. Perhaps the business portion of faculty meetings can be done through memos, and that time can be channeled toward grade-level meetings. Perhaps a pupil-free day can be devoted to literacy professional development and grade-level planning.

■ Question the constraints that have already been embedded in your school's schedule. For example, if your school has two fifteen-minute recess times, consider combining them. Can you schedule a common prep period alongside lunch to create longer blocks of time? Could your school district send children home at noon one Friday a month? Could you tap community volunteers and not-for-profit groups to lead clubs one afternoon a week so that teachers have more time to plan?

Of course, you'll need to find ways to support collaborative planning that fit into your culture and your contracts. If you have gone to great lengths to give teachers more time to plan, you may also feel comfortable asking teachers to devote some of their prep times to collaborative planning. In different schools, different assumptions develop around teachers' prep time. In some schools, that time is personal time, and teachers call the realtor or run out to the dry cleaner. In other schools, some portion of prep time is designated as time for grade-level planning meetings and for collaboration with specialists. You'll want to open conversations with your teachers about what the assumptions will be in your school.

Make sure that collaborative groups go well.

It will be easier for you to protect times for grade-level planning if those times are extremely useful. Suggest that teachers at each grade level talk together about their experiences with grade-level planning groups that worked well—and those that didn't. This will help them harvest insights about how to make their discussions as productive and inclusive as possible. They'll probably develop a list that is a bit like this one:

One Grade-Level Team's Agreement to Make Its Meetings Productive

- If we agreed before the meeting to bring student work, or to read something, we actually bring it, read it. We set up reminder systems when we need to.

- We arrive on time, stay the full time, and are all-in while at the meeting. That means no cell phones and no correcting student work.

- We start by either making an agenda or reviewing one that's already made. We check in on prior to-do's, rank which items on the agenda are the most important, and prioritize our time.

- One of us watches the time, moving us along through the agenda (e.g., reminding us if we only have ten minutes and two more items left).

- One of us keeps notes on a Google doc open to all.

- We avoid taking undue air time. We bring out quiet voices.

- We try to stand back from negativity and help each other do so. If the group gets into venting, someone says something like, "What positive steps forward can we take?"

- Just prior to the ending of the meeting, we list to-do's and clarify who is doing what.

Dignify on-the-job learning.

You are the best person to dignify on-the-job learning, but doing so takes courage. We've seen countless principals do this all-important work, and the results are breathtaking.

The more insecure you feel—and the more transparent you are about that—the better. We remember the story of Jamie, a principal in an upper-middle-class Connecticut school. Before we began work in the school, we'd heard that "Jamie knows nothing about this." That, of course, was far from the case, but that was the buzz.

A few weeks after the writing Units of Study were launched in Jamie's school, he agreed to try teaching a minilesson in front of his fourth-grade teachers, asking them for feedback. The plan was that the school's coach would set Jamie up to do this, and all the fourth-grade teachers would agree to teach the same minilesson in rotation, moving together as a group from one fourth-grade classroom to the next. Jamie chose that grade because the teachers there were already collaborative, and he felt a bit safer teaching in front of them.

The coach later told me that Jamie was sweating bullets as he prepared his minilesson. It was no easy thing for him to take his seat at the front of a class of nine-year-olds and in front of his fourth-grade teachers and to teach publicly, aiming to keep the minilesson brief. The coach assured him that there would be no down side. The worse he was, the better it would be for sending the message that theirs is a school where people take risks. Jamie knew the important thing was for him to be public about messing up, to be vulnerable in front of his teachers, to welcome feedback, and to help that group of teachers be willing to do likewise.

We didn't hear all the details of Jamie's minilesson, but we know that after almost twenty minutes, he abruptly ended it, aware that he'd botched things up. "Awww, this is so hard," he said. The teachers and Jamie went into the hall and talked, with everyone supporting Jamie, laughing together about how someone had tried to signal to him at this or that point, regaling each other with reminiscences of the various turns his teaching had taken. They strategized together over how the minilesson could have been done differently and then proceeded to watch one of the teachers reteach the same (now improved) minilesson in another classroom, and again, there was debriefing, and then the group moved to a third fourth-grade classroom, and yet another teacher took a go.

That team of teachers became a close-knit community. Often, they brought two classes together and jigsawed a minilesson, so they could support each other. Before long, Jamie had worked with teachers from other grades in similar ways, and after the school was two years into this work, we brought principals from seventy-five Connecticut schools to a study group at Jamie's school. As part of that visit, Jamie opened every classroom in his school, encouraging visitors to watch any and all of the school's reading and writing workshops, roaming between classrooms to see whole-school implementation.

The point is this: too often, we brace ourselves against seeming vulnerable. We armor up. We are cynical and disengaged and defensive—all versions of that armor. We wear masks. We think that showing vulnerability reveals weakness. We don't want to let others—especially our colleagues and our leaders—know that we are sometimes not sure how to do something.

Brené Brown, author of *Daring Greatly*, points out that we protect ourselves against vulnerability, yet vulnerability is the cradle of all we most long for in life—authenticity, wholeheartedness, real relationships. She says that when we protect ourselves against vulnerability, we protect ourselves against all-in engagement and emotional connection. "To foreclose on our emotional life out of fear that the costs will be too high is to walk away from the very thing that gives purpose and meaning to living" (2015).

To foreclose on our emotional life out of fear that the costs will be too high is to walk away from the very thing that gives purpose and meaning to living

(Brené Brown 2015).

We think she is right. For a moment, consider the times when you have been vulnerable on the job. Perhaps those were times when you voiced an unpopular opinion, took a risk, tried something new, went public with something important to you, threw yourself heart and soul into a mission you cared about. Were those times of weakness? Probably not. Probably those were, instead, times of strength.

The important thing for you, the principal, to keep in mind is that your people's learning curves will never be sky-high if they don't feel safe enough to take risks, to try something new, to admit confusion, to ask for help. When messing up on something that's hard is not okay, when failures along the way are not okay, then you can forget about your school being a place where teachers or kids innovate and learn.

Tony Wagner, a great twenty-first-century scholar, talked to us at Teachers College about what's needed in this world of ours. He emphasized that we need to embrace the F-word (*failure*) and cited the "Fail early and fail often" principle widely adopted by software developers.

When Roland Barth visited TCRWP years ago, he said, "In a good school, everyone's learning curve is sky-high. So I ask you, what are you (as the principal) learning on the job?" People told each other what they were learning. Then Roland pushed another step. "Who knows about your learning?" he asked. He added that it isn't enough to be a learner, that school leaders need to be *public* learners.

Hopefully, your talk is full of language like this:

"Yesterday I got some pointers on how I can . . ."

"Talking with you is making me realize that I need to rethink . . ."

"I've got that on my reading list."

"Would one of you be willing to coach me on how you . . . ?"

"Can I try out an idea with you. If . . . is true, does it make sense that we . . . ?"

"My head is spinning. I learned so much by watching you . . ."

"One of your kids just gave me a seminar in . . ."

You not only need to be a public learner, you need to help your team be that, as well. Ask your AP to go into a classroom and ask the teacher if she would be willing to let him try conferring with the kids. Perhaps the teacher would be willing to give him some feedback. Do this in ways that not only position your fellow administrator as a learner, but that also empower a teacher whose expertise has perhaps been overlooked before. If your colleague, the AP, has a background in the upper grades, then he can certainly learn in leaps and bounds from a first-grade teacher. Channel your fellow administrator to ask for some coaching—perhaps on shared reading, or on conducting and scoring running records, or on working with a beginning reader.

My point here is that to make learning on the job something that the most powerful people in your school do all the time, it's important that you and your team are public learners. It is a good idea to exaggerate the visibility of your stance as a learner—perhaps you and the other administrators agree to carry notebooks or iPads around with you and to take notes on techniques you learn from watching kids and their teacher. You and the others in your team will make a big impact if you snap pictures of student work or of great homemade charts as you go through your days or if you film kids when they are doing something beautiful, and tell parents and other teachers about your learning.

Then, be accustomed to asking teachers, "What are you learning?" Say to them, "Talk to me about the new risks you are taking." Give little pep talks often about how Google asks its employees to choose goals for themselves and then is unhappy if they meet *all* those goals because the hope is they are ambitious enough that they choose goals they can't fully meet. Your message needs to be, "Together, let's all reach for the stars."

Anticipate resistance from some teachers and work to dissipate it.

You can count on it—one teacher will roll his or her eyes at another. A teacher will act out during a grade-level professional development session. She'll put her very large bag up on the table, shielding her from whoever is leading the discussion. Or she'll pull out her cellphone while someone else is speaking. Your resistor's gestures and tone will drip with contempt. You've seen this before.

This is on you, and you cannot remain silent. In the prologue of *Blink*, Malcolm Gladwell tells about psychologist John Gottman, who, in fifteen minutes of observing a married couple, can often infer the likelihood of whether they will stay together (2007). One telltale sign? Eye-rolling. It is one of those seemingly small moves that indicate utter disrespect. If you see this kind of behavior, you must take it on, and the rest of your teachers need to see you doing that. You needn't address the problematic teacher publicly, in front of everyone, but if you remain silent and look the other way, you are complicit. You are condoning the behavior. You might start by saying something like, "I've got to go to another meeting but before I go, can I just remind everyone that this school needs to be a community of kindness and of respect? We need to hold ourselves to the same behaviors we teach our students. Check yourself because it is okay to disagree. It is *not* okay to be rude to each other." And perhaps for your first intervention, you can just give that one teacher the eagle eye.

But if the behavior continues, even if it is a little milder, this next time you need to address the person one-on-one. Say, with firmness, in front of the group, "May I speak with you?" and pull that person from the room. Tell the person in no uncertain terms that this behavior is not okay. You might name the specific behaviors that are unacceptable, such as arriving late, not bringing agreed-upon materials (like student work), or using her cellphone during the meeting. Then, schedule another time for the kind of conversation that might help there to be an actual reset. "I can see from your crossed arms and stone expression that you aren't happy with how things are going. Help me understand what's going on for you." Remember that for a time, you may need to tell that person that he or she will need to do the professional development (PD) in a one-to-one relationship with someone (you? the AP?) because that person's presence in the group is not helpful.

In Chapter 13, "Leading Adults Can Be Tricky: Responding to Trouble," we talk in greater depth about dealing with resistant teachers. It isn't easy. But for now, it is enough to say that you need to address the problem, so that it doesn't derail everything. Your teachers need you to be their moderator and guide, helping them stay the course when the going gets choppy.

Celebrate early successes in ways that energize.

Think about times when someone you respect, someone with power, has seen and celebrated your work. Chances are that when you felt seen and recognized, your energy soared. You worked harder, longer, better. You even walked through your day with a lighter step, with more grace and generosity.

David Rock, a neurologist who studies the brain to help all of us become better coaches, points out that many people go months before receiving any positive feedback at all. On top of that, we all tend to recycle any negative feedback we *do* receive, rethinking those harsh words over and over, making them even harsher. We hear, "You're late again," and we translate that into "You're lazy." We burn with indignation. We hear, "What was going on in your room yesterday?" and we translate that into, "You can't control your class," and we are filled with shame.

Shame and guilt erode the load-bearing walls of a person's self-concept. They make a person less capable, less responsive, less energetic.

If you can only do one thing to lift the energy level in your school, make a point to compliment your teachers. On Sunday night, sit in front of your computer and grab a teacher's name, and type that into the address line of an email. Then dive into an appreciative email. Don't worry about deciding first on what you can say. Just write, "Dear Joe." Then start the next sentence. Take any of these as your sentence starter:

> I wonder if you have any idea how beautiful (or inspiring) it is when you . . .
>
> I wanted to send you a quick note to tell you how much I admire . . .
>
> I've been thinking back over last week and remembering that child from your room who . . . I know that's a reflection of your beautiful teaching and I just wanted you to know that . . .
>
> The other day, I walked into your classroom when you weren't there and just stood there for a moment, taking in the way you . . . I wonder if you have any idea how rare and how special it is that you . . .

You will make a teacher's day, year, life with an email like that. When complimenting someone, remember to be as specific and as detailed as possible. At TCRWP, if our office staff has just pulled off the behind-the-scenes work on a giant institute, we don't write them and say, "Thanks for all you did. It was marvelous. You were perfect. Thanks so much." Instead, we write something more like this, "Saturday morning, at 6:45 a.m., I saw you literally running down the hall to get something—the agenda I think it was. I couldn't help but think, 'Yep, that's Lisa for you.' Thank you for being the sort of leader who'll tear through the halls of TC to not keep a teacher waiting." Specificity—details—matter in all writing, and a compliment is a kind of writing. You send the message: *I see you*.

You might also walk the halls of your school with a pack of Post-its in hand, jotting brief compliments to teachers as you go. Visit a classroom, leaving behind a Post-it in which you glow over a precious detail. Did a child reread and cross out her own work? Wow, how beautiful that children in this school are growing up with a revision mindset. Did a child tell you what she is learning from a character? It's amazing when books begin to help kids grow into the people we hope they become.

You will want to show your support and celebrate your teachers by your actions, as well as by your words. What a difference it will make if you hang a child's writing up on your bulletin board or begin a faculty meeting by reading

Jordan,

I just read Griffin's essay about Gatsby. You've gotten that boy to love that book—and to write with passion. Beautiful.   Todd

Molly,

Loved the way Savaria taught that student-led small group! She taught like a pro. Hoping we can catch it on film next time and share with others!

Dina

Caitlin,

Holy moly. The essays outside your room have such voice. I didn't need the kids' names as their quirky personalities shine through.

Can I include one in my next newsletter? They'll convey so much about our teaching to the parents.

Lara

aloud some of the things that children have told you about their reading. Take pictures of your teachers and kids, immersed in learning, and send them home in a school newsletter, showcasing these pictures as your pride and joy. Hold a meeting in a teacher's classroom and channel other teachers to take in the beautiful environment.

Name the small details that you see in ways that make them holy, that imbue them with significance. Remember the bricklayer at a cathedral who described his work not as "I'm setting bricks into cement," but as "I'm building a cathedral to the Lord."

8 Provide Teachers with Professional Development

*P*rofessional development will engine your school's forward progress. Districts that minimize support for professional learning make a mistake. How important it is for you to figure out your goals and to organize the professional development that will help you move your school toward those goals! There are lots of different ways to help teachers become more proficient at the handful of methods that undergird any reading or writing workshop, or at any of the topics that merit further inquiry. You'll need to fashion a plan that takes advantage of the resources and people that you can access. The plan will of course be different for different grade levels and for teachers at different levels of proficiency.

Develop expertise by linking with TCRWP.

We encourage you to consider connecting in some substantial ways with "the mothership"—that is, with Teachers College Reading and Writing Project. There are many ways to do this. Our deepest and closest partnerships are with approximately a thousand schools in which we provide on-site professional development across the school year. These schools are in more than forty countries, and they include private schools, International Baccalaureate (IB) schools, charter schools, and university lab schools, as well as public schools. Generally, we are in those schools for ten days across the year (five, if they are small or our focus just spans a few grades, as is the case for most middle schools). While we are there, we often lead three cycles of professional development such as those described

IN THIS CHAPTER, YOU'LL FIND . . .

▶ Avenues to support your teachers' ongoing development, including:

  ▶ Connecting with the TCRWP

  ▶ Linking with other districts doing this work

  ▶ Engaging teachers in a cycle of professional development

  ▶ Building the capacity of site-based literacy coaches

  ▶ Developing assistant principals and other administrators as lateral leaders

  ▶ Setting up a learning culture in which teachers share with and learn from each other

in this chapter. This partnership usually also involves TCRWP staff developers leading learning opportunities such as site-based coaching institutes, curriculum-writing retreats, workshops on specific new topics, and so forth. Best of all, when we are in a building regularly, we are able to provide professional company for school leaders and coaches, sharing our impressions, suggestions, resources, insights, questions, and ideas about next steps.

It is also vitally important to send key people to institutes. TCRWP leads a dozen three-day mini-institutes during the academic year and four weeklong institutes in New York City each summer, with the large ones involving well over a thousand people. When people come to TCRWP, you learn in the classrooms and lecture halls where John Dewey and Martin Luther King Jr. taught. You sit alongside teachers and school leaders who have come from around the globe for the opportunity to study together. The learning culture is contagious. Send your most willing and eager teachers to us, and we will send you back grade-level leaders and future coaches. And send us your naysayers, too; usually they come away with new insight into the curiosity, intellectualism, and research that inform this work. Some of your most resistant teachers will end up being your best practitioners. We know. Some of them work for us now, as lead staff developers.

The advantage of coming to Teachers College is that you and your teachers are brought backstage to glimpse the deep inquiries, the heady mix of expertise, and the cycle of teaching and reflection, of innovation and exploration, and constant critique that goes into the curriculum—a curriculum that can look, to an outsider, like a prepackaged, teacher-proof kit. When you and your teachers are merely given a printed scope and sequence, that document doesn't convey the back-and-forth conversations that informed the document. It's beneficial when you and your people can be part of conversations that might begin like this:

> **Q:** "Why did you sequence the second-grade units . . . ? We would have preferred . . ."
>
> **A:** "Actually, we 100% agree with your preference, but so many grade 2 teachers pleaded with us to . . . so we altered. . . . But if you prefer . . . , you should know that we agree with you. And in any case, the important thing is that you and your colleagues weigh the options."

We especially encourage you to send your experienced teacher-leaders and your coaches to Teachers College. Those people will be in good company—many participants in TCRWP institutes are attending their fifteenth or twentieth institute. Veterans learn more than others, because the more a person knows, the more a person can learn. Many districts find that it is especially important to send school-based literacy coaches to TCRWP's coaching institutes, because our methods for coaching teachers haven't been written and aren't publicly available, yet they are as important as methods for teaching children.

Every summer, we also lead more than a hundred homegrown institutes on-site in districts dotting the globe. And districts that are just getting started with Units of Study often ask us to staff a one-day launch for their K–2, 3–5, and 6–8 teachers—that can be done with small groups of twenty-five teachers, or in auditoriums with a thousand. We aim to say yes to any invitation for a single day, because that one day can set your school/district on a productive pathway.

We also lead a number of professional development opportunities that are specifically designed for school leaders, including a Leadership Institute every October and leadership sections in our summer institutes. You'll benefit from the opportunity to look at leadership issues and leadership methods together with school leaders from around the world. Your spirit and energy and vision shape your school. Your teachers aren't the only ones who need to be lifted up!

Develop expertise by linking with other districts.

We have also seen schools become proficient at this work by linking with other schools that are farther along. If fact, if one were to make a map of places in the United States where reading/writing workshops are especially flourishing, in every one of the places, there are districts and specific people who are at the center of that hub. And at the Project, we hear time and again of the generosity of those hub schools.

There is a contagious quality to this work, when it goes well. Teachers are bursting to share their insights and ideas, tools, and texts. It's considered a blessing to host visitors (as well as to visit). Children rise to the occasion of being spokespeople and gladly take visitors on tour of their classrooms, explaining the charts and student work, the rituals and responsibilities that make their classrooms hum.

The Project's enthusiasm about school visits actually began two or three decades ago when I visited Jerry Harste, an important literacy leader in Bloomington, Indiana. I asked Jerry if we could pop into a classroom in which the teacher was teaching literacy well, according to Jerry's image. Jerry picked me up at the airport, and we drove several hours to get to the classroom of Karen Smith, arriving just an hour before the end of the school day. As I remember the day, we spent four hours of driving for an hour in a classroom, and I continue to think of how well spent that day was. That one hour in Karen's classroom is still with me, thirty years later. I don't think I ever, in my life, learned as much, as quickly and intensely as I learned in that hour.

Karen is a magnificent teacher, and that is part of why I learned so much from that visit. But more than that, Karen's teaching illustrated the principles that Harste elaborates upon in his books, so it was especially valuable to see a living illustration of all the theories and explanations he champions.

People who visit TCRWP strongholds are able to do the same—watching the instruction and aligning it to all that they have read in the books that TCRWP puts out into the world. That combination of theory and practice makes these visits especially potent.

When one visits a TCRWP stronghold, visitors are able to see teacher after teacher, classroom after classroom, all doing similar work—and yet, doing the work differently. Teachers each have their own pulse, their own quirks and strengths and beliefs. When visiting an entire school, it is helpful to see ways in which the teachers at a grade level are similar—and ways they are different. One classroom will represent the epitome of efficiency, with kids literally running from meeting area to desk, diving into their work without wasting a second. Other classrooms will have a relaxed, authentic feel, with children almost ambling between one activity and another. Both classrooms can be equally wonderful, and both can have limitations too—my point is that it is helpful to see the handprints of individual teachers on their teaching.

The added advantage of teachers from different schools visiting each other is that soon, collectives form between districts and those relationships sustain everyone. In many hubs of this work, leaders from a collection of places have formed support groups for each other. Sometimes those collaboratives involve directors of ELA meeting across districts, sometimes they involve literacy coaches, sometimes school principals. Either way, these informal support structures have been invaluable.

For example, in Texas and Georgia, district leaders have worked together to develop crosswalks between reading and writing workshops and their high-stakes tests. In California, leaders from seventy-five districts recently spent three days together in one district—Palo Alto—visiting schools together and talking together about statewide challenges. That led to the five TCRWP leaders and a dozen California leaders with special expertise in ELL meeting to develop an instrument that details the ways in which every unit in the entire Units of Study series supports English language learners. In a dozen places, teachers from neighboring districts have convened for a summer Make-It, Take-It Toolkit Day in which they work side by side to start toolkits to support their teaching. As the 2018 school year got underway, I spent an hour or so in video-chats with collectives of school leaders from districts across Iowa and South Carolina. When neighboring districts form collaboratives, they can share their access to TCRWP. For example, in a couple of states, a dozen or so districts are currently talking about co-sponsoring a coaches' institute in which literacy coaches from all their districts gather together once a month to learn from a TCRWP staff developer—and especially, from each other. That sort of collective is inexpensive and invaluable.

Provide your teachers with cycles of professional development.

Whether an in-house coach provides professional development for your teachers, or you bring in an outside expert, you'll probably want to provide these teachers with cycles of support, not just isolated days. You'll need to be very clear about your goals for a cycle of staff development, so that you have a way to measure the effectiveness of your support for the teachers. If you don't know what you are hoping to achieve, it is hard to check on whether the professional development actually made a difference. (And in this country, all too much of what occurs in the name of staff development doesn't make a lasting difference.) Of course, the goals for a cycle might well be selected by the teachers, although an expert can help lift the level of those goals, making it more likely that the work is high leverage.

Consider an example of a cycle of professional study.

Imagine that the decision was made to help teachers provide readers with additional practice in high-level comprehension skills by tapping the power of the read-aloud. The hope could also be that if teachers take a reading skill—interpretation—that they are teaching in a unit, and they invent ways to reinforce that skill by demonstrating it and providing kids with guided practice using it during the read-aloud, teachers and kids will "own" that reading skill more. Kids will also have opportunities for repeated practice, and especially for transference. The cycle could also help teachers learn more about how to teach in ways that help kids transfer the reading skills they are practicing during the read-aloud to their independent books. Teaching needs to be different if it is going to support that sort of transference.

That sort of thinking about the goals of a cycle of staff development matters. If professional development doesn't have ambitious goals, it is not apt to make a big difference.

While thinking through all the goals of a three-day cycle of professional development, the leader of this professional development will also want to plan the work that the teachers will do together. It helps to have a plan upfront for all of the days of the cycle, so the leader isn't just inventing cool things to do. Ideally a cycle of study has a storyline, much as a good unit has a storyline.

The general plan for a cycle of staff development, as for a minilesson, follows the "I do, we do, you do" rhythm repeatedly as the work grows in complexity. This particular cycle might begin with the leader showing teachers how the leader plans a read-aloud that is designed to support higher-level comprehension skills.

The leader of this work might have gotten hold of a read-aloud that the teachers at that grade level were already working within—say, *Tiger Rising*, if this involves fourth-grade teachers. Participating teachers could watch as the leader reminds herself of the skills that are on the fourth-grade teachers' anchor charts for reading, and then read a page of that book herself, spying on herself to see when she used any of those skills, authentically, in her effort to read that excerpt well. She could then mark up that page with Post-its to remind her of ways she'd want to pause and think aloud as she read that page. For example, when the main character repeats something, she might decide to pop that out, asking "Why might the author be repeating this? Could this have something to do with what the book is *really* about?"

The leader could show teachers how she plans places in that page where she'd demonstrate by thinking publicly, and she could plan places she'd channel the kids to do some skill work. ("Wait a minute. This is reminding me of an earlier part. Let me reread that, then will you talk with your partner about how these two parts go together?")

After the leader demonstrated this sort of preparation for a read-aloud, the participating teachers could practice doing that same work with that same page, and then they could work together to do similar work on the next page or two. They could then all go into a classroom together, first to watch the leader read aloud to one small group and then to disperse, with half of the teachers reading those two pages aloud to another small group of kids while the other half of the teachers watch, getting prepared to take over. Before the baton is passed from one partner to the next, however, the observing partner could debrief the other and the leader could debrief all the teachers so the next round of work was ratcheted up a notch.

After the teachers try the read-aloud work, the leader could demonstrate how to help kids transfer that work to their own independent books, with teachers again watching in preparation for doing this themselves with other kids. Teachers might carry this read-aloud book with them into the reading and writing workshop and practice drawing on the book to show kids work they can do with their independent books and drafts.

Notice that a good cycle of professional development, like a good unit of study, follows a sort of story arc. The work of one day builds on the next, and across the course of the work, teachers tackle a problem and invent ways to grow and grow. It is helpful for the end of the cycle to contain almost a send-off that makes it likely that the learning continues on and on into the future. The cycle I've described here might end with the suggestion that similar work could be occurring in social studies and science, planning read-alouds in similar ways. Or, it might end with teachers making a pledge to spy on themselves reading another text, to mark it up in preparation for reading it aloud in ways that engage kids in watching and trying out particular skill work and then in transferring that work to their own books. They might say, "We promise to bring our well-marked-up books to our next meeting."

> *Notice that a good cycle of professional development, like a good unit of study, follows a kind of story arc.*

Explore topics on the frontiers.

You may wonder, "What topics will especially pay off for experienced workshop teachers to study in a cycle of professional development?" One way to glean some insights is to look at the advanced section titles for TCRWP summer institutes, because those will suggest some of the frontiers that we are especially excited about. Here are a few topics that we think merit continued study:

- Lifting the level of students' talking, thinking, and writing about reading

- Transform phonics instruction into the writing workshop

- Developing a revision mindset: partner work, tools, and reflection

- Teaching grammar inside and alongside workshop

- Historical fiction and nonfiction research—immersion and independence

- Bringing the best literacy methods to social studies and science

- Helping learners to be more analytical as readers, thinkers, writers

- Turning students into lifelong researchers—and in so doing, supporting new kinds of reading-writing connections

- Using mentor texts to support writers becoming more ambitious and independent

- Developing toolkits to support assessment-based small groups

- Tapping the power of series books to help readers with the all-important skill of working between parts and whole texts

- From inference to interpretation: developing deep understanding of skill progressions

- Tapping the power of nonfiction read-alouds to provide guided practice in minds-on-fire reading

- Thinking about how record keeping makes us into minds-on-fire teachers

- Scaffolds need to be temporary structures: reexamining our efforts to support students who struggle with reading or writing

Use site-based literacy coaches effectively.

We have found that site-based literacy coaches are far more helpful to other teachers if you set them up to do their jobs effectively. This begins with establishing a schedule for the work and setting up expectations for what the coach will do and what the participating teacher will do during their time together. In the end, the coach's goal must be to enable and empower the teacher, so it is important that the plan mobilizes the participating teacher to do as much work as possible.

Channel coaches to support cycles of professional development.

In many schools, a coach may, at any one time, be working with at least three or four groups of teachers. It is possible for a coach to support that many teachers, because even when a group of teachers is working with the coach in a cycle, that cycle needs to contain spaces for independent practice within it. For example, if the coach is working with all the first-grade teachers to help them transfer their phonics instruction into lean coaching during the writing workshop, the coach might start by showing teachers ways to carry tools from Phonics Units of Study with them as they confer with young writers, drawing on those tools in writing conferences as appropriate.

If the coach helped teachers do that work on Monday, she'd want to give the participating teachers a day or two to try that work in their classrooms before the group met again on Thursday to debrief, to hear the coach's tips for next steps, and to practice the new work together. Again, the teachers would use the interval before they reconvened with their coach to integrate the coach's tips, perhaps with the coach briefly coming into their classrooms to give feedback.

The next week, the coach might lead this same group to do similar work supporting transfer to writing workshop only, this time with a focus on small-group instruction. Before the cycle of staff development was over, the group might have made some new tools, written a new minilesson or two, and worked to transfer phonics not only into writing, but also into reading. Meanwhile, this same coach might be working with a different grade level of teachers to lift the level of analytic thinking within a literary essay unit.

Note that even when a coach is working one-to-one with a teacher, it helps if that work is designed as a course of study rather like the cycle described above. When collaborations between a coach and participating teachers have a predetermined beginning and end, a defined coaching/learning plan, and achievable goals, you set higher expectations for everyone.

Set the coach up to teach the teacher, not the students.

Usually the principal needs to establish an informal sort of contract for how the relationship between a literacy coach and a classroom teacher (or a group of teachers) will go. That is especially important if the coach is working one-to-one, because teachers are apt to think of the coach as either a substitute for them or as a specialist (like the roving art teacher) or as an assistant (four hands are better than two).

You might, for example, tell a few teachers that you have asked the coach (say this is Lea) to work with them individually (or as a group) to help them get started leading effective writing workshops. You could suggest that Lea work for an hour, twice a week, in the classrooms of each of the participating teachers and also meet with each of those teachers during their preps several times during those weeks. You might say, "Lea is not coming into your room as an extra pair of hands so that together you can reach more students. That'd be a worthy goal but she's actually coming in so you two can help each other, and so she can help you. So I'm going to ask that you and Lea take turns teaching in front of each other, observing each other, giving each other feedback, and talking about the hard parts. And Lea, I hope you will demonstrate some of the methods you learned at the TCRWP summer institute."

If your hope is that Lea is working with teachers to help them be more reflective practitioners, you need to make that clear. She is not a glorified substitute. Let participating teachers know that Lea is there for them, not really for their kids. Lea's presence in the room is not meant to give teachers a chance to work on student papers, on bulletin boards, or even to reach more kids. You might say to them, "I'm going to ask you two to both read the chapter on small groups in the reading workshop, and then Lea is there to help you strengthen your methods of teaching, putting the content of that book into practice."

This is a tricky relationship. It won't always work. Lea needs to have stronger skills than the teachers with whom she is working, and she needs a personality that makes her a pleasure for them to learn with. She will be vastly more effective as a coach if she has been taught methods of staff development. The TCRWP leads regular institutes for coaches, and you might see if Lea can join one of those. But the important thing is that even if Lea has all the skills in the world, she'll only be able to work this way if you set her up to do it and if you are involved in making this sort of on-the-job learning occur. You are going to need to visit the classrooms when Lea is working with a teacher to see whether they are joined at the hip most of the time. If they aren't—if they are each in different corners of the room—plan to talk with them at another time and ask how you can help make their time together more focused on professional study and less on simply reaching more kids. They may point out that for now, there's an urgent need to get more kids on track, and they may be right. But you will still want to establish some ground rules, making it clear that before long, you hope their side-by-side work shifts, so that Lea is actually functioning as a coach for the teacher.

Communicate that you'll evaluate your coaches by noting teachers' learning curves.

Certainly as part of this, you need to clarify with Lea that her goal is for the participating teacher to become the most effective and happy teacher possible. Lea should know that if the kids cheer when *she* enters the room, that is a bad sign. She is not in that classroom to be the Charismatic Teacher. Her goal is to make it so that the kids cheer when *their teacher* says it's time for writing or for reading.

To help Lea make the shift from being the teacher-of-kids to being the teacher of teachers, tell her that you'll visit the classroom to give her feedback—and point out that you'll visit on a day when she is *not* there. Just as a classroom teacher is assessed based on students' work, you can assess Lea based on the teachers with whom she works. This means that if she complains to you about the teachers, saying things like, "He's just putting in his time before he retires," you'll want to say to her, "What do you think you could do differently, so you have more success with him?" That is, show her that the progress that teachers are or are not making is on her—just as kids' progress or lack thereof is on their teachers and actually, on us as the people who lead those teachers. If a coach tells you that the teachers at a grade level are especially difficult, respond by saying something like, "When you reflect on what hasn't worked with them, what insights do you have about yourself and the ways you've worked with them so far?"

Of course, I'm being tough, and I don't entirely mean what I am saying. Of course, you also need to be company for the coach, and yes, some cohorts of teachers are much more challenging for us all. And yes, you need to be a team with the coach, to stand by her. And the truth is, you, like that coach, need to see evidence that teachers are not growing as a reflection of *your* leadership—their growth is not only a reflection of your coach's success or lack thereof but of yours.

The work we're describing is not easy to pull off. It will help a lot for you to talk with your entire staff about this image for how your coaches will work. You don't want your coaches to be left roaming the halls, trying to bribe teachers into letting them come into the classroom! It needs to be clear that you are mobilizing them to help teachers do work that you think is really important.

Make sure building-based coaches work with experienced as well as novice teachers.

A word to the wise: Your teachers will not want to work with coaches if you only send coaches in as emergency interventions to help the novice or struggling teachers. You need to be sure that some of a coach's time is spent helping your strongest teachers become even stronger. Those strong teachers may not want to work one-to-one with the coach, but you and the coach could rally a group of strong teachers to take on a topic that is challenging for everyone and to work shoulder to shoulder as a team to do some pioneering work on that topic. For example, perhaps you might suggest that a team of those teachers could take on the task of helping kids lift the level of their writing about reading. The participating teachers could read chapters from our books and other books on that topic, revisit relevant minilessons from across a sequence of years, and plan some small-group work. In the company of each other, they could try their hand at leading those small groups, studying the results, and then thinking about how that particular small group could be even better—and try that new iteration. The important thing about this work will not only be the topic-based insights that the group harvests. You will also send a critical message that on-the-job professional study is for everyone and that working with support from the building-based coach is a good thing for one and all.

Developing Lateral Leadership—Lead Teachers and Other Administrators

Who was it who said that great leaders make more leaders? That's an absolutely key insight to remember. I once heard that if one wants to make sure that all children have the best possible start in life, it helps to count how many adult advocates each child has. Does this child have a swim coach rooting for her? A grandma? A pastor? A big sister? Kids flourish if they have half a dozen or more active and important advocates.

Teachers who are engaged in the all-important work of outgrowing themselves need a similar number of advocates. When visitors come to TCRWP stronghold schools in late October, we always take them into the classrooms taught by brand-new teachers, suggesting they watch the teaching for ten or fifteen minutes and study the student work. We don't mention that these are new teachers, and afterward we ask the visitors how long they believe those teachers have been teaching. The visitors' mouths drop when they hear they've just observed a brand-new teacher. "How is that possible?" they ask. To answer that question, we pull that teacher from the classroom and ask her to list the sources of support she has gotten in her first few months on the job (and during the summer before the job officially began).

You can only provide your teachers—the experienced as well as the novice teachers—with lots of support if you distribute the role of providing leadership for this work. It is especially important to distribute that role if you do not have a literacy coach, but either way, do this! When you tap the talents of your people, you not only allow those people to form a supportive infrastructure for your learning community, you also give those fledgling leaders new ways to spread their wings.

Rally people to take on leadership roles.

At TCRWP, our staff developers focus on a grade band—either K–2, 3–5, or 6–8. Some can work across two of those bands, but becoming deeply familiar with this curriculum for three grade levels is, in and of itself, a lot. In your school, think about the in-house leaders and ask, "Who can help with K–2 writing? With phonics? With K–2 reading? Who can help with 3–5 writing? With reading? 6–8 ELA?" You may have one person supporting reading, writing, and phonics in grades K–2, and another doing similar work in 3–8, but it is unlikely that any one person can lead all of this terrain. If even the staff developers at TCRWP—people who devote their entire lives to literacy leadership and who themselves receive a full day a week of high-level PD—rarely work across the whole span of K–8, it is unlikely that any of your people can do so either.

If you have an assistant principal, we strongly encourage you to assign that person to take a lead role with one segment. Too often, assistant principals get few opportunities to be engaged in curricular leadership, which is a shame because experience doing so will make them vastly more effective when they become school principals. If someone—let's say, Jacob—is going to take a lead role in K–2 reading, Jacob will need to read the *Guide* for K–2 reading, watch those orientation videos, and participate in grade-level unit planning meetings. This will help him figure out which teachers in those grade levels can be his informants, so he can spend time learning from those teachers. Then, he'll need to function as Johnny Appleseed, going into other teachers' classrooms as a sort of junior coach and as a vulnerable, open learner of teaching. Jacob may not have a lot of expertise in K–2 reading, but he can read the chapter on small groups, study the small-group write-ups in the Units of Study books, and then join his teachers in trying to put some of what the books say into action. In so doing, he can dignify what it means to learn on the job and rally teachers to participate in a learning cycle together. Jacob, as well as the teachers, will benefit from the shared study.

Systematize what it means to lead a segment of the school's literacy learning life.

Of course, you yourself can do similar work with another segment, and you can rope in your ELL teacher or your reading specialist to do similar work in another segment, as well. The important thing is that the work you do with your own segment can be a model for what a wholehearted, deeply joyous investment in this work looks like. By doing so, you will send a critical message to those who are working in parallel ways alongside you.

At the Project, we find that it's unbelievably important to formalize the relationships between those of us who are trying to do similar work. That is, if your AP leads K–2 reading, you lead 3–5 writing, and the English department chair leads 6–8 reading, make sure that you take advantage of the fact that the three of you are doing similar work. You have different topics, sure, but similar roles. To lift the level of the work the three of you are doing, it will be important to align what you do in those roles. For example, the ten of us at TCRWP who each leads a cohort of staff developers, all try to align the ways in which we work with our people while they are engaged in staff development in schools. We articulate our goals so that we all agree that we intend to help the staff developers in our cohorts set clear goals, develop their own learning lives, address issues that interfere with their effectiveness, and capitalize on and share their strengths. Early in the school year, the ten of us all try to do one shared visit together at one of our schools, so that we democratize our methods for doing this work. It's hard to schedule all ten of us on a morning to do this, but the impact of that one shared morning is incalculable.

Recently, for example, when ten of us visited Alissa as she did her professional development, one person—Brooke—took primary responsibility for the pre-visit planning time with Alissa. Brooke talked us all through the conversations she had with Alissa prior to our visit, so that we could pitch in ways that our pre-visit conversations are similar and different. We realized that we had different views about whether a pre-visit conversation was a time to give feedback to the plans. As it turned out, some of our feedback to Alissa related to the plans she'd made for her work with teachers. We decided that in the future, we generally will want to help a staff developer revise his or her plans *before* the visit, giving input early on in the process and thinking together about the plan for the PD so that we agree on and take shared responsibility for the hypothetical plans for the PD, knowing that, in fact, both we and the staff developer may end up rethinking those plans once we are actually in the school.

A score of other questions came up as we tried to align our ways of giving feedback and to learn from each other's best ideas. For example, if we see twenty things we want to compliment, do we want to share all those compliments? Do we want to give more compliments after some visits and fewer after other visits, or do we aim to equalize the sheer volume of compliments we give? What about suggestions? If we have ten tips we might give, do we give them all, assuming that the staff developer will want to learn, learn, learn, or do we try to hone in on a few tips? (We decided on the former!) You and the others who are mentoring teachers in ELA and in different curricular areas will want to norm your supervision in similar ways, democratizing your ways of supporting teachers.

In similar ways, if there are a dozen people leading in-district study groups or work groups or PD sessions or parent meetings or anything else—it might be valuable to gather together, doing a case-study example of this work together so that you can learn each other's best practices and build an image of the work that is better than that which any of you might have done on your own. The learning culture in your school needs to exist not only for kids and for teachers but also for you and other leaders.

Locate examples of best practice and shine a spotlight on them.

The general principle that I'm advocating is this: locate examples of best practice and shine a spotlight on them. Suggest that everyone doing similar work learn from those examples. If one substitute teacher is especially helpful, for example, consider asking all your substitutes to observe that one person, and afterward get together to develop a coda for being a great substitute teacher in your school. Do the same with bus drivers!

You'll find that some people have strengths in scheduling, ordering, working with parents, interviewing potential teachers, writing newsletters, and so on. As much as possible, democratize your people's knowledge by making your school into one where everyone learns from others, and people in every line of work aim to develop a shared understanding of best practices.

Your role as principal is to keep a wide-angle lens, taking in the whole school. You are apt to find that good work is happening in one part of the school—and your job is to democratize that work, to make sure that if grade 1 knows A and grade 4 knows B, in the end, those two grades each come away knowing both A and B. You will want to culminate knowledge across any one grade level, between grade levels, and you will want to do that same process across your leadership team.

Helping Teachers Benefit from Each Other's Company

Rufus Jones, the great American Quaker, once said, "I pin my hopes on the small circles and quiet processes in which genuine and reforming change takes place." We too pin our hopes on those small circles.

Some people say that you are what you eat. That is a scary thought. In contrast, at TCRWP, we have found that we are the sum of our conversations, our partnerships, our small circles. We teach youngsters that by talking with others about their writing and their reading, they learn to dialogue with themselves. If a child shares a story she wrote and hears a classmate ask, "Why did you end it that way? How else could you have ended it?" then we know that another time, this writer will pause in the act of writing, shift to rereading, and ask herself, "Why did I end it this way? How else could I have ended it?" When teaching children that the conversations they have with each other become internalized as conversations they have in their own minds as they read and write, we're teaching them what thoughtful reading and writing are all about. The same is true for teachers and for teacher-leaders. The conversations they have with each other become internalized as conversations they have with themselves, as they shift from doing to reflecting.

Give novice teachers mentors, channeling novices to teach in sync with those mentors.

Your novice teachers will benefit enormously when they are partnered with teachers who can help them think about their teaching and their students. The conversations between a novice and an experienced mentor can provide that novice with invaluable support and guidance. The mentor teachers you choose are not necessarily your longest serving, but they should be those you regard as your best. Those relationships may be challenging to finesse, because sometimes the teachers who'd actually be especially good mentors are second- or third-year teachers, not your veterans. Chapter 2, "You Can't Be the Only Leader—But the Job of Delegating Leadership Is Yours," includes tips for how to approach this work.

Mentor teachers will be vastly more powerful learning partners if they and the novice teacher are actually teaching in sync with each other—teaching in the same grade, using the same curriculum, and following a similar curricular calendar. There are few investments that will pay off more than you financing the mentor teacher to spend a day with the novice during those final days of summer, just before school starts, helping that novice teacher to plan her first week or two of school. If your novice teachers start their year teaching in ways that at least aim to be aligned to their mentors, the novice teacher is much more likely to continue under the influence of the master teacher for the duration. Cement this relationship by freeing some of the novice teacher's time, so that she can spend some time observing in his or her mentor's classroom. Encourage the two teachers to occasionally bring their classrooms of children together to coteach a workshop. It's also surprisingly powerful for the teachers to simply swap places, each teaching the other's children for an hour. Think how the conversations that ensue will be dramatically different as a result of that hour!

Support other social structures that help everyone's learning curve stay high.

When my colleagues and I lead the TCRWP summer institutes, each of us is assigned a partner who checks in with us on how the day has gone, providing some morale-boosting and an extra hand. In their first two years, staff developers have mentors who are paid a token amount extra to work with their mentees. A group of especially senior staff developers receive mentoring in public speaking, and another group, in writing. And we're about to start a system in which every staff developer has a mentor—and sometimes the mentors can be far more junior. For example, I will have a new staff developer who will mentor me in incorporating technology into my work. Mary's mentor will be a staff developer specializing in K–2 phonics.

When social structures flag, either abandon or revitalize them.

One challenge is that you will sometimes launch social structures and they—like kids' reading logs—can dwindle down to nothing. For years at TCRWP, each of us took on "a job." Our jobs involved giving of our time and talents in ways that made the community stronger. One person's job was to organize birthday celebrations, while another's job was to help people handle their calendars. But eventually, people began to not really do their jobs. Administrators had to hound them. Feathers got ruffled.

The leadership team at the Project needed to make a decision. We did not want to leave a structure in place that was increasingly ignored, because we knew that doing so teaches our team to ignore structures in general. Leaving a structure in place that was becoming a sham would convey the message that our plans and assignments can be freely ignored. We didn't want to get to the point where leaders' words began to mean nothing. So we met and talked about whether we wanted to breathe new life into that old ritual, or to announce that it had served its time and would be abandoned.

We reincarnated the ritual, this time altering the title of the ritual from "Jobs" to "The Gift of a Day." In this reincarnation of "Jobs," we made a huge effort to ask people what special gift they wanted to give to the organization. We tried to make people's gifts represent their passions and talents. Shana Frazin, who is passionate about books, agreed to select the summer reading books that would be given to us all, and to also help the organization choose books that we'd give to our principals periodically throughout the year. Lisa Corcoran, whose talents in art dazzle us, agreed to lead a team of artists-in-residence who would be on-call to help staff developers who wanted help making a PD tool particularly beautiful and enticing. Gary Petersen, who is especially known as someone who lifts our morale, agreed to lend a hand to the office staff on a day when we all knew their work would be especially overwhelming. The ritual was given new life, and we were reminded that rituals, like people, need to be nurtured.

9

Rising to the Additional Challenges of Particular Populations

As the principal of a school, one of your goals is to help your colleagues provide all children with the richest possible learning environment to help ensure their success. Of course, this is quite a challenging, complex goal, when your school is full of diverse and beautiful students with a wide range of needs. In this chapter, I'll provide suggestions on ways that you can help your teachers succeed in teaching reading and writing workshop to English language learners and to children with disabilities. I'll also discuss some special considerations for teaching reading and writing workshop in the primary grades and in the middle school grades.

Helping Teachers to Provide Support
for English Language Learners

The TCRWP team works with thousands of classrooms around the world that are full of language learners, and we are fully aware that English language learners are one of the fastest-growing demographics in this country. We are also centered in New York City, and for thirty years we have taught reading and writing in diverse classrooms, chock-full of students with a variety of home languages and literacy experiences. We have been fortunate to collaborate with experts in language acquisition, who have helped us study the kinds of instruction and the kinds of theoretical stances that support language learners. Our work is fueled by a beautiful imperative, to fulfill the democratic covenant of equal access to education for all children.

> **IN THIS CHAPTER, YOU'LL FIND . . .**
>
> ▶ Advice on helping teachers to provide support for students who are language learners
>
> ▶ Advice on helping teaches to provide support for students with disabilities
>
> ▶ Special considerations to support teachers of grades K–2
>
> ▶ Special considerations to support middle school teachers

Research has long shown that it is crucial for teachers to recognize language learners' strengths and to build on these as they learn a second or third language. Researchers such as Kellie Rolstad, Kate Mahone, and Gene Glass (2005) and Jim Cummins (1991) have written about how important it is that teachers validate and draw upon students' existing knowledge of the language(s) they speak while teaching them a new language. It's also important that language learners participate in complex, rich study of content as a way to learn a new language (Bernhardt 2011; Hakuta and Santos 2012).

In each *Guide*, I detail some significant ways that teachers can support students' language growth inside a workshop curriculum. Be sure to refer teachers with English language learners to these resources. On our TCRWP website, you'll also find toolkits of supports for ELLs that we've created, specific to each grade level K–8 and to reading and writing. Although some of these toolkits specifically address California standards, the strategies included in each will be transferable to classes around the world with English language learners. Teachers can see, for instance, ways in which each session within each unit is particularly supportive for English learners, as well as ways teachers can add in additional supports, perhaps breaking down their demonstration into specific steps or providing language stems to support students' talk. The Up the Ladder books for grades 3–6 also include similar suggestions within each session.

As a principal, you'll want to develop a few ways to efficiently and thoughtfully assess the level of literacy instruction English learners are receiving in your school. You might invite teachers to join you as researchers in their own classrooms, thinking about modifications they can provide so that English learners can be full participants in each workshop.

To better support English language learners, you might suggest that your teachers consider using these strategies with their students:

- **Provide consistent structures.** The fact that workshop classrooms are organized in clear, predictable, and consistent ways is very helpful for ELLs, because the predictability allows children to quickly become comfortable participating in the work of each day. When teachers follow these routines day after day, students can focus their energies on trying to figure out how to do their work, rather than on worrying over what they are expected to do. You might stress to teachers of ELLs that it is particularly important for them not to skip parts of a workshop, and to keep their expectations for what students will do during each part of the workshop consistent.

- **Use consistent teaching language.** Workshops are characterized by specific, repeated instructional language. The consistency of this language scaffolds learners' classroom experience, making it easier for a child who is just learning English to grasp the unique content that is being taught that day. You might check that teachers of English language learners begin minilessons in a predictable manner, perhaps by saying "Readers," or "Writers," then by reviewing a previous minilesson, perhaps also by referencing that day's Post-it on the anchor chart.

- **Use visuals and gestures whenever possible.** For example, teachers might embed gestures within their minilessons. A teacher might say, "You want to choose a seed idea that is small," squeezing her two fingers together, "not a big large watermelon topic," lifting her arms and making a big circle. Or she may show children what zooming in is by closing her fingers around her eyes, imitating binoculars.

- **Tailor instruction and expectations, based on students' home language facility.** Some children are literate in their first language, others are not. If a teacher knows that a child is literate in his first language, the teacher will want to encourage the child to read and write in his first language, as well as in English. Do not worry if neither you nor the teacher can speak or read the child's first language. This is irrelevant. If those of you who are native speakers of English and I were to live in a nation where people did not speak English, even if we needed to spend six hours a day in a place that did not allow English and even if no one could read what we wrote in English, we would still want to read and write in our first language—and so, too, should children.

- **Facilitate social support for English language learners.** Researchers have a consensus around this: to promote language acquisition in general, it's best if teachers involve children in a rich classroom culture of talk and play, of interactive read-alouds and interactive writing, of structured and unstructured conversations with peers and teachers. Many researchers caution wariness of pull-out instruction that gets in the way of ELLs receiving critical social support. As you check in on classrooms, you might look to see that ELLs are integrated into the social fabric of classrooms, and that partnerships are in place to support ELLs' language development. In many cases, such as when children are in the silent stage of language acquisition, triads would be especially helpful, in which an English language learner is grouped with two proficient speakers of English who act as models.

- **Focus especially on English language learners' vocabulary development.** ELLs benefit from explicit instruction to build their vocabularies. Check to see that teachers are providing vocabulary instruction to English language learners, perhaps introducing a few high-leverage vocabulary words at a time, or specifically teaching words students will need to know for a content study.

Helping Teachers to Support Children with Disabilities

As the principal of a school, one of your responsibilities is to make sure that you and your colleagues move heaven and earth to give all kids access to the richest possible learning environment. Your teachers will look to you for signals that will guide the entire school culture, and it will be important that you demonstrate that providing access to each learner is a moral imperative.

There are some obvious places to start. For example, it goes without saying that in classrooms with two teachers, one a licensed general education teacher and one a licensed special education teacher, both teachers need the curriculum—in this instance, the Units of Study books—and both need to be part of the same staff development. It is also important that you set up structures so that the two teachers take shared responsibility for the curriculum. That is, we find if one teacher becomes the reading expert and takes responsibility for that part of the curriculum, while the other becomes the writing expert and teaches all the writing lessons, the result is often teachers using inconsistent language and methods with students.

Classrooms that contain students with disabilities are distinctively individual, as are the students within those classrooms, but there are a few commonalities that generally hold true across classrooms. Certainly in self-contained special education classes—that is, in classrooms in which every child has an IEP and the teacher-student ratio is lower—the pace of the curriculum is often altered. If your teachers are using the Units of Study, it can help for you to suggest they prioritize sessions that feel most important to their students, so that units of study don't drag on forever. For example, some teachers may elect to skip the third bend in a book.

Then too, if a particular session teaches a big idea (for example, writers notice the techniques an author has used) and mentions a collection of related subordinate ideas (writers notice techniques such as show don't tell, repetition, figurative language, symbolism), the teacher will probably decide to drop out mention of some of those subordinate ideas, focusing more on the main point of the lesson. Those subordinate ideas can be taught during small groups or one-to-one instruction to students who are ready for them.

The Up the Ladder units will be especially helpful for teachers in upper-grade classrooms who feel as if their students need repeated opportunities to practice what is being taught. One of the advantages of that series is that students are channeled to write on kinds of paper that are especially supportive, borrowing from some of the decisions that primary teachers make. For example, some older students benefit from sketching before they write and from writing in booklets instead of on long sheets of notebook paper. You'll probably find that it's helpful for teachers of students with disabilities, especially those in the upper grades, to have the K–2 Units of Study in addition to the grades 3–5 set of books.

Before each school year begins, encourage teachers to survey their libraries next to their list of reading levels for their incoming students. It can be devastating to a student's self-esteem and reading identity to have to visit the coach's office or the bookroom to book shop because there aren't any books on that student's reading level in the classroom. Help teachers make sure they have books in their classroom libraries that represent the wide variety of students in their classrooms. The TCRWP Below-Benchmark Classroom Libraries will be especially useful resources if teachers are looking for lower-level high-interest books.

Your teachers might benefit from professional development that explores coteaching methods. Often in classrooms that have two teachers (a general education teacher and a special education teacher), one teacher leads the minilesson, while the other teacher positions herself where students might need the most support and coaches those students. One teacher might also research individual children to figure out what they are learning from the minilesson and how to support them learning even more. The two teachers most often rotate this role. Sometimes teachers parallel teach, with both teaching the same minilesson to half the class, so students have opportunities to access the same content in smaller-sized groups. One of those teachers might, however, teach the minilesson to children who are standing up, using whole-body actions to support concepts in the minilesson. Alternatively, if the level of the minilesson doesn't feel appropriate to the entire class, teachers might create more homogeneous groupings and model different strategies appropriate for different writers. If, for example, the minilesson is about ways to add dialogue to writing, the teachers can model different ways to do that with varying levels of sophistication—adding speech bubbles, using quotation marks, using paragraph indents, and so on. Your teacher teams will benefit from shared planning time to think through which coteaching methods will be the highest leverage in different situations.

A guiding principle should be flexibility. If some learners find it difficult to sit on the floor during a minilesson, those children might be assigned to chairs on the periphery. If some need to be holding an object while listening, then by all means, provide them with the appropriate object. If some benefit from software that encodes their speech, then secure that software. The goal is to give all learners the opportunity to learn.

Special Considerations for the Primary Grades, K–2

Support teachers with scheduling and time management.

Most of the contents of this book are equally applicable to teachers of primary and of upper-grade students, but primary teachers have special worries about the schedule of their day. There are many components of balanced literacy that are important to young children, and teachers will rightly wonder whether all of these can be shoehorned into a ninety-minute literacy block. The answer, frankly, is no.

In the end, you and your teachers will need to make decisions about the amount of time that is dedicated to fostering your children's literacy. We cannot make that decision for you, but certainly we can emphasize that teachers are correct if they think we advocate them devoting time beyond the reading and writing workshop to phonics (twenty to thirty minutes), shared reading, interactive writing, and read-aloud.

I will also say this: I believe that kids benefit from consistency whenever possible. Morning meeting should generally run for about the same amount of time each day, as should reading workshop, writing workshop, phonics time, shared reading, and the rest.

The following chart summarizes approximate amounts of time we recommend teachers allot to each subject or activity. Of course, these amounts of time can be tweaked based on district requirements, or by individual teachers based on the needs of their class.

SUBJECT/ACTIVITY	MINUTES
Reading	45–60
Writing	45–60
Phonics	20
Read-aloud	15
Shared reading	15
Interactive/shared writing (often merges with morning meeting and/or science/social studies)	10–15
Math	45
Choice/science	45
Phonics extensions/transitions	5–10
Specials/other	40–45

In each *Guide*, including the newly released *A Guide to the Phonics Units of Study*, we offer specifics for teachers on how they might organize their daily schedule so as to fit in everything.

Provide students with the books and the paper they need.

Providing time for read-aloud, shared reading, and phonics—as well as for reading and writing workshop—matters, but so, too, does the provisioning of materials. Kids can't read and write up a storm without having access to lots and lots of within-reach books (and poems, songs, signs) and to lots and lots of paper. Now is not a time to jealously guard paper supplies.

Time and again, we have seen an entire curriculum rollout derailed because teachers don't have the supplies they need to pull off the curriculum. Although teachers theoretically could write Donors Choose grants and race through tag sales and library closings to secure the books they need to provide a welcoming classroom library to their children, the truth is that teachers barely have time enough to prepare for the next day. They can't turn the world upside down in an effort to provide their students with at least a barely minimal classroom library. This needs to be the job of the school leader.

How many books are enough? Many more than you might imagine. Start with the idea that each of your thirty kids will need at least ten books in his or her book bag—that's 300 books at the levels your students are reading today. Presumably you'll want books remaining in the bins after kids have chosen their books, so now you're thinking at least 600 books. Of course, they'll be reading those books early in the year and eventually they'll progress to an entirely different collection of books, so now you are imagining that number of books at higher levels: 1,200 books. And that is just for *one* of the classrooms at that grade level. By second grade, children will read longer books so these numbers can decrease.

Answer primary teachers' predictable questions.

Primary teachers ask a few predictable questions that you can help them with. First, they wonder when they can start the units of study in reading, writing, and phonics. Some suggest they need a month to socialize students into workshop etiquette or to teach letters and sounds prior to launching the units. Teachers can, of course, make that decision, but the units are designed to be launched at the *start* of kindergarten, first, and second grade. The only exception is the second-grade writing units—we've provided an entrance ramp to that unit in the second-grade writing online resources for teachers who think that might be helpful.

When teachers ask questions about when to begin the units of study in reading, writing, and phonics, these questions all relate to teachers' uncertainty over how there can be a reading and writing workshop "if kids can't yet read or write." The units will help with this; we especially encourage teachers to read the sections in the front matter of each reading unit that detail children's literacy development during this stage.

Primary teachers also ask about how to schedule guided reading groups. Channel those teachers to read chapters about this in *A Guide to the Reading Workshop*. The short answer, however, is that usually teachers include guided reading as one of several forms of small groups that are held during the reading workshop, while some children read independently. These groups are kept brief, and teachers also lead strategy groups, shared reading groups, and interactive and shared writing groups.

Special Considerations for Middle School

Considering the Middle School ELA Schedule— and Ways to Change It, if Needed

In a presentation at a recent conference in Seattle, Doug Reeves posited that a middle school schedule is a "moral document." In fact, the schedule for any child's school day is a moral document. Your schedule needs to reflect your beliefs and values about what's important for kids' learning.

We suggest those of you who lead middle schools take a moment to peruse your students' schedules, asking yourself, "How many minutes does a middle school student in my school get each day, each week, for ELA?" Then ask yourself, "How many minutes do students get for soccer?" Many principals who undertake this challenge find that kids are getting many more minutes each week to get better at a sport than they are getting for reading or writing. Kids may get more or equal time for band or for art. That might make sense if you are a specialized school, training future professional athletes, musicians, or artists. You may decide it makes less sense if you are hoping your students will thrive academically.

My colleagues and I strongly believe that every content class, every high-stakes exam that your students will take in high school, has, as its underpinnings, a hidden curriculum of reading and writing. Your students can't study science unless they can read science texts. They can't do well on math exams unless they are fast, adept, and analytical at reading word problems. They can't answer those history questions unless they can write quickly and with complex organizational skills, as they need to shuttle between facts and interpretations, and to show how information illustrates ideas.

Kids who have emerged from our Units of Study in middle school are turning out to be terrific at the kinds of high-stakes exams that they are expected to take in high school. When they have to generate an essay inside of an hour for an AP exam or the SAT, they are confident, having written on-demand pieces at the start and end of every writing unit, as well as flash-drafts inside the units. When they have to read steadily and analytically for an hour, they have the stamina and expertise to do so, having spent many hours reading like this.

So, what's an *ideal* schedule for middle school? It is best if students receive between 90 minutes to 120 minutes a day for reading and writing workshop, separate from science or social studies. That allows teachers to teach a full curriculum of five to six writing units and the same number of reading units. It means kids are always writing and always reading. It means teachers have twice as much time, with half as many kids, compared to teachers who are teaching inside of a forty-five-minute schedule.

Of course, middle school schedules vary, and many schools must cope with having just forty-five minutes a day for language arts, or combining language arts and social studies, sometimes in one forty-five-minute period a day. If that is the schedule in your school, one suggestion is to channel your teachers to alternate units month by month, teaching a writing unit one month and a reading unit the next month. At the same time, don't be too accepting of such a schedule, because it truly doesn't offer enough time. If you can cobble together even just another one or two forty-five-minute blocks a week for ELA, then while the kids are deeply engaged in a reading unit, they could be working on independent writing projects, meeting once or twice a week to get feedback from a teacher and each other. In a month when writing is front and center, the kids could pursue favorite genre studies on their own and meet once or twice a week in book clubs that support that independent reading. Even that is not enough time, however.

You'll want to look at your schedule, and if you're not satisfied with it, think about how, over the next year or two, you can change it. Almost always, you need to involve parents, and your parents need to understand how deeply committed you are to their kids' academic achievement, to their education.

If you want more opportunity for kids to do music, art, and sports, consider a rich after-school club program, where kids can work on those without compromising their academics. I'll offer, once again, a Finnish example: in *The Smartest Kids in the World*, Amanda Ripley looks at Finland, where schools are sites of academic instruction, and all other instruction happens immediately after the school day in clubs (2014). Perhaps you might have a shifting schedule, and arts and music teachers offer classes before and after school for kids who want to study more seriously?

As you think about your schedule for middle school ELA, we caution you to resist the trap of thinking that it will work for middle school kids to read and write at home, coming to school to learn about that reading and writing. For example, one thing we know for certain is that for kids to read more *outside* school, they need to read more *inside* school. There is a direct correlation between how much kids get to read inside of school, and how much they read outside of school.

We strongly encourage you to take your schedule seriously, get a team to look at it, and plan for the schedule—and the academic achievement—that you want.

There are a few questions that pop up again and again in our conversations with middle school teachers. We're often asked whether kids really gather together in a meeting area for minilessons in middle school, and our answer, is "Yes, absolutely." We've found it makes a world of difference if kids are huddled together, close to the teacher, for a short chunk of time before dispersing to spots around the room to read. The entire tone in the room shifts. That doesn't mean that all kids need to be sitting on the rug, cross-legged, before the teacher begins. Teachers might have a small rug area, surrounded by chairs or benches, where kids convene, or even a makeshift meeting area where kids gather with chairs if there isn't a rug. Consider working with one teacher in the school to create a model reading or writing workshop classroom environment, helping him reorganize one day after school and perhaps providing a budget for that teacher to purchase a rug, lamp, book shelves, and bins. Then, you might encourage that teacher to invite others in to visit so they get a vision of what's possible.

Teachers might also have questions about read-aloud. Due to scheduling constraints in most middle schools, there isn't time for a separate read-aloud each day, as we recommend in K–5 classrooms. Instead, you'll see teachers reading aloud to students at the start of each bend. They might read aloud an article, a short story, an excerpt from a nonfiction chapter book. Especially if they are reading from a chapter book, chances are that they won't have time to read the whole book aloud. Students won't need their own copies of the book, since the teacher will be reading aloud, and since they'll have their own independent reading books to dive into during the workshop time.

Turning Content Classes into Sites of Intense Reading, Research, and Writing

Especially if your students' time for literacy instruction is brief, you'll want to consider how you can recruit your content-area teachers to understand their role in supporting literacy instruction. An accessible way to start is to encourage content-area teachers to remind kids to use reading strategies they learned in reading workshop, such as previewing a text, embracing the complexities of a text and seeing that there may be more than one main idea in a passage or chapter, reading closely to gather evidence, and synthesizing information on a topic from a variety of sources. You might also look at the volume of reading your students are engaged in outside of ELA. In all of our middle school content classrooms, we seek to engage students in a high volume of reading, so they learn *how* to read science and social studies texts while learning content.

In some schools, ELA teachers will teach a nonfiction reading unit, perhaps *Tapping the Power of Nonfiction*, early in the school year and then pass the unit to a science teacher, who will reteach Bends II and III, this time inviting students to study texts related to climate change or a similar topic. In other schools, content teachers take complete responsibility for one of the grade-level nonfiction units, and they divide up the bends across the year, where relevant, perhaps first inviting students to read longer nonfiction chapter books about the American Revolution during the first unit, and then inviting students to research topics related to the Civil Rights era during a later unit. There are even schools where the content teachers dive into *Historical Fiction Book Clubs,* curating collections of texts on eras they study and inviting students to bring their content knowledge to bear on their books. Encourage your teacher teams to study the grade-level units of study and make decisions about who will take on which units collaboratively.

Similar decisions can be made with grade-level writing units. Sixth-grade social studies teachers might decide to take on the *Research-Based Information Writing* unit and incorporate relevant content. Or, if the unit is taught in ELA, social studies teachers could bring out relevant charts and writing checklists from the units the next time they ask kids to engage in information writing.

One way to engage your content teachers implicitly with literacy work is to suggest they study student notebooks in social studies and science. When teachers study the work of kids who are getting top scores on Advanced Placement and International Baccalaureate exams, they frequently notice that almost all of them have amazing notebooks. They don't just take notes, they often share them in study groups. They go back in and annotate. They use their notes for projects and studying. Often, when you get your content teachers studying notebooks, that leads into a curiosity about kids' reading work, as well as into what kind of writing is happening.

All this means that content teachers need to be invited to professional development, whether it's done in-house or provided by TCRWP. Inviting content teachers to cycles of staff development on accelerating progress for kids reading below benchmark or on teaching kids to write well-crafted informational texts. Doing so will ensure there's a shared set of teaching methods and expectations in the building. Make sure that access to professional development is shared across the staff in your building.

Establishing Structures across the School and Community

PART THREE shifts from a focus on classrooms to a focus on your school community as a whole. In this part, you'll think about the structures you can put into place to support literacy in deep, lasting ways, including: setting up feedback cycles through instructional rounds and targeted conversations, putting into place rituals and traditions to support your school community's unique character, and staying the course in the face of new initiatives.

◆ ◆ ◆ ◆ ◆

10 Data-Based Instructional Rounds in Reading and Writing Workshops

*I*n most of the districts in which my colleagues and I work, instructional rounds are an important structure. They provide a way for you, the school principal, and other leaders to focus on the quality of instruction in your whole school and to gather energy around tackling a few especially high-leverage schoolwide problems of practice. Teacher-leaders often participate in these inquiries, perhaps involving a representative from each grade. Often instructional rounds that occur early in the year are done in-house, and then the superintendent, other principals, and other district leaders join instructional rounds later in the year. Some districts even conduct instructional rounds that circle through the schools in the district—or in a subgroup within a large district.

Instructional rounds aim to take the pulse of instruction in a school or district. The two terms—*instructional rounds* and *walk-throughs*—are sometimes used interchangeably, but in fact, instructional rounds are intended to be more structured, more focused, and more data-based than walk-throughs or learning walks. The term *round* captures the fact that the team walks 'round to classrooms, investigating within them. It also captures the cyclical process, the rotation between studying data, observing in classrooms across the school, analyzing the now-broader set of data again, tackling a problem of practice and then, two months later, repeating the process. In this chapter, I'll focus on instructional rounds that target literacy instruction, on helping you study the literacy instruction in your school to find high-leverage problems of practice to tackle. A not of thanks to my colleague, Janet Steinberg, for critical input in this chapter.

> **IN THIS CHAPTER, YOU'LL FIND . . .**
>
> ▶ An overview of the Instructional Rounds Cycle including what it is and is not, possible goals, and how a cycle might unfold over time
>
> ▶ Descriptions of the first step of instructional rounds: ways to study results from reading and writing tests
>
> ▶ Lenses observers might use in instructional rounds, including what data to collect in classrooms and ways to study it, with examples
>
> ▶ Examples of problems of practice selected by school teams based on data collected in classrooms

An Overview of the Instructional Rounds Cycle

As mentioned above, the cycle starts with a probing look at a school's data, broadly defined. The analysis of data is generally started before participants convene—by an appointed "analyst" from the participant team. Then, participants mull over the analysis, generating questions and perhaps some hypotheses. These hypotheses provide a focus for the ensuing classroom visits, always mindful that to presume learning is happening, one needs evidence. Therefore, observers look at evidence of instruction and learning, such as class-made charts and student work. People observe students at work and interview individuals. During visits to classrooms (and corridors), each team member observes with one particular focus as the group proceeds through classrooms and corridors, across the entire school.

For example, a review of the data may have highlighted that many students struggle with nonfiction texts. The participants in the instructional rounds might then look to see the following:

- What is the volume of nonfiction reading that selected kids (perhaps a low-, medium-, and high-level child) have done so far in comparison to their volume of fiction?

- What percentage of the books in the classroom are nonfiction? How are they organized and "marketed" to kids, and how does all this compare to the classroom's fiction books?

- If a few representative readers are asked to read aloud a bit of their nonfiction books, can they do so with fluency, accuracy, and comprehension? If they are asked to do this with their fiction books, are the results similar? If nonfiction fares less well, is the issue mis-leveled books or readers who read one level in fiction and another in nonfiction?

- What strategies do one or two students report using to read a nonfiction text? Do they overview the text? Notice if it is narrative or expository and adjust accordingly? Notice text structure? Pause to recall and to ask, "What is this mainly about?" If pressed, can they name and show *only* strategies they use?

- What strategies from ELA does a selected kid seem to draw upon when he explains how he reads a social studies or science text? Does he orient himself to the text, chunk the text, and pause to rethink and monitor for sense?

- What has been the ratio of fiction to nonfiction read-alouds? If you can ask the teacher or see evidence about the nonfiction read-alouds, what do you learn? Is there evidence that the teacher plans stopping spots, demonstrates skills, supports conversation? Is reading aloud similar or different before fiction and nonfiction?

- What is the ratio of time spent on information writing units versus narrative writing?

- When you assess selected students' narrative and information writing, do they seem stronger in narrative than in information writing or vice-versa?

- What do kids say they do to write a good nonfiction text? Do they name: introductions and conclusions, text boxes, graphics, sources for their information? Is there evidence that instruction in information writing has "stuck"?

- When you survey students to learn their favorite genre/texts in reading and writing, what patterns do you see that illuminate the group's central focus?

- When you scan the classroom/corridor to see the lessons that the physical spaces teach, the messages being sent about the relative value of nonfiction, what do you note?

Although participants will observe specific lenses, you'll want to keep in mind that the goal for an instructional round is to see cross-school patterns. This is not a time to generate and give individual feedback to specific teachers.

Whatever the assigned lens, observers probe, zooming in on one individual and then another, going through the contents of an individual's desk or notebook, digging for evidence like a detective, asking follow-up questions. For example, if the observer asks a child what she is doing as she reads, and the child says, "When we read, we . . . like . . . we . . . divide it into parts, and then we stop at the parts to think about what it said," the observer would press, asking, "Where was the last place that you stopped in this book you are reading now?" The observer might suggest the child continue reading while the observer moves to another child, saying, "Come get me when you reach another stopping spot," and then, later, the observer might ask, "What are you thinking now that you have stopped at this place?" That is, the observers press a point far enough to find and collect evidence about what the work and learning entail.

While these observations must be detailed, each classroom visit is only ten minutes. The important thing is that each observer maintains a focus and collects only that information, intensely, in many classrooms.

Again, instructional rounds are not meant as a way to evaluate a particular teacher. It's outside the boundaries for someone to visit a classroom and say, "That teacher needs . . ." Instead, the point is to think about what the patterns across the grade level and the school show about ways to help *all* teachers be more effective. If there is an evaluation going on, the observers are mostly evaluating those whose job it is to lift the level of teaching and learning. The effort aims to unearth overarching patterns in instruction, and especially those that merit attention. If two teachers at a grade level are considerably less effective than the others at that grade level, the team of observers will likely be thinking, "What has the school done to be sure that *all* teachers get the support they need? Which structures exist to allow the less experienced teachers to grow?" The rounds are designed as a way to generate a direction for improvement for a school, and that focal point is often called the *problem of practice*.

After the instructional rounds, the participants will gather to debrief, pooling all the traces of instruction and evidence of learning they have found that might yield an understanding of a problem of practice that feels especially high-leverage for that school. Together, they analyze the evidence and make a decision about what to try as a next step. They also decide how to communicate what they have learned to the rest of the school and think about what the work forward might entail.

After another eight or ten weeks of schoolwide work, after everyone has wrestled for a bit to address the targeted problem of practice, there will be another set of instructional round classroom visits. At that point, participants will again collect focused data to see how the improvements are taking root and what the *next* steps might be.

This cycle continues until the next year, when usually, school leaders reexamine the data widely once again and decide on a new, high-leverage problem of practice, in the light of the prior year's work.

It can be thrilling to inquire deeply, to look analytically at the instruction across a school or district to find opportunities to improve—but it's not at all easy to know what to study or even how to look to see high-leverage problems. It isn't easy to know *how* to look at classroom teaching, student work, and school culture in ways that produce insight. In the rest of this chapter, then, I lay out what you and your team might look at, what lenses you might take, what questions you might ask, to uncover and select a deeply rooted, high-leverage problem of practice in your school.

Before you read on, you might flip to the end of this chapter to examples of problems of practice. This will give you an idea of the scope and breadth of some problems of practice that have proved to be fruitful for schools we know well.

A First Step: Studying the Results of the Reading and Writing Tests

Before the whole team gathers for instructional rounds, a data analyst (and this could a teacher or a teacher-team or person with relevant experience) looks analytically at the reading and writing test results.

Studying Reading Test Results

When studying the reading testing results, the analyst will want to question any packaged report the school will have already received from the state or the testing company. Often, such analyses attribute students' errors to a particular reading skill deficiency when actually, much of time, the issue is something completely different. When looking at where many students in the school or the grade level went wrong, it will be important to look beyond the packaged report that often comes with the scores.

This issue may be a particular passage's overall **level of difficulty**. The report may suggest that students struggled with specific questions about a passage because the students were not able to name character traits, for example, but it may be very clear that the source of difficulty was the text complexity of the passage.

The analyst will also want to look at the **wording of the questions** that students mostly missed. Might the issue be that the test-maker uses different terminology than the children are used to? For example, in a recent New York State test, kids were thrown off when the test asked, "What quality about Ben Franklin is emphasized in both articles?" The children hadn't known that *quality* can be a synonym for *trait*, and therefore, they were confused.

It is also helpful to consider whether kids in a school struggle more with understanding one **genre** than others. For example, perhaps the questions that threw kids off were those that involved narrative nonfiction passages, although students scored well with fiction and with expository information texts.

Perhaps the problematic passages were last on the test, and **stamina** could have been the problem. There will also be instances when the students (especially the more proficient ones) **didn't read the directions**, or **take the time to read everything**, including the front matter and the captions to the illustrations. Those issues can sometimes reveal themselves on closer examination of test data.

Of course, the data analyst will also search for **skill-related patterns**. It is common to see kids struggle with some of the more analytic questions, such as those about author's craft, and questions about the way a specific passage connects to the larger text.

Sometimes kids are confounded by questions that seem to adults to be easy—such as questions about the setting—and the analyst will probably end her data analysis with questions that need to be explored, as well as with some hunches about possible sources of difficulty.

Studying Writing Test Results

Of course, it is equally important to study the writing data. Most states give schools legal permission to look at the students' actual writing (done in testing booklets or on the computer) for instructional purposes. It's a lot to ask an analyst to study *all* the kids' writing, but it will be useful if, prior to this day, the analyst:

■ Zooms in on a few writing samples that represent three levels of proficiency (low, middle, high) from one grade level, for starters. Ideally the teacher may have identified those students as representative.

- Rereads the prompt or question and, if the prompt references texts, rereads those texts as well. To study students' responses, the analyst almost needs to take the test himself or herself, becoming familiar with the prompt and with the texts that are referenced in it.

- Studies the exemplar answers that the state provides.

- Turns to the mid-level writers and reads what they have written, trying to figure out if the issue that kept them from achieving more is a writing issue or—if this is writing about reading—a reading issue. Part of the issue may be that the passages were written at high levels of text complexity and studying the students' writing won't illuminate the problem. If it is a writing issue, the analyst will look between the state rubrics and each of the samples, asking, "What do these mid-level kids seem to be missing? What have they succeeded at already?"

- The analyst does similar work with the lower- and higher-level writing samples, and in that way emerges with some hunches and some questions about instruction at that grade level.

- The analyst does similar work with another grade level and then thinks about patterns emerging between them.

For example, the analyst may find, as my colleagues and I have, that sometimes students who are especially strong writers don't score well on passage-based written responses, because they draw too much on their own thinking and not enough from the test passages. Then again, sometimes we have found that these kids can be so creative and so long-winded that we suspect their evaluator didn't see their writing's structure (the sheer volume of writing, the lengthy lead, made that hard for an impatient evaluator to see at a glance), so the evaluator missed the fact that they actually *have* answered the question. Sometimes these kids need to be taught to be more constrained, more structured, more accurate, and more concise. They need to learn to draw upon the passage more, to include citations and facts. They also need to be very obvious about their text structure, relying on paragraphs and very explicit, prominent transitions.

In the 2018 New York State test, fourth-graders were asked to write an essay that developed similarities and differences between two nonfiction passages that both addressed the same topic. In an award-winning Title I school, the kids were able to look between the two texts, noticing what was the same and different between those texts. However, the kids' introductions and conclusions lacked any of the craft elements that could give them extra points. That is, the kids had done the hard parts that were called for, but still needed to write introductions and conclusions that would be equal to the analytic work they'd done. Interestingly enough, the kids in that school were found to have a matching challenge in reading: they tended to focus on the particular part of the text that was before them, and they didn't integrate that part with the beginning and ending of the passage, ignoring those as readers, just as they gave short shrift to introductions and conclusions in their writing. The problem of practice for that school became the goal to work across *whole texts*, integrating parts together.

Studying Test Results for Patterns in Subgroups

It will be important to look at the big picture of all this data, across the field of the whole school. What percentage of kids are below benchmark at each grade level, at each classroom and, most of all, how has that changed over time? Are there more below benchmark in a certain group than there were a year ago? Do high-performing students show at least one year and ideally more than a year of growth, or do high-performing kids seem to flat-line from year to year? What patterns can one see when looking at the schoolwide data? For example, have kids in one classroom or one grade level made much more (or much less) progress than kids in another room or at another grade? If there are kids who are regressing over the years, is there any apparent commonality that may indicate an area in need of schoolwide attention? For example, are these the boys, the ELLs, the most proficient students, the kids with IEPs, the kids in a specific classroom, or some other group in need of a schoolwide focus?

The data you and your team gather doesn't control the next steps, so much as it engines and directs the inquiry. It will give you and your team hunches about what the high-leverage problems of practice might be, helping you to develop lenses for observing and gathering information about instruction in classrooms.

Planning for the Classroom Lenses Observers Might Use in Instructional Rounds

It would be easy to assign roles during the observation that are like this: one person looks at writing notebooks, another at reading Post-its, another at small-group work, another at conferring. The problem is that if the assignment to "look at" something is that open ended, the viewer could end up looking at almost anything or everything. Say the viewer was asked to look at student writing, for example. Is the viewer looking at sentence length? Spelling? Genre characteristics? Revision? And is the viewer looking at strong students? Less proficient students? ELA writing? Writing across the curriculum? A tighter focus will yield more insights and make it more likely that the viewer actually brings the same lens across classrooms.

To settle upon lenses to bring to the instructional rounds, it helps to look at places and ways in which kids aren't progressing—in either reading or writing—and ask, "What could be holding them back?" It also helps to compare those places or instances with success stories and to ask, "What's different in instances where the kids *are* doing well in contrast to instances when they aren't doing well?" It will be by putting the two side by side, that insights emerge.

Remember that in a day devoted to instructional rounds, each observer will take a different lens into all of the visited classrooms to gather wide data with that specific lens. To give you the big picture, let's look at the variety of lenses that observers brought with them on one instructional round.

Example: Lenses Taken by Observers in One Early Instructional Round

After looking over the data analyst's conclusions and discussing implications about instruction across the school, participants in this instructional round developed the hunch that kids in their school might not be actually performing as proficiently as the pieces of writing and teacher-noted reading levels suggested. They wondered if learners across the school might be overly scaffolded and therefore not receiving enough opportunities for repeated independent practice.

To confirm or disprove this particular hunch, one of the observers in the instructional rounds agreed to look at the **running records** in each classroom. She more specifically studied the records of a few higher-level readers. Had teachers taken into account comprehension, as well as word accuracy, for those readers? Were kids holding high-level books but not comprehending them? Were they using reading skills that one typically sees in readers of far less complex texts?

Meanwhile, a different observer looked at the **writing about reading** that a few especially strong readers had done, looking against the learning progression from Units of Study. This visitor tried to see if, for example, the student's reading level was on par with the thinking level revealed in her writing about the books, as described in the learning progressions. This visitor had a partner who joined into this investigation, and the partner specifically looked at the same

reader's written responses in the content areas, noticing again the level of comprehension work the child seemed to be doing in that context. For example, if the child seemed to be thinking about character motivations in ELA, was she also thinking about why people did things when reading history? Was there any evidence of transfer from ELA to social studies reading?

Yet another visitor compared the student's **on-demand writing**—or any one day's writing—with that child's **published writing**. This person also looked for evidence of adult input. Was there more or less adult input for more or less skilled writers? Were there particular areas in which the adult input seemed especially dominant? Was the adult input helping writers with next-step improvements or was it aimed far above the writer's reach?

Yet another observer looked at **evidence of the writing process** to see instances in which kids assessed and improved *their own* drafts. The visitor interviewed students to ask them, "If you were going to make this writing even better, what might you do?" to see kinds of improvements in their writing that students seemed able to envision.

Another observer in this round **talked to teachers to understand more about her** goals for her students, and her plans for helping students meet those goals. To what extent has the teacher calibrated goals for her students? Were the goals for the less proficient learners ambitious yet within reach for them? Was there evidence that the teacher believed that with work, those students could meet those goals with independence—or were the goals for the less proficient learners so high that it seemed unlikely those students could reach them without a lot of scaffolding?

Another observer **listened to each teacher teach**, focusing on whether the teacher was supporting kids in doing the work themselves, allowing for productive struggle, or was scaffolding (or even doing) work the learner needed to be doing. This observer also noted wait time.

Of course, that instructional round was shaped by hunches that the observers formed from a study of their data, and different data will lead to instructional rounds in which participants approach their visits with very different lenses. It might be helpful to imagine an array of possible ways in which a visitor could look at any one thing. In the upcoming sections, I lay out a repertoire of possible ways to look at running records, reading performance assessments, writing folders and notebooks, and to look at and interview students as they read or write. This is meant as a menu of options, although there will be times when it will especially pay off to look at two or three of these indicators in relation to each other.

Lenses on Running Records

In most K–5 balanced literacy classrooms, teachers will conduct running records as a way to understand readers' ways of reading and to track readers' progress over time. There are lots of different angles to bring to a study of running records, starting with some initial questions:

- How often does the teacher conduct them?

- Is this the only way for a reader to progress to new levels of text complexity?

- What does a running record entail for this teacher? How much time does the teacher spend conducting them?

- What information does the teacher draw from these?

Try to ascertain what the spoken or unspoken policies are that guide how (and how often) these are given and what is involved in giving running records. Is there some consistency across K–2 classrooms, grade 3 classrooms? 4–5? Is the consistency related to grade level or to readers' proficiency levels? Look beyond running records to see whether beginning readers in different classrooms are all assessed similarly. That is, do all readers working with level E texts participate in a developmental spelling inventory, in addition to running records? In an assessment of their command of high-frequency words? Or does that only happen for the younger children who are reading at these levels?

See if there are any patterns between how running records are given and the number of times they are given. That is, do teachers who do extremely complete jobs with running records only give them three times a year, whereas teachers who shortcut the process give them vastly more often? Note, too, whether the only way for a reader to move into a higher level of text complexity in a classroom is through the teacher seeing a certain score on a running record, or whether teachers use other indicators to signal that children are ready to tackle more complex texts.

Note the weight that is put on a reader's comprehension. Are some teachers using running records only to determine levels of text difficulty at which readers read with accuracy, or is there a schoolwide commitment to at least basic levels of comprehension?

When you study students' running record levels, you'll again want to look between one thing and another. One of the most telling things to look for will be whether a child's running record score generally aligns to the scores that child receives on the high-stakes test. To ascertain this, a viewer will need access to both sets of information. Do the running records suggest that this child is reading below benchmark, at benchmark, or above benchmark level? Does that match the score the reader received from the high-stakes test? If the teacher's running records suggest a child can handle level T texts which mean the child is at benchmark for that grade level, but meanwhile the reader received a 1 on the state test, the running record data and the test data don't match. That requires investigation. (Teachers may be inadvertently inflating the running record scores by looking only at accuracy, not weighing comprehension, thereby sending students to books that aren't actually at their just-right levels.)

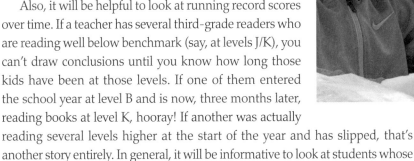

Also, it will be helpful to look at running record scores over time. If a teacher has several third-grade readers who are reading well below benchmark (say, at levels J/K), you can't draw conclusions until you know how long those kids have been at those levels. If one of them entered the school year at level B and is now, three months later, reading books at level K, hooray! If another was actually reading several levels higher at the start of the year and has slipped, that's another story entirely. In general, it will be informative to look at students whose running record levels are remaining flat or regressing.

It will be telling to study the correlation between the level of text complexity at which readers are reading (as shown by running records) and the actual reading work they are doing. For example, perhaps readers are reading level U texts, but instead of doing the work that one would expect at that level of text complexity, such as considering how a character changes and wondering if this is connected to bigger themes in a story, they seem to be doing the work that one expects at levels K/L/M, such as simply naming the traits of the main character. This discrepancy will be evident if you compare the relevant learning progression from *Reading Pathways* to students' Post-its, reading notebooks, and other reflections of their thinking and think, "Are these readers doing the work that texts at this level of complexity ask readers to do?"

The previous questions get at the heart of the consistency, usefulness, and effectiveness of running records across a school, which will be intimately tied to many literacy problems of practice.

Lenses on Reading Performance Assessments

In addition to running records, you will also want to look at performance assessments. The previous section, of course, already highlighted ways in which you can look between running records and students' Post-its and jottings about their reading. Studying such writing about reading is a form of performance assessment. In the grades 3–5 reading Units of Study, we have also included more formal performance assessments that can be conducted at the start and at the end of each unit. Again, an observer in pertinent grades might note how different teachers use that form of reading assessment:

- Do all the teachers across a grade level have a common way of conducting those assessments?

- How much time do different teachers designate to these assessments and their analysis?

- What sort of scoring process does each teacher undertake?

- What does each teacher report having learned from these assessments?

- How do these assessments influence instruction?

Just as the observer who is looking at running records tried to see spoken and unspoken policies informing their use, this observer will want to try to ascertain what policies are guiding how (and how often) these are used. If there are some teachers who report that these performance assessments have been worthwhile, requiring relatively small amounts of time and yielding a lot of help for their instruction, what do these teachers do with the performance assessments that seems to make them pay off? If other teachers report these are too time-intensive to be worthwhile, are these teachers conducting or scoring the performance assessments differently?

The person who is studying performance assessments might want to dig deeper by homing in on a particular skill. It could be that the observer looks at a particular skill in every classroom—say, she looks at students' work with character traits. She might interview two students in every classroom—a proficient and a less proficient reader—to learn what they think good readers do when thinking about character traits. Then this observer might look between the work these readers are doing in relation to character traits and the expectations for character trait work that are embedded in the performance assessments they have been engaged with. Does it seem that the performance assessments have shaped students' notions for the character trait work they should be doing?

Alternatively, the visitor might interview teachers to learn what the teacher has taken from her analysis of the performance assessments. The visitor might ask the same question in every classroom: "What have you gleaned from your study of the kids' work on the performance assessments?" By collecting teachers' responses to that question, the visitor might see patterns that suggest the extent to which these assessments are guiding a teacher's teaching. Is that happening more at some grade levels than others? More for teachers who have participated in a lot of PD than for teachers who have had less help? In general, it will be interesting to see the extent to which teachers regard students' progress or lack thereof as feedback for the teacher about his or her teaching.

A visitor may also approach this topic as a vehicle for learning teachers' relationships to curriculum. Did this teacher see the published performance assessment as a suggestion, and did he or she feel comfortable making adaptations? Did the teacher discuss those with other teachers at his or her grade level, assuming that the teachers across the grade level should be in sync with each other? Was there any discussion among teachers at a grade level prior to giving the assessments, prior to scoring them?

Lenses on On-Demand Writing, Writing Folders, and Writing Notebooks

When looking at student writing on instructional rounds, observers will harvest insights if they compare and contrast one piece of student writing with another. For example, it is always useful to look at the on-demand writing that students did at the very start of the year or at the start of the unit and compare it to writing that students have done most recently. How has the student's writing improved? Might it be that the work the student produced in an on-demand assessment earlier in the year is actually better than the work the student produced today— and if that is the case, what explanation is there for that apparent regression?

Although it will be interesting for the observer to notice ways the more current writing is better than writing done earlier, it is equally interesting to ask the writer to talk about how he or she thinks the more recent writing is better. This research, of course, will be especially interesting when one looks at these patterns across teachers on a grade level and across students from varying levels of skill proficiency. Might it be that in all the classrooms at this grade level, the strong writers are able to talk about ways in which they are working to make their writing better and the less proficient writers seem to have very little language for talking about their writing? Or might it be that the stronger writers are more apt to talk about work with structure and the less proficient writers seem to think only about mechanics and content? If there is a pattern, is it equally true in every genre? If the inquiry yields exceptions and spotlights, for example, teachers for whom the less proficient writers are very articulate about their work with the structure of their writing, that will help the school respond to the specific problem of practice.

Of course, the example given previously is just one of many patterns that an observer could see when looking between the on-demand writing and the most recent writing that a student has done. The observer could also (or alternatively) look at any one of these patterns:

- How has this writer's fluency, stamina, volume, or expectations for productivity increased over time? What seem to be volume expectations at different grade levels?

- Has the writer done the work that instruction has highlighted in charts and checklists? To what extent, when discussing the writing, does the writer refer to and show awareness of the past teaching? Is this different for more or for less proficient writers? Across grade levels?

- When looking at the on-demand and current work for several mid-level writers in the class (or several of the most proficient writers in the class), what similarities do you see between those students' work? Do those similarities feel as if they are evidence of instruction and therefore seem positive, or do they seem to be evidence of overreliance on scaffolds and therefore seem like a problem?

- Ask the teacher to direct you to a low-level writer, a mid-level writer, and an especially proficient writer. What are the primary differences in their writing skills? Is it structure, elaboration, volume, understanding of genre, application of the teaching? Look at the different strands of the writing rubric/checklist to see if any particular aspect of writing is holding students back more than others.

You might also look to see whether there is (or isn't) a general correlation between the on-demand writing scores and the writing test scores. For example, the Smarter Balanced Assessment Consortium (SBAC) scores suggest skill areas that need improvement; these may or may not echo the areas for improvement that are revealed in students' on-demand writing. Keep in mind that there will be instances when the on-demand writing scores are not strong predictors of scores on the writing components of high-stakes tests. There are several explanations for this. First, high-stakes tests will value some but not all of the criteria that are valued when assessing on-demand writing. For example, in some states, spelling is counted, while in others, it isn't. Then, too, in some states, scores are elevated when kids use decorative words—lavishing adjectives and adverbs into their sentences. In some states, citing the text and then discussing the citation is especially key. Still, using the on-demand writing assessments will absolutely help you to track students' progress as writers, and that progress will have carryover onto the high-stakes tests.

You may also want to channel observers to study the students' grasp of writing process as it relates to the problem of practice. To do this, a participant will need to look over a student's writing folder and/or writer's notebook, with some of these questions in mind:

- Are writers in the primary grades revising their writing nearly every day as intended by the Units of Study? Or are they waiting to be told to revise, and only revising just before they officially publish a piece of work?

- Are writers in the upper-elementary grades rereading some of their entries, and writing more from them, revising some and bringing others to publication? Or, does every piece follow the curriculum and the minilessons lockstep though the process, with no sense of organic motivation, inspiration, or innovation?

- Is the writing in the writer's notebooks and folders more inspired or better than the on-demand writing that students do at the start of each unit? Has teaching raised the level of the writing work?

- When you compare the writing in the folders or notebooks to the anchor charts on the classroom walls (the evidence of the teaching), do you see that the teaching has had an effect on the writing?

Lenses to Use Observing and Interviewing Student Readers

The observers who are using the lens of focusing on the kids and their reading work may want to start with the basics: what are students reading, how much and how deeply? Can students read the texts in their hands with 95% accuracy? When you ask about the book, can the reader explain the gist of the story in a way that makes sense to you? When pressed, can the reader talk about how earlier sections of the text fit with whatever the reader has read most recently, in ways that suggest the reader is accumulating and holding on to information as he or she reads?

Observers can ask questions like, "What has the teacher been teaching you to do as you read?" When the reader responds, the observer can press, saying, "Can you show me a place where you did that?" Alternatively, if you are assigned to observe and interview student readers, you might act as if you don't know about the skills the reader has said the teacher has been teaching—say, prediction—and get the youngster to teach you about it. You will be trying to understand if the reader has some work he or she is trying to do as a reader and if the reader has some grasp of what that work is. This may involve the reader referring to tools or charts, which would be great.

If you are observing, carrying this lens, you may want to notice how children keep track of their reading, how they track things like number of pages and amount of time spent reading, and how they record their thinking about their reading—Post-its, flags, highlights, logging the pages read, writing in a notebook. Hopefully, indications are that writing about reading is done quickly and doesn't intrude on reading time, and hopefully, kids look back over their records of their reading to talk with others about those thoughts, elaborating on and defending them.

Of course, it will be all-important to notice the volume of reading the child is doing. It should be about two thirds of a page a minute—if it is half a page a minute, that's in the ballpark. But if kids are reading just a few pages a day, that will sound alarm bells. (In general, when reading books at levels J/K, you can expect eight books a week, when reading N/Q, at least two or three books a week, and above R, approximately a book a week.)

If the teacher is doing a read-aloud when you observe, you can ask, "Does the read-aloud draw *me* in?" and look for signs of engagement and for indicators that teachers are aware of student engagement. You can note the opportunities for kids to talk and think in the midst of reading aloud.

If your school has been using Units of Study for Teaching Reading for several years, you might also consider the following:

- Unless the pre-observation discussion has led you in a different direction, you'd be wise to start by focusing on the less proficient readers, asking whether they can read the texts they are holding with 95% accuracy and with fluency and expression that reflect comprehension. As mentioned previously, you'll want to ask about the book, checking to see whether readers can explain the gist of the stories.

- As mentioned in the discussion of running records, it will pay off to see whether readers are doing the level of thinking that their texts are asking them to do or that instruction is asking them to do. Often readers turn complex texts into simpler ones, either by being plot readers only, ignoring nuance and complexity and figurative language, or going overboard with personal connections in ways that draw them away from the text. To understand the work students are doing, you might ask, "What has the teacher been teaching you to do as you read?" and then follow up the child's response by saying, for example, "Can you show me a place where you did that?"

- When you examine the writing that students are doing about reading, it will help to think about whether it is making readers' thinking deeper. Do students show a knowledge of what good writing about reading entails, and are they working toward those goals? Sometimes students think their writing-as-they-read should resemble literary essays, which it needn't.

Lenses to Use While Observing and Interviewing Student Writers

Earlier, we listed lenses you and your team could bring to on-demand writing. Keep in mind that it is also valuable to watch writers at work and to talk with them about their process. If you see children writing, notice their comfort level. You'll want to sense that kids' hands rush to keep up with their thoughts, that their pauses come at the ends of thought-chunks, so their writing is fluent instead of being a stop-and-go, word-by-word ordeal. Writers at all grade levels benefit from writing with fluency, and this is a byproduct of time spent writing.

It is helpful for observers to talk to students enough to learn whether they feel their ideas and stories are important. It is immediately obvious, for example, that in some classrooms, children assume you'll want to hear their writing, and in other classrooms, one senses that writing is corrected, but never read for pleasure. Observers can ask students to share writing with a partner and then watch to see whether, when one writer shares with another, the listener responds with warmth and interest.

It will pay off for observers to ask, "What are you working on as a writer?" and "Can you show me that?" Writers may point to passages in their own drafts or in a mentor text. Do they have goals as writers, a language for talking and thinking about good writing, and a sense of when writing reflects that goal? Is the writer attempting to achieve particular effects as he or she writes, and shifting between writing and self-assessing, drafting and revising?

If your school has been working with Units of Study for several years, observers might also research to see if kids are now able to sustain working for large chunks of time, moving between a task that the teacher has initiated and ones they self-initiate. For example, if the minilesson called students' attention to their lead, do they move from that to work on other aspects of their draft? Do they have the ability to reread their own writing, to decide on next steps, and to get busy doing those steps?

Observers of teachers who have worked with Units of Study for multiple years might also look to determine whether writers know the specific kind of text they are trying to make and have some sense of the qualities of good writing that characterize that kind of a text. "What sort of thing are you writing? Oh, so you are writing a literary essay? What makes for a good literary essay? How could you make this draft into an even better literary essay?"

Overall, your team will go through several cycles of instructional rounds. You will often look back at the same kinds of artifacts and look through the same lenses that you used in the first instructional rounds—the ones that proved to be the most revealing—only as the year progresses, you will focus not just on what you see there, but on growth and change in what you see now compared to what you saw earlier.

Examples of Problems of Practice Selected by School Teams

Once you and your team have discussed the testing data and hunches brought by your analyst, once you have planned your lenses for instructional rounds and visited all the classrooms, collecting data across your school, you'll then meet back together to debrief and decide on a high-leverage problem of practice to tackle to support for your students' growth. Some examples of problems of practice that school teams have chosen are as follows:

How can we give students more opportunities for sustained, engaged reading and writing?

Reading and writing are skills that are developed in use. The amount of time that kids spend engaged in actual reading and writing matters tremendously. Kids who read more have better vocabularies, more fluency, more general knowledge, and read higher levels of text complexity than kids who read less—and even ten more minutes a day of actual eyes-on-print engaged reading matters. The statistics are similar for writing.

Readers and writers who have not had lots of opportunities to read and write often come to a classroom without a lot of stamina as readers and writers. When they read and write slowly, in word-by-word ways, and are accustomed to doing both reading and writing for only a short bit of time, this becomes a self-sustaining cycle. It is hard to be very interested in what one is reading or writing when the work is word by word, amounting to a few paragraphs or a few pages a day. A reader and a writer's volume and stamina are not everything, but without these, it is hard to go further. The best-selling author Stephen Covey suggests that leaders put first things first—and it makes sense for a school to prioritize increasing the volume of reading and writing that students do, and as part of that, increasing their stamina.

The pathways forward to this will include cajoling kids to push themselves, as runners do who want to get stronger and faster, but it will be even more important for teachers to convey the joy that people feel when reading a great book, when writing a great story. It will be important for teachers to go to great lengths to model and demonstrate and support a culture of loving reading and writing. In reading, this will mean finding ways to bring more high-interest, easy books front and center in a classroom; giving book buzzes that celebrate especially "hot," easy books; encouraging kids to share their favorite books; establishing fan clubs for favorite authors and genre; starting traditions that celebrate books; and reading aloud more often and with more energy and joy than ever. This will also mean creating lots more opportunities for kids to talk in authentic fun ways about books, sharing favorite parts, reading those parts to each other, acting them out, delving into series books, anticipating what the next book in a series might be like.

In the same way, it will be important for teachers to model and demonstrate and cultivate a love of writing. This will involve teachers bringing their own authentic writing into a classroom and storytelling about their own involvement in writing. It will involve teachers working on giving compliment conferences that develop students' identities as writers, that make writers famous for what they can do, that celebrate writers' strengths. It will mean developing traditions that champion and celebrate writing (writing buddies across grades, bigger splashier author celebrations, more energy around writing partners).

Then, too, to support more reading and writing, whole-class talk needs to consume less time. Teachers need to learn to make their minilessons briefer, and they need to revise their schedules to give kids more opportunities to actually read and actually write across the whole day, not just during ELA.

How can we help our students be authentically engaged rather than compliant and dutiful as learners?

There is a sense that learners across some schools have learned to "do school." They follow directions willingly, they do as they are told, and that results in a lot of productive work and learning. But for this learning to turn kids into lifelong self-initiating and joyful learners, the school needs to support more authentic engagement. This will mean giving learners more choices and invitations than assignments. It will mean more radical candor conferences that challenge students to be more ambitious, risk taking, and invested. It will mean the teacher demonstrating in ways that show more true personal engagement. Language needs to shift from "I need you to . . ." to "I want to invite you to," and expectations, from "They won't do it unless I make them" to "If I can tap into her dream of . . . then she'll pour herself into this." Classrooms need to be more joyous, work more varied, and more student-sponsored.

How can we avoid overscaffolding and instead provide learners with opportunities to do the hard work that will yield growth?

Across some schools, there are many instances in which teachers scaffold students so that they are freed from perseverating. For example, teachers ask a question and then give little wait time before helping the student answer that question. When the work is challenging, such as writing an information book, teachers often decrease the challenge with worksheets that spell out and assist with each step. These schools may decide to embrace the value of productive struggle, giving kids the opportunity to do the hard work that will help them to get better, step by step.

To do this, teachers need to calibrate expectations, so learners are being asked to do work that they can actually do with independence, even though those expectations may not yet be for grade-level work. Teachers need to learn ways to take the actual work that kids produce on their own and to think, "How can I help learners to make *this work* one notch better?" and then they need to teach kids to do the hard work of improving that work.

Embracing the importance of productive struggle will mean giving kids more wait time. It will mean kids working with independence on challenges that are within their reach—so some will work on different writing paper, and read different books, than others. It will mean that during small-group instruction, the kids are the ones doing most of the work and the teacher is observing and coaching. The work that a student generates after a reading and writing conference will last half an hour, not half a minute. Teachers will assess their own teaching by noticing if the child's appetite for work goes up, not down.

In general, teachers will need to learn to create opportunities for kids to work with heart and soul, independently, on meaningful work. If a child's gotten started reading a novel in school, the teacher might suggest she finish the book that night. If a youngster needs to add dialogue into a part of a draft, the teacher might suggest the child reread the entire draft for dialogue—and then see if there are other things to add as well.

How can we give equal opportunities to all our learners?

In some schools, there is a sense that lots of the kids take initiative, assume leadership roles, embrace challenges, and engage in multistep work without needing teacher input at all times, and others do little of this. Too often, the kids who show this level of engagement are, for the most part, the most academically proficient students. And meanwhile, the less proficient students tend to perform assigned tasks, answer rather than ask questions, follow rather than lead, and do work that asks little of them. It is not okay if more proficient learners are given a thinking curriculum, characterized by opportunities for collaboration, problem solving, student initiative, meaningful projects, and a growth mindset, while less proficient learners are more apt to be channeled to work alone, on low-level, teacher-assigned tasks, with few opportunities to think, talk, problem solve, or to set their own goals and self-assess.

These schools may decide to work on bringing a growth mindset to all learners, supporting initiative, problem solving, leadership, and identity building in all learners. This will probably mean that the wells of knowledge that less academic students bring to the classroom become more valued in the classroom. Perhaps songs and graphic novels and chess become more valued. It will mean that images of good work become more inclusive and expansive. It will mean that process is valued as much as product: a writer who is less proficient at, say, spelling, could be the model for risk taking, self-assessment, or bold revision.

Teachers will examine their assumptions and expectations. This might mean that more teachers engage in record keeping that involves recording oneself, assessing oneself. Do they give equal wait time to less proficient learners? Do they inadvertently talk to some students differently than others, showing only their more proficient students that they believe they want to work hard on projects of personal importance? Most of all, teachers will inquire into how their teaching and students' learning change once teachers work deliberately to give equal learning opportunities to all.

How can we prioritize reading comprehension?

Sometimes in the press to move students ever-upward in levels of text complexity, a school can end up turning reading into something less than it really can and should be. Reading is all about comprehension. Reading *is* thinking. If a learner holds a thick, hard book and correctly decodes the words in that book but doesn't laugh aloud, develop and follow theories about the people and events, or think about the book later and apply its lessons to the reader's own life, then really, the reading that student is doing is only a pale imitation of reading. Comprehension is everything, and helping kids to think more, question more, learn more from a text is absolutely essential.

Too often, kids *hold* hard books—books that can give the reader lots of opportunities to note foreshadowing and flashback, symbols and layers of meaning—and yet read those books as if they are just simple, straight, plot-driven stories. The reader may be reading a book that is level T, but the work the reader is doing is similar to what readers of *Poppleton* do!

Some schools, therefore, will decide to prioritize higher comprehension. This will start by making sure that when conducting running records, teachers are taking into account comprehension. If a child isn't grasping the gist of a story enough to retell the story and to answer basic questions about what happened and why that happened, the child would be better off to be channeled to read easier books for a time, learning to expect and demand a level of meaning from whatever he or she reads. Readers absolutely need to monitor for sense and to pause and problem solve (reread) when things aren't making sense, and they'll only do that if they expect a book to add up as they read.

The first step in highlighting comprehension, then, involves teaching kids to choose just-right books and to monitor for meaning.

It will also be helpful for readers to know that harder books ask them to do new kinds of thinking as they read. Teachers will probably lead a version of guided reading groups to support kids as they move from reading within one band of text complexity to another and will help kids to know that now, when reading these more complex books, the texts will be asking them to do new kinds of thinking. Teachers will draw on the bands of text complexity (see *Reading Pathways*) or on their knowledge of books to convey higher levels of expectations for comprehension. A reader reading a level T text will be thinking about minor as well as major characters, asking why the author gave this or that character certain objects or roles, noticing how a character is different in different relationships.

The standards for comprehension today are considerably higher, the expectations more rigorous, than those from even just a few years ago.

The standards for comprehension today are considerably higher, the expectations more rigorous, than those from even just a few years ago, and teachers need to teach in ways that support analytic interpretive comprehension at all grade levels. The learning progressions in the Units of Study can help teachers become more familiar with strategies that support higher-level thinking, in part by trying those strategies themselves in reading groups with each other.

How can we take advantage of every moment of instructional time, explicitly teaching not only during minilessons but during all parts of our teaching?

Minilessons are one good vehicle for teaching, but there are many other equally important ways to teach, and students will learn more if teachers across a school think about ways to be effective teachers during other forums as well.

For example, sometimes we aren't taking full advantage of the read-aloud as an opportunity to teach. It is helpful to ask, "What skills do I want to be supporting through reading aloud?" and to realize those could be the same skills that are highlighted in a unit, or they could be the skills that were taught in a previous unit and need to be kept in the forefront. Once a teacher has decided on skills she wants to highlight, the teacher could plan a read-aloud to demonstrate and give guided practice in those skills, and then that read-aloud book could be referenced in small groups and conferences when the teacher is explicitly teaching.

Teachers can embrace a study of small groups as well, making sure that kids are doing most of the work during them. These are not times for teachers to talk but rather for teachers to channel kids to do some work that will benefit them, perhaps with a new tool or lens (or an old one that the learners may have forgotten) while teachers observe and coach.

A school that decides to take full advantage of instructional opportunities might think also about the extra moments at the end of the day, about lineup times, or snack time, or times when kids are waiting for the eye doctor or the dismissal bell. Of course, thinking about taking full advantage of instructional time also means thinking about how to reduce wasted time.

Finally, for instructional time to be used to the max, teachers need to have more sources to draw upon for content to teach. It can't be that the content of that day's minilesson is the only content that is taught. Teachers will benefit from forming collaborative communities of practice and generating ideas, for not only *how* to teach but also *what* to teach.

All in all, as you wrestle with uncovering and selecting a high-leverage problem of practice, remember that all roads lead to Rome. That is, no matter which area of teaching and learning you and your team choose for intensive focus, no matter which plan of action you implement, your school's improvement in that one area will also bring improvements in other areas. So, we advise this: don't belabor the choice so much as labor to build improvement in whatever problem of practice you have chosen.

Create Rituals and Traditions that Hold the Heart of Your School

A few years ago, the Teachers College Reading and Writing Project held its ninetieth Saturday Reunion. If you haven't been to one of these extravaganzas, you'll want to come soon. For each of these days, the College opens its doors to any and all. There is no registration and no cost. Teachers pour in from all corners of the country—usually as many as 3,500 of them. Many teachers leave their homes at 3 A.M.; others come for two days, visiting schools on Friday. The actual event begins with a world-class speaker at Riverside Church, with thousands of people in attendance, followed by four cycles of workshops, with almost thirty workshop choices during each hour. The entire staff of the Project helps to lead the 120+ workshops and keynotes. Always, a few special friends from the world of literacy leaders join us to lead the day: Lester Laminack, Kathy Collins, Carl Anderson, Pat Cunningham, Jack Gantos.

To mark the ninetieth of these events, I used my opening keynote as a time to pause for a moment and to reflect on what can be learned from the very presence of these Saturdays as part of the rhythm of our years. It occurred to me that the only way our organization has been able to pull off these events is that they have become traditions. Because we always know that for one Saturday in October and one in late March or April, there will be a Saturday. We don't need to pause in the hectic pace of our work to initiate the idea of holding a free Saturday conference for all. We don't need to ask, "Where will we hold this?" or "How will it go?" We only need to think, "How can the upcoming Saturday can be even better than the last?" We don't need to secure workshop leaders because the same presenters (TCRWP staff) know this is part of their lives, and they live with this expectation in mind, learning toward these events. School districts, as well, plan for their teachers to attend. Because these Saturdays are traditions, districts budget for bus transportation and mobilize participation long in advance.

The fact that these Saturday Reunions are traditions not only makes them worlds easier, it also means that they help shape the character of our organization. They make a statement. These Saturdays announce to the world that teachers are so enthusiastic, they gladly devote their weekend and travel for miles for the chance to gather together to learn more.

> **IN THIS CHAPTER, YOU'LL FIND . . .**
>
> ► Descriptions of the ways that traditions and rituals help give each organization its character
>
> ► Examples of school-wide systems for creating and showcasing best practices

Traditions and rituals help give any organization its character.

In today's start-up culture, leaders often launch a start-up by first identifying the values that will be important to the company, and then settling on a few rituals or traditions that will crystallize those values. For example, a company that values innovation might place a suggestion box by the front door, asking people to share ideas for innovations. A committee might review those suggestions once a month and lead a companywide conversation about them. Or awards might be given every quarter to the person with the most innovative suggestion. Perhaps the CEO's newsletter contains an Innovations Column. Our point is this: traditions bring values to life.

Google employees have a tradition of meeting in "pizza-sized groups"—groups that are small enough to share a large pizza. Another tradition is that everyone at Google, including the leader, chooses OKRs (objectives and key results) for themselves. These are public for all to see. The message is that at Google, employees need to reach for the stars. Their OKRs need to be ambitious enough that they can reasonably hope to meet some of them, but not all.

Other companies have other traditions and rituals. At Facebook, for example, when managers conduct employee performance reviews, they carefully consider peer reviews and self-reviews as an important part of the evaluation process. This provides 360-degree feedback for each employee. And it works both ways—through direct reports, employees also get to review their managers.

As the seventeenth-century poet John Dryden said, "We first make our habits and then our habits make us." Scientists estimate that at least 40% of what we do each day is shaped by our habits, our traditions, our rituals.

In schools, traditions and rituals sometimes grow organically.

When Carmen Fariña was principal of PS 6 (she went on to be NYC's Schools Chancellor for many years), she wanted to strengthen the alignment from one classroom to the next within each grade level. To achieve this, she organized her grade-level teams so that at each grade level, one person was a writing lead teacher, one the reading lead, one social studies, one science. Then the writing lead teachers from preK to grade 5 constituted the writing articulation team, and similar articulation teams were developed in every discipline. The lead teachers for each discipline were sent to extra professional development on their topic and helped to lift the level of that work across their grade level. When the parent-teacher night came along, the writing lead teacher talked to *all* the parents from *all* the classrooms at that grade about the writing curriculum that their children *all* would experience (no matter which classroom they were in) and the same was true for lead teachers of other disciplines. That practice continued, and in relatively short order, a schoolwide tradition had taken hold.

Carmen used the K–5 articulation teams to help teachers think about how to be sure that as kids proceeded through the curriculum, one grade level was building on the work of earlier grades. These committees wrestled with the inevitable questions revolving around teachers at particular grade levels who wanted to fend others away from reading aloud their key books. Because every teacher led cross-grade articulation related to one subject or another, teachers tended to give the leader in one area or another a bit of a break. That is, there was a sense of "I'll scratch your back, if you scratch mine."

Because grade-level articulation was a priority for Carmen, she created other traditions that supported that as well. For example, every May, teachers across the school would teach a full day to the children who would be their incoming students the next year. That is, fifth-grade teachers taught in the fourth grade, while those fourth-grade teachers were teaching in the third grade, and so on. On these days, the visiting teachers taught according to plans that represented typical work, and they participated in the structures, rituals, and expectations of that earlier grade. Teaching a typical day, at the preceding grade level, allowed teachers at every grade level to get a sense for what their incoming students were already accustomed to doing.

The impact of this is more than you might imagine. How often we have seen teachers at one grade level totally underestimate what their new students can do! How often we see second-grade teachers start their year, asking incoming students to read for only ten-minute stretches of time because they are sure those little ones don't have more stamina than that. Meanwhile, by the end of first grade, six-year-olds were easily able to sustain reading for half an hour.

In other schools, every year the teachers at one grade level meet with those from an earlier grade level, asking the teachers who know their incoming class, "What aspects of the curriculum I'll be teaching will be easy for our incoming kids, and what will be challenging?" For example, seventh-grade teachers bring their reading units of study to a meeting with sixth-grade teachers. Together, the teachers across the two grades skim through the seventh-grade units, with the sixth-grade teachers explaining which aspects of the curriculum will be old hat for these kids and which will pose challenges.

Just giving the seventh-grade teachers a set of the sixth-grade teachers' anchor chart Post-its allows the teachers in that later grade to make little bookmarks and reminder charts that help them hold kids accountable for prior instruction. (Anchor charts are on the Heinemann online resources. Extra sets of anchor chart Post-its are sold separately.)

Traditions can showcase best practices.

Mark Federman, the principal of East Side Community High School, says that when he interviews potential teachers, he tells them, "We have our East Side ways, and I'll want you to participate in those ways—in 90% of them. But we also want you to bring your own 10% to East Side. And we want that 10% to be shared, so that in the end, some of that becomes part of 'The East Side Way.'"

Mark's school has established a tradition of sharing expertise through best-practices mini-workshops. Each year, Mark asks teachers, "What is your best practice?" Teachers identify an area of expertise, then they work with Mark to plan a course of study to develop even more expertise in that selected area: debate, guided reading, record keeping. During the first two bimonthly half days that Mark has established as times for teachers to study together, teachers each do a five-minute trailer workshop on their best practice. Six teachers at a time, each working simultaneously in a different corner of the school library, do these brief bits of PD for their colleagues. Attendees receive a map of the room, showing topics and names for the mini-workshops, each of which is given several times. After participants attend one mini-workshop, they can continue to go from workshop to workshop. "These are brief, deliberately," Mark says, "because the whole point is to start conversations. People can follow up on them later if they want."

Later in the year, Mark also asks each teacher to showcase his or her best practice in his or her classroom. An announcement will go out: "Mary Beth is demonstrating debate, her best practice, during the second half of periods 2, 3, 6, and 7 today. Anyone is invited to stop in, even just for five minutes." Mark adds, "If a teacher can't get any free time to stop in on a 'best practice' and you want me to cover your class, I'll try to do that." He points out that teachers rarely take him up on the offer, but that making the offer is a way to convey the value he places in people learning from each other.

Other schools have other traditions. At PS 158, toward the end of the year, one teacher from each grade is elected to participate in the schoolwide walk-through, and the goal of this is to help establish a sense of next steps for the upcoming year. The committee, comprised of the principal, AP, math and literacy coaches, a TCRWP staff developer, and a teacher representative from each grade, assign each person to observe a particular activity across every classroom. One observes small-group work, another asks kids to take them on a tour of their writer's notebooks or portfolios, another asks kids to tell them about the sort of revision they might do. Yet another asks kids to talk about recent books they've read and the thinking they've done in those different books.

The powerful thing is that this group visits a classroom (randomly selected) at each grade level, preK through grade 5. Afterward, they meet to share what they heard and saw, without judgment, followed by asking "I wonder . . ." questions. The discussion leads to the group beginning to coalesce around a few possible next-step schoolwide goals for the upcoming year. The grade-level representative from each grade then recounts the conversation with others from his or her grade level, then shares the list of possible next-step goals, getting additional input from grade-level colleagues.

This process has led PS 158 to identify next-step goals that influence what they do in their schoolwide faculty meetings and help shape some of the PD work that TCRWP and a math organization does with the school. Several years ago, the goal was to put assessment, goal-setting, and reflection in the hands of kids. Another year it was to make sure that kids—not the teacher—are the ones working the hardest in small groups. Yet another time, it was to help the school move from compliance to a more passionate and authentic engagement in literacy, starting from teachers themselves being engaged in the work they were asking kids to do.

Evaluating and developing rituals and traditions for your school.

Your school probably already has cherished traditions and rituals that help shape the character of your organization—traditions that embody the values important to your school and community; rituals that bring your teachers, staff, and students together to work toward common goals; or a few time-honored traditions that simply help celebrate your school's achievements on a regular basis and infuse some fun and energy into your building. If these traditions create value for your school, you'll certainly want to continue them and enrich them further with ideas from your school community. I hope that you and other principals in your district gather regularly to share these traditions, building on each other's ideas—and I can't wait to learn about them as well.

12 Giving and Receiving Potent Feedback

*L*eadership is all about helping people grow faster, and that happens often through talk—and sometimes, through hard conversations. The test of a conversation is how long it resonates afterward. The question for those of us who aim to give good feedback is, "How can we hold hard conversations in ways that actually get results, that lead to positive changes?"

My colleagues and I have been studying this topic for a long while, as have many of you. We've found it is easier to read theories about effective feedback than to actually put those theories into practice! Sheila Heen, who has spent more than twenty years with the Harvard Negotiation Project, developing negotiation theory and practice, and is the coauthor of *Thanks for the Feedback* (Stone and Heen 2014), has pointed out that those who give feedback think they are successful about 50% of the time. But the *receivers* of feedback report that feedback almost never leads to positive change. Many say things like, "I told him I would change just to get him out of my face, but I truthfully haven't given it a thought since" (Teachers College, September 27, 2017).

To improve your ability to give helpful feedback, try doing something Sheila Heen did with us. She put us into role-play partnerships, with one person assigned to deliver a specific sort of feedback to the other. The giver of feedback meanwhile passed his or her cell phone to the receiver of feedback, who filmed the interchange so the two of us could replay it afterward while reflecting on our efforts. This was enormous fun and for many of us a wake-up call.

IN THIS CHAPTER, YOU'LL FIND . . .

▶ A call for offering appreciation first and foremost, setting the stage for later feedback

▶ Explanation of the power of thoughtful, focused feedback–and the need to solicit it

▶ A list of ways to deliver feedback to make it more likely to be powerful, with examples

My larger point is that I hope you get some coffee before reading this chapter. Sit up taller. The information I'll be sharing can actually make your leadership worlds better. I say this with all humility, because the chapter reflects what I have learned that has made my leadership better. It draws on many books about feedback and on several deeply significant days we have spent with Sheila Heen, and with David Rock, author of *Quiet Leadership* (2007).

Separate appreciation from feedback.

When Sheila worked with us, the first thing she said is that when we think about feedback, it helps to separate appreciation from feedback. Give both, but give them at different times. Remember that appreciation is most potent if it is specific and detailed. And remember that when we give appreciation, we create a context within which we can also provide feedback. Sheila's example to us was this: Imagine that over the weekend, you receive an email from a teacher. It is laden with a million suggestions for how you could do your job better, and the teacher has taken no responsibility for what she could do. Just looking at the email exhausts you. You know you will need to have a hard conversation with the teacher and that she won't love all of what you say. But before you give her your thoughtful feedback, you can offer some appreciation. You can still write an email right then and there, saying, "I got your lengthy email. I can tell you put a lot of your weekend time into thinking about our school, and I want to thank you for that investment of time and thought. I'll have time to read your email carefully during the week and will be sure to schedule a conversation, but meanwhile, I want to appreciate the fact that you took time on this beautiful Saturday morning to think diligently about how things at our school could be even better."

Similarly, if you do a classroom observation and have thoughts swirling around about what exactly to say, you can write an immediate, appreciative email thanking the teacher for welcoming you into her classroom and for all the obvious hard work she put into her teaching. Celebrate particular details as specificity matters. And you can also suggest that you'd love to sit down with the teacher another day to talk over your feedback.

Separate appreciation and feedback, and remember that appreciation builds a context in which feedback can be heard.

So #1: separate appreciation and feedback, and remember that appreciation builds a context in which feedback can be heard.

Value feedback—and help others do so.

The research is clear that feedback can accelerate a learner's progress in important ways. Apparently when a learner takes on something new, he or she has a strong learning curve for a while—say, when talking about new ways of teaching, the teacher who is new to this kind of teaching steadily improves for a year or two—and then he or she plateaus. For a learner's learning curve to continue to accelerate, the learner needs to engage in deliberate, goal-driven practice, driven by an awareness of what he or she needs to work on. That deliberate practice is most apt to occur if learners are given good feedback.

John Hattie, whose book *Visible Learning* synthesizes research on the factors that influence achievement from hundreds of meta-analyses involving 20 million students across a huge range of fields, has found that many reforms occupying a lot of national attention don't have a large effect size (2009). Some say those reforms amount to little more than shuffling deck chairs on the *Titanic*. Decisions about whether or not to ability-group, assign homework, or adopt uniforms, and even decisions involving smaller and larger class sizes have a negligible effect on levels of student achievement. One thing, however, has gigantic effect size—and that is the presence of high-quality feedback. Hattie suggests, in fact, that powerful feedback is eight times more effective in influencing achievement than small class sizes, for example. Figuring out how everyone in a school can receive quality feedback—and even more, can *learn from* quality feedback—will have dramatic payoff.

Hattie suggests that effective feedback is really a cycle. The learner is working toward a crystal clear goal—say, a diver is learning a new dive that he has seen on a video. The coach observes and notices progress the learner has made. Often the learner has made that progress without being aware of it and without even grasping what he or she has done differently that works. The coach names the progress, accentuating what, exactly, the learner has done that is paying off. "The way you are swinging your arms is giving you lift. Great! Keep doing that, always," the coach says. The coach also thinks to herself, "Which next step can I suggest—one that is ambitious and yet, with hard work, obtainable?"

Then the feedback becomes teaching as the coach demonstrates that next step or shows the learner someone who is doing that next step, helping the learner crystalize his image of an effective dive so that the next step is crystal clear. The learner then sets to work, using repeated practice to approximate and then over time to master that next step.

This insight about how to help learners push past their plateaus not only reminds leaders that we all need to get better at giving feedback, but also that we need to organize our lives, so we receive the sort of feedback that makes us better at our work as well. We need to ask ourselves, "Who gives *us* feedback? What systems do we have in place so that we get the feedback that allows us to accelerate our own development as leaders?" Generally, the higher we are in our organizational flowchart, the fewer people have permission to give us feedback.

Of course, the reverse is also the case. The higher we are in our organization's flowchart, the more people have feedback to give us, and of course, they are giving that feedback all the time to anyone who'll listen—in the staff room, the hallways, the bathrooms. The question is just whether they give that feedback to *us*.

At the close of Sheila Heen's recent day with us and with the 300 principals closest to us, Sheila said, "I have one parting suggestion. It really helps to go to the people with whom you work and to ask, 'What's the one thing I could do differently that would really help you do your job better?'"

That seems like a doable suggestion for every school leader to keep in mind. Sheila isn't nudging us to ask for a head-to-toe critique or a 360-degree assessment. We'd just be letting the people around us weigh in on the one thing we could do differently that would really help them do their jobs. But if we can hear that one suggestion from a person, if we can be gracious about taking it in, we not only learn from the feedback, we also set the tone for our community. We demonstrate that even we, the people in power, want to learn ways we can improve.

The most important part of this may not be that we are *successful* at reforming ourselves. We can also make progress even just by being more self-aware. Humility, self-effacing humor, and public apologies go a long way. We can ease tensions even just by 'fessing up to the work that we still need to be doing. For example, it would be a valuable thing for many of us leaders to say, "I know there's unspoken stuff about race and gender that we need to be talking about. I'm not great at that talking, but I know you all can help, so I'm wondering if we can schedule some time to put those concerns front and center. I'm probably going to bungle along a bit, but with your help, I think I could do some important learning and we could move things forward."

It is also important to keep in mind that we have a choice to make day in and day out as to whether we regard *our* results as feedback. Let me explain what I mean by talking first about teachers. You all have teachers in your buildings who continually resist assuming responsibility for their kids' progress. They'll say

something like, "Half my kids fake read. They just hold the book and pretend to be reading." They honestly say that as if it is an indictment *on their students* and not a reflection of *their* teaching. The truth is, when half the class of children are "fake reading," that is all about the teacher. And probably the first step to addressing this issue is for the teacher to assume major responsibility for the problem.

If half the children in that classroom are fake reading, however, that is *also* all about *you* as a school leader. And especially if the teacher thinks that problem is all about the kids being somehow deficient (and not about her teaching), *you* aren't doing an effective job helping that teacher.

I know, I know. You may have led your school in ways so that the kids in two-thirds of the classrooms are on fire as readers. This may be a final holdout classroom, and so forth. But my point is that we actually are being given feedback on our leadership *all the time*.

Schedule a faculty meeting for 3 p.m. Are the teachers in the room at 3 p.m., ready to work and learn, or do half of them straggle in seven minutes later? Do they come with paper and laptops in hand, ready to take notes because they expect to hear something valuable, or do they bring the contemporary version of "their knitting"? The way your teachers cross the threshold to that meeting is feedback on your leadership. You might look into your own heart and think about whether you regard results as feedback on your leadership.

You might think, too, over whether you are attuned to early signals that all isn't well, or whether you wait until the trouble is undeniable. For example, if a few parents write emails asking where the parent meeting will be held, do you take note that if three parents ask the same question, you can ascribe to the helpful adage, "Where there's smoke, there's fire" and assume your school probably has had trouble communicating with parents? Or do you wait until the fire alarms are going full blast?

You could also notice what you tend to do when you do see such a pattern. Do you jump to solve the problem yourself—say, in this instance, by writing a letter to all parents reminding them of the time and place for the upcoming meeting? That solves that day's problem, but it doesn't address the systemic, behind-the-scenes problem—that communication with parents isn't as thorough as it should be. Or, instead of responding yourself, do you forward those emails to the parent coordinator and then after a bit, check a bit later to see whether she has taken note of the pattern and sent out another notice about the time and location of the meeting? If she doesn't do that without your reminder, do you sit down with her and talk about the value of living by that adage, "Where there's smoke there's fire"? Do you suggest that you'd be glad to meet with her again to think together about systems she might develop so that during the year ahead, she becomes super-attuned to small signals, taking them as feedback to address problems before they become larger?

My bigger point here is that the research suggests we only get better at our jobs through deliberate goal-driven actions, and receiving feedback that helps us to aspire, to act differently, to self-assess is essential. We can interpret day-to-day life itself—the comings and goings of our school—as feedback and be engaged in a continual cycle of self-improvement, or we can act as if the problems around us are all someone else's doing. We can say, "My kindergarten teachers are lock-kneed in resistance to this work," or we can say, "I haven't yet learned how to bring around my kindergarten teachers. I need help learning how I can work (or set someone up to work) with teachers who seem like their knees are locked in resistance."

Remember that the recipient of feedback is in control.

The book *Thanks for the Feedback* (Stone and Heen 2014) develops a further question: When you and I receive feedback—either direct explicit feedback or indicators of problems on our watch—how do we respond to that feedback? Are we quick to shift blame—it's coming to us on the wrong day, in the wrong way, from the wrong source, and delivered poorly? There are lots of things that trigger a person to reject feedback, or to hear only the headlines of the feedback and never really take in the message, but if we brush aside feedback, we deny ourselves opportunities to grow. Meanwhile, we also make it all the easier for teachers and kids to do likewise.

There has been a lot of emphasis on leaders learning to "give good feedback," but the truth is, even if the feedback isn't perfect, the recipient can benefit from it, if he or she chooses to do so. You might want to remind teachers that the recipient of feedback has all the power in the interaction; the recipient decides what the results will be. Will he take the feedback to heart, turn to it often, and alter his actions and thoughts because of it? Or will he be made of Teflon and let the feedback roll off him? Worse, will he use the feedback in ways that diminish his capacity, that fuel his anger or passivity or disengagement? In the end, the learner will either take in the feedback and run with it, or he won't.

Reduce fear so the recipient of feedback can learn from it.

To make it more likely that the recipient of feedback uses the feedback in helpful ways, you'll need to decrease the recipient's fear. As David Rock (2007) reminds us, human beings are mammals, and in some core and essential way, we are hardwired to fight for survival. We perceive everything that comes our way as either a threat or a reward. To survive, we avoid threats and move toward rewards.

If we are afraid for our lives, we freeze or we flee. When we are afraid, we are not in a state of mind that allows us to think in nuanced ways. Imagine a bear approaching you in the woods. Imagine how you might react to that bear coming closer and closer. In that imagined state of panic, chances are good that you are not great at being self-reflective. You probably aren't thinking with nuance and insight. You don't make subtle connections between things, and your ability to process goes down. Your fear will probably make you good at a repetitive action, such as running fast, but it wouldn't make you good at problem solving. Your peripheral vision goes way down (which is why you may find yourself jerking your head this way and that way to see to your side).

Fear also gets in the way of a person using feedback productively. When giving feedback, your goal will be to help the teacher be more reflective so as to come to new insights about herself, so you need to start by decreasing her fear. First, make sure you aren't issuing a social threat. If your feedback to a teacher comes wrapped in social shame, if it challenges a teacher's status with other teachers, that will amplify the threat level. It turns out that the old saying, "Sticks and stones can break your bones, but names will never hurt you," is exactly opposite of the truth. The truth is that sticks and stones can break your bones, sure, but it's *names* that can *really* hurt you.

David Rock suggests that one way to decrease the threat level is by increasing the teacher's sense of certainty. It helps to signal that the person is doing fine, that the talk won't be a tsunami of feedback but just a pointer or two, and even to let the person know what the topic will be beforehand. "I loved that visit to your class and at some point, I want to tell you all the things I loved, but I also have a question about your kids' writing about reading. Could I share a few musings and get your thoughts on them, if you have a few minutes to talk?"

It also helps to give the receiver of feedback as much autonomy as possible, even if some of that autonomy is somewhat imagined. You might ask, "Is this a time to talk that would work for you, or would after school be better?" The teacher is given a sense of some control, leaving her feeling less vulnerable and helping to reduce her fear. She can say, "Could I swing by after school instead?" maintaining a small measure of control over the timing of your conversation. Then, too, in the conversation, you might say something like, "Would you prefer to get started by giving me some of your thoughts, or would it help for me to just dive in? Which would work better for you?"

Convey solidarity with and confidence in the recipient of feedback.

David Rock, who stresses the value of certainty and autonomy, also highlights the importance of giving the receiver of feedback a feeling of relatedness. The receiver of feedback is thinking, "Are you with me or against me?" and you need to help her know you stand with her. Convey that you see her, you see her goals, and you are 100% behind her intentions. At a recent conference, Tony Bryk, president of the Carnegie Foundation for the Advancement of Teaching, said that if we want an innovation to take hold, participating teachers need to feel that the innovation "fits them." They need to feel as if this work is "their kind of thing." That sense of identity matters.

Toward the start of a feedback conference, you'll want to help teachers know that you recognize their efforts and you believe this huge, important work is 100% within their reach.

This is not the same message as "give two compliments before you give a critique." Think of all the times someone has begun their feedback with little compliments that feel so trivial they drive you crazy. If you are anything like me, you listen impatiently as the person says the equivalent of, "I love that nice jar you have for your pens," and all you are thinking is, "Yeah, yeah, just get to the point!"

Instead, I'm suggesting that at the start of the conversation, you truly need to convey, "I see you." I see your hard work, I see the challenges you are dealing with. I see the boatload of new things you are being asked to do, all at one time. I see the standards that feel impossibly high and your frustration when the kids seem miles away from those standards. Convey, also, "I believe in you." I have seen the deep, life-changing work you did with that one learner/topic. I know that's what's in you. I have seen the great wells of energy you bring to what you do, and I know that when your teaching taps into your passion, there's no stopping it. I have seen your willingness to get help and outgrow yourself, the courageous way you . . . , and I know you can show the rest of the school the power of on-the-job learning.

Those two messages need to be front and center in your feedback. I see you. I believe in you. Don't perseverate over these messages—they can be delivered in a few minutes. But don't waffle either. Make your words get through to this learner. Be intensely present as you convey these messages.

For a moment, try thinking about the times when you have received feedback that has made a world of difference to your life, feedback that has helped you grow in leaps and bounds. Chances are, that person conveyed that he or she saw more in you than you see in yourself. There is an important quote by Goethe: "If you treat a person as he is, he will remain as he is. But if you treat a person as if he were what he ought to become and could be, he will become what he ought to be and could be."

I once heard another tip—and have long since forgotten the source of it, but it's valuable advice. "When we don't know what we are capable of, we err on the side of caution. We set goals well within our capacity—goals we can easily achieve. We grow from committing ourselves to more ambitious goals."

So early on in the conversation, express solidarity with the person's efforts, convey confidence in the person's ability to do this important work, and help the person to see this as work that matches his or her personality and talents.

This part of the exchange might sound like this:

> Watching you today, I started just listing in my mind all the things you have needed to learn in the last month. I mean, so much of what I saw you doing today is really pretty new for you. What a learning curve you have been on!
>
> I love the way you have relied on other people. I see you listening to . . . and really taking in what she is saying to you, asking for help, and that's not easy to do when you get to be our age. I mean, this is making *me* have to learn a lot too, and sometimes I find myself wanting to just go back to the old stuff. So my hat's off to you for being so willing to learn.
>
> The next stage that I'm gonna suggest is that you bring your energy and focus on learning from professional reading, because the truth is, there's no one in the school that can take you as far as you are ready to go. I'm *hoping* you'd be willing to start learning from the books themselves, and then bringing what you learn to the rest of us. Lots of times, I sense you just need even more content knowledge, we all do. I'll send you to whatever PD I can, but I also think you could learn stuff from the books and help the rest of the school do that, too.

Or it might sound like this:

Wow, you have been working hard, haven't you? I was exhausted just watching you today, racing to reach everyone, to give everyone a leg up. Phew! This work is not for the weak of heart, is it? Your work ethic is so gigantic that I can't help but think you are destined to really rock in this kind of teaching.

Or perhaps like this:

I've been thinking about the work we have done so far—you as a coach, me as the principal, and I feel like together, we've gotten this thing off the ground. I mean, it's hard to imagine that just a year ago . . . A lot of that progress has been due to your blood, sweat, and tears. Whew! It's been a lot, hasn't it? I'm thinking that we're ready for a whole new stage, and the thing is, this new stage is absolutely perfect for you. I'm remembering the work you did two years ago with . . . You . . . This time, you need to bring that same intensity to all the teachers across a grade level.

Name clear and ambitious next steps.

This is the hardest part. The time comes for you to come out with it. You need to clearly say whatever it is you have to say.

This can be scary to do, so coaches do all kinds of things to avoid this. You—we—ask leading questions that are intended to make light bulbs go off. Perhaps the hope is that the teacher will arrive at the insight himself, herself, and save us from needing to spell it out. Then there are the fuzzy, vague, general tips that we say in such convoluted and obscure ways that no one has a clue what we mean. Or the teeny tiny detail that we fixate upon, hoping to make a more general point, but without ever getting around to that point.

So here is specific advice for this part of the conversation:

- First, you'll want to keep in mind you are talking about development, next steps. So plan to focus 80% of the conversation on the future, on solutions, and work to tap people's emotions so they feel excited to rally around the future.

- Yes, you'll name that there were some problems. Stuff happens. But I suggest that your message be this, "Let's put that in the past and focus together on where we can go from here."

- Then, when thinking about next steps, you'll want to think first about what the really important and big steps or revisions are that you hope this person will do. Mull over your options and choose this with care.

- Figure out how to say what you hope for in the clearest possible words. Imagine this will be four or five sentences, not forty. Plan on *radical candor* (the term is borrowed from Kim Scott's book by this title).

- Be ready to immediately shift to saying, "What ideas do you have for how I could help you tackle that important next work?" and be prepared to listen and support a conversation about the future. That is, 80% of the talk is about next steps, about ways forward.

These pointers are, of course, easier said than done. You may want to try this little exercise:

- Jot down the names of the key people who help you move the literacy work in the school forward. These may be APs, reading specialists, coaches, teacher-leaders, ELL support teachers, Directors of Special Ed. Star the three or four of these who are most important to the work.

- Now try thinking about what the suggestions might be for how each person could do his or her job better. What next steps do you have in mind for each of them?

- Reread your next steps for those people, asking yourself, "Does that add up to my hopes for literacy in my school? Does my vision for their work add up, in total, to the huge, important, compelling next step dreams I have for my school?"

You'll want to give these questions some thought. Time and again, when I ask school leaders to think about the feedback they'd give to their coach, their AP, the feedback seems so minuscule, I wonder why it is even worth the trouble of giving it. I want to say, "*Really?* You think that will take your school to the next step?"

Here is a way to think about it: When working with people on their writing, we will often give someone the feedback that they have added too much elaboration (too many examples, say) to a mere twig of a thought, and they need to rethink that. It is okay to elaborate on the tree trunk or on the two main branches of your thinking, but adding pages of detail to a tiny point in an exposé just doesn't work.

As with writing, we find that people sometimes want to make their feedback be about a twig. So let's say the AP works with an articulation team of lead teachers from across the grades, and you hear that those team meetings have gotten bogged down because one person is dominating too much. Suppose your feedback is:

> Brian, I want to give you feedback on your work with literacy. I hear that the grade-level articulation meetings that you semi-lead (and attend) are getting mired in debate, because Celia is being especially contentious.

That bit of feedback will help Brian in less than 1% of his work. Instead, you need to back up, take in a broader landscape, and think about the patterns that inform this. Perhaps your feedback would instead go like this:

> Brian, last year, you and I worked hard to get some systems into place—the grade-level meetings, the mentoring. Those systems are generally going now, so your focus can be on lifting the level of work inside them. I think your next particular challenge is to make sure the social relationships work, so that teachers want to do this learning.
>
> My suggestion is that you and I talk more about how you can work on your leadership skills so that you do all you can to be sure teachers' energy and zeal are on the upswing. It's worth mulling over how you can engineer social relationships so that when things are getting derailed, perhaps by one contentious colleague, like what happened with Celia last week, you can keep teachers' energy from spiraling down. It will be tricky work.
>
> It is really about breathing vitality (or helping teachers do that) into the structures we've got in place. It won't always work, but it's important that you and I both work toward helping teachers feel that the structures like grade-level meetings and mentorships give them energy. I'm wondering if we could meet later this week, so I can hear your thoughts about how I can help you begin to tackle this.

When giving people this sort of feedback, it can help to remember that people want to be engaged in big and important work. People want to be given significant challenges that matter tremendously. Don't shy away from that. You convey your trust in the person and your optimism when you define the next steps in ways that feel like they are projects worth living toward.

You'll probably find it hard to come right out with it, saying what is on your mind. Kim Scott's book *Radical Candor* (2018) addresses the importance of clarity, suggesting that the best feedback you can give to someone comes from a high degree of care and a high degree of candor. That struck home for my colleagues and me when a few years ago, Kathleen Tolan, the Senior Deputy Director of our Project, died suddenly, unexpectedly, at the age of fifty-one. It seemed that the entire world came out for her memorial service, and literally hundreds of people spoke about how Kathleen had helped them more than anyone else had. Yet we also talked about how scary she'd been for us all. Kathleen was the most intense and forthright and direct person any of us knew. Staff developers shared stories of the feedback she'd given them. Kathleen had said things like this:

"Your staff development was like a mist. Go into this next room and make sure your input doesn't just float away.

"This morning at Starbucks you had so much energy. Just now, as a staff developer, you were flat. Bring all your beautiful energy to your PD.

"Listen. Really listen. You can't listen if you keep talking."

Kathleen's feedback was brief, direct, and incredibly helpful. When you go to give feedback, follow her example—don't belabor what isn't working yet, what needs to happen next. Say it and be done. Say this in declarative sentences, not questions. You may find that the teacher listens to you with a blank look on her face. You aren't sure she has really heard you or that she believes your critique is merited. You may find yourself wanting to reiterate the problem, to cite example after example to justify your point. If we do that, we too often find ourselves digging deeper and deeper into a hole. We say things in more extreme ways and layer on yet more complaints. Don't do this. Trust that if you were straightforward and direct, the person heard you. Be solution-oriented.

Another time, the person may ask for examples, for explanation. But usually it is best to plan on this conversation being focused on positive next steps, not on the autopsy of what is now history.

Focus on the solution, not the problem. Coauthor the solution.

Think about times when someone has come to you for advice on next steps and you've been brilliant. You've thought of one thing after another, your mind racing as ideas tumble out. You end up saying things you hadn't even thought of before you began the conversation.

That sort of forward-thinking, solution-oriented conversation creates energy. It pumps dopamine into the speaker's system. The high is not just emotional, it is also biochemical. The problem is that the person who needs this high is the recipient of feedback, the person who is being asked to change.

If our feedback conversations are going to energize learning in ways that support courageous next steps, it is helpful to orchestrate the conversation, so the *learner* gets that chance to think of brilliant next steps. Donald Murray, Pulitzer Prize–winning writer and "father of the writing process" once said to us, "In a writing conference, the writer should leave wanting to write. The writer's energy needs to go up, not down." That is true not only of writing conferences, but also of teaching conferences.

In a conference about someone's teaching, it is the recipient of the feedback who is being asked to do difficult work. Outgrowing oneself is not for the weak of heart. This means that it is important that the recipient of feedback, the teacher, needs his or her energy go up, not down. The teacher should leave with renewed energy, ambitiousness, direction. One of the best ways you can make that happen is to put the learner into the position of generating his or her own brilliant ideas for next steps.

So after suggesting the next step, after laying out the major challenge, you'll want to ask, "What ideas do *you* have for how I could help you do that?" or some variation on that. You could take yourself out of the equation and say, "What ideas do you have for what this might look like?"

The important thing is that you give the learner time to generate his or her own ideas. There is a wise saying: "Ideas are like children. There are none so brilliant as your own." Whatever the person suggests, nod and write it down. Now is not the time to haggle over the details. This is brainstorming. Take any suggestions, and add some of your own.

Suggest next steps, leaving decisions to the learner.

When you ask the teacher/learner, "What ideas do you have for how I can help you?" or "What steps do you think you could take to get started on this?" you need to be prepared in case the teacher looks back at you blankly. You will have just sprung something on her, and she may not have any thoughts yet for ways to proceed. You can, of course, simply postpone the rest of the conversation until she has had time to gather her thoughts on the topic, but another option is to use this as an invitation to help shape her images of possible next steps. It can work to say something like this, "Would it help if I told you what some others have done, when they were working toward this same goal? Then you could tell me if any of those ideas fit with you—matching your personality and your sense of what might work well?"

Notice that in that instance, you are still leaving control in the teacher's hands.

When you do suggest next steps, focus on the big-process steps that can actually make a difference. So, for example, if your charge was for the coach to go from a compliance way of leading to a way that feels more invitational, your suggestions might sound like this:

- You might gather teachers and let them know that you want to draw a line on how things have been proceeding—and that you want to shift from you pushing them into this work toward you tapping into their ideas for next steps. And you could then suggest that you'd love to interview each of them, tapping their minds for next steps. If you do those interviews one-to-one, that would still allow you to synthesize their suggestions, culling out some that seem especially important and putting your own spin on them.

- Another way to go might be for you to spend some time thinking about which relationships you already have that have made teachers feel all-in. Then you could think about identifying a few next-people and trying to replicate what you've done with that first group with yet more people.

- Then, too, you might take a day or two to visit a coach from another school who has worked on this exact same thing, and the two of you could form sort of a support group for each other in doing this.

- Another option is that you might take a topic and a group of teachers and do everything you can to lead those teachers, that topic, in ways that lift teachers' energy and ownership. (For this option, you could also suggest the coach watch and participate in your effort to do similar work. The two of you could debrief often, noting what you did that worked and that didn't work, and then she could try parallel work with a different group of teachers and a different topic.)

My bigger point is that again, when translating feedback into an implementation plan, don't let the vision become too tight, too restricted, right away. You won't want the to-do list to become too ticky-tacky small right away. You are asking for this person to take a big step forward, reaching for a change that will actually make the world of difference. Don't sell this process short.

Follow up!

Finally, of course, feedback needs to be part of a process, and following up on the feedback is as important as giving it. If you go to great lengths to give great feedback and then never ask, "How's it going?" and never work with learners on the hard parts and celebrate the small successes, the feedback will be for naught. So make sure that as part of giving feedback, you set up a system for supporting follow-through.

13 Leading Adults Can Be Tricky: Responding to Trouble

*J*ust as teachers often have a student who keeps them up at night, principals often have a teacher who keeps them fretting. There is no one profile for such a teacher, such an adult. Sometimes teachers act in ways that seem overtly rude. Some may act that way just during professional development sessions; others seem to act that way constantly. Other teachers pose other challenges. Some just seem to struggle as teachers, leaving us unclear what the underlying issues are. As Tolstoy wrote in *Anna Karenina*, "Happy families are alike, each unhappy family is unhappy in its own way."

Those of us who lead the TCRWP are not psychological counselors, nor are we experts on dealing with the union in your district or on the formal processes in your district for writing teachers up. But we are leaders of a big, complex organization, as you are, and over the years we have struggled with our own versions of these challenges. We've brought in leadership coaches who have helped us have the difficult conversations that are sometimes necessary. We've also had the advantage of being able to watch and learn from fabulous principals and district leaders over the years. We'll share our insights on this topic and invite you to challenge and extend our thinking with your own ideas.

We think it is helpful to categorize the sorts of trouble that different people pose, and then decide which difficulties we should tackle and which should be outsourced. Certainly one place to start is with responding to teachers who fit into the category of being resistant. Often these teachers act rudely to professional development and sometimes to everything. Sometimes, they just ignore any efforts you make to bring the school toward shared ideas about teaching and learning.

> **IN THIS CHAPTER, YOU'LL FIND . . .**
>
> ► A list of steps to take and approaches to try with resistant teachers
>
> ► Ways to learn from resistance
>
> ► Recommendations for supporting struggling teachers including common profiles and possible suggestions and interventions

Responding to Resistant Teachers

Imagine the scenario. Your school's coach is working in the classroom with teachers, and she asks them to gather close, so they can overhear two students as they talk in pairs. Two teachers instead stand toward the back of the room, arms folded, making side comments to each other. The group gathers afterward in the library, and one of the two puts her giant bag full of student work in front of her on the table so that her view of the coach is entirely blocked.

The principal throughout all of this says nothing. Our question is this: what gives? Why is this allowed to continue?

Or, in every grade save for fifth, children spend time in a writing work-shop, drafting and revising their writing. In fifth grade, instead, the teacher lectures and kids take notes. The only writing those students do is done at home. Again, we wonder, why doesn't the school leader tell that fifth-grade teacher that teaching by lecture isn't okay?

Sometimes the challenge isn't curricular, it's social. There is a gigantic rift between teachers on one grade level. Two of the teachers don't get along and they display their displeasure with each other regularly. The other teachers on that grade level try to stay out of it, but the tension is palpable. It often seems almost impossible for the teachers at that grade level to function as a team.

Our question, again: what gives?

Sometimes the issue is less overt, but still, morale seems intractably low and everyone is constantly complaining. You feel as if a third of the staff can be counted on to bring down everyone's morale.

What can be done? It's hard to imagine saying, "I need you to be cheery," or "I need you to be nice."

Still, as leaders, we can offer some tentative advice, some of which we are ourselves are also struggling to follow!

You'll want to decide if this is a systemic problem that will require you to gather your people, confront the issue as a staff, and attempt to turn the page in some dramatic, public way—or if this is a smaller issue that relates to particular people, to specific combinations of teachers, which requires a more surgical response.

If the problems are systemic, rally your people to repair the culture.

If this is systemic, we absolutely think that you need to look for an opportunity to tackle this directly, openly, and with your whole team. You'll presumably need more help than we can give you. Our instincts would be to first, get that help, either by hiring a coach or by reading books that can function as distant coaches. We recommend *Difficult Conversations* by Douglas Stone, Bruce Patton, and Sheila Heen (2010).

Our instinct is to gather your people in ways that signal that you are asking them to convene for an important conversation. Let some suspense build by not discussing the content of the meeting beforehand. And then, when people have gathered, be ready to shoulder full responsibility for the culture of the school. Tell people you have messed up and you are sorry. You are asking them to give you a chance to start again.

You are probably flinching at the notion of taking full responsibility. After all, *you* have not instigated the trouble. Still, the truth is that as leaders, it is our job to lead in ways that create a community of care, and yes, if things are awry, that is on us. Furthermore, coaches will tell you that in life, you can't change the other guy. You can only change yourself. Taking responsibility for your role in this, saying "I'm sorry," can go a long way. Hopefully others will respond in kind, also saying "I, too, had a role in this and plan to change." Even if the toxicity isn't systemic, there is wisdom to the approach we're outlining, and it can be done on a smaller scale, with teachers within just a specific grade level.

Invite teachers to bring problems into the open.

In any case, after apologies, you and the group will need to set to work. A leadership coach once pointed out to us that it can help to bring complaints out into the open. Things fester in the dark.

One way to do this is to tell your people that complaints are masked requests and suggest that the organization make a commitment to making requests in more straightforward ways. So instead of saying, "Geez, it's hot in here," it helps to say, "Can we open the window?" You can suggest that people try to make requests rather than complaints, but people will still complain. You might suggest that others turn that complaint around by saying, "What is it you are asking?" or "What positive steps could we take?" And when people complain in ways that don't necessarily seem to be suggestions, you can say, "Why are you telling me this? What is it you'd like me to do?"

> *Tell your people that complaints are masked requests and suggest that the organization make a commitment to making requests in more straightforward ways.*

There will be times when people need to be able to vent, but of course, prolonged negativity doesn't help anyone. So, try saying up front, "Let's take five minutes to put our concerns and worries out on the table." After those five minutes are over, turn the conversation by saying something like, "Now let's draw a line in the conversation and start thinking together about some positive steps forward we can take."

Notice small steps forward.

After the group has made New Year's resolutions, resolving to be a kinder community, you are apt to see people making small steps to contribute to the social fabric of the group. Be ready to recognize and support those small steps forward with comments like these:

"I watched you step back from an argument today. You're my hero!"

"Whoa. What finesse you used today when you helped that conversation turn a corner!"

"I was really touched by the way your supported Carmen today. She's lucky to have you in her corner."

"I just loved the way you put your struggles out there for everyone to see. That sort of willingness to be vulnerable can transform a group. I'm going to try to follow your lead."

"You did this small thing today that was just so beautiful. You took notes on your colleagues' ideas! It might seem like a tiny thing, but you are sending messages that make a world of difference. Thank you."

"I keep thinking about the way you used humor to lighten things today. You have such a deft way with people. I'm in awe!"

Plan and rehearse for how you'll confront people who act out-of-bounds.

It also helps to have a plan in mind for how you will respond when a staff member acts in a way that is beyond the boundaries of acceptable behavior. Usually this doesn't catch you totally off guard—it is likely someone who does this fairly often. You need to be ready with a response, because when you allow someone to be rude or to undercut your leadership in an in-your-face way, it doesn't help to avert your eyes from the offensive behavior. It's not as if the rest of your people avert *their* eyes.

So what do you do? It doesn't work to create a spectacle, hoping to heap social shame onto the person—but it also doesn't work to say or do nothing. If you've emphasized that a study group begins at 3 p.m. sharp, and a teacher who

is constantly late again arrives late again and doesn't even apologize, you need to respond.

You can try using humor and a light touch to engage the group in helping. "Geez, Marybeth, what are we going to do about your timetable? Okay, everyone, I think we have an 'all hands on deck' challenge. What can we do to help Marybeth get here on time? Raymond, you pass by Marybeth's room. How about if you make a point of stopping by en route to our meetings, so you can escort Marybeth here. Marybeth, we'll try giving you an honorary escort. Or what better ideas do we have?"

You can, alternatively, defuse the late arrival by channeling the group to work in pairs while you then pull the latecomer to the side and engage in a conversation about that action. It would probably help to ask Marybeth, "What suggestions do you have for how we can turn around your late arrivals at meetings—because your lateness is undermining the group's morale." Alternatively, you might ask, "Can you explain what gets in the way of you coming to grade-level meetings on time? I'd love to know how I can help you so it doesn't happen again."

Then again, you may decide to just be clear that the behavior isn't acceptable. "Marybeth, I'm not sure I've been clear with you that your late arrivals at these meetings are a problem. The chance to work together as a team is super-important. If everyone did as you've been doing, we'd end up with very little time together. It is disrespectful to your colleagues and to our values as a school for you to always be late. So I'm going to ask that after this, it not happen again."

You might press on and also say something like this. "Can you and I talk now about what we'll do if it *does* continue happening? One option is that we could make something of a contract that if you are more than five minutes late to a grade-level meeting again this year, you just don't come. Instead, that day after school, you and I can work together. If you have a better plan, I'm open to hearing it. What is *not* okay is for you to continue being late."

The bigger point is that you can't be afraid to take these things on. If a teacher isn't a strong team member, then you will want to let that teacher know that foremost on your list of goals for that teacher is that you expect to see her functioning as a strong team member. You can ask her to let you know how you can help her do that, and you can spell out the sorts of actions that you think would be helpful.

Ultimately, if a teacher's behavior influences an entire group of her colleagues, you will need to pull her away from those colleagues. If she cannot participate in grade-level planning meetings without taking the group off focus, you can ask her to plan with you or with the AP in a one-to-one arrangement instead. You won't want to free her entirely from doing the work, but you can't expect her colleagues to police her behaviors, and you need to remember that one bad apple does, in fact, spoil the barrel.

Be aware of research suggesting that one bad apple can spoil the barrel.

There is some fascinating research on the effect of a "bad apple"—an individual who acts out in negative ways—on a group. For a long time, people thought that when a group overall had positive social norms, those norms would overwhelm the effect of a single negative individual. But in "How, When, Why Bad Apples Spoil the Barrel: Negative Group Members and Dysfunctional Groups," researchers Will Felps, Terence Mitchell, and Eliza Byington show that even a single bad apple can negatively affect an otherwise positive group in significant ways (2006). You can listen to a discussion of their research in the first seven minutes of a mesmerizing Ira Glass podcast from *This American Life*, called, "Ruining It for the Rest of Us" (2008). We've sometimes seen principals channeling a group of teachers to listen to that podcast together, using it as the invitation to talk about their own processes.

"Ruining It for the Rest of Us" suggests that bad apples really do have a negative effect on groups, even when the rest of the group is working well. In the interview with Ira Glass, Felps talks about three kinds of bad apples: the aggressive jerk, the depressive pessimist, and the slacker. Listen to the descriptions and see if you recognize anyone in your school! The aggressive jerk speaks loudly, makes sweeping gestures, seems angry, and introduces rising tension to every discussion. What's troublesome about <u>aggressive jerks</u> is that their norms are inevitably contagious. Soon others are speaking louder and getting upset. What's perhaps worse, though, is that this behavior silences others who might otherwise have contributed something original. The depressive pessimist expresses that everything is too hard, that it's not going to work. Their mantra is "Yeah, but . . ." or "I just feel so overwhelmed." They see obstacles everywhere. They are depressing—as is the slacker, who shows up late, puts her head in her hands sometimes, says things like, "I'm just so tired." Soon others are exhausted.

✦ What matters most about this research is that it turns out a bad apple affects the group in three ways: lowered morale, lowered productivity, and lowered innovation. Not good. You're probably asking yourself, "So, what do we do about this?"

Simply listening to the podcast with your staff or your cabinet can be helpful. When we listened to it with our staff developers and in our coaching classes, it was such a relief for people to say, "Oh my gosh, that's what happened the other day in my meeting!" Even if you are just saying in your mind, "Oh, you're the depressive pessimist," that helps you get a little power over the situation. Once your staff has listened to this podcast, you're able to talk about avoiding "bad apple" behaviors. But there is more. Being able to name a behavior also gives you power to defuse it by talking about its effect on the rest of the group. You can not only think, but say polite things like, "When you come in late, it's demoralizing for the rest of the group. I'm thinking maybe you should skip these meetings until we get you more support for your schedule . . ."

The main thing is, a bad apple isn't just an unhappy colleague. He or she is a negative force, and you need to recognize that force, name it, and tackle it.

Make concerted efforts to bring resistant teachers on board.

Sometimes, problems arise because one or more teachers are simply resistant. They may be resisting the implementation of reading and writing workshop because they favor another approach, and they may resent that their ideas and practices aren't given equal spotlight. Sometimes resistance to this curriculum springs from interpersonal troubles, not intellectual ones. When that's the case, wallpapering over the trouble is not apt to work.

When you encounter this kind of resistance, you might try talking one-to-one with a resistant teacher. You might try leading with a heartfelt apology—surely there is something you have done that hasn't helped, and owning up to that can make the world of difference. Then, you might shift into an encouraging request for collaboration. The conversation might go a bit like this:

- "I know this conversation is long overdue. I think I've been afraid to have it, and I'm sorry for that."

- "Listen. It is clear to me that you are resisting . . . There's palpable tension in the room when . . . and sometimes you are even acting in-your-face rudely. I know that isn't your usual way of being and that long ago, I should have taken you aside and asked you to help me understand. So anyhow, belatedly, that's what I am asking. What's going on for you? Help me understand."

- "I don't think I've really said to you that you have every right to question . . . I agree that this approach isn't perfect. It has lots of holes and gaps. But I do think that in the end, there's never going to be a perfect way to teach reading and writing, and that we, as a school, will be better off if we are all aboard something that is shared, helping each other do that shared work better. I want you as part of this community, and I want your thinking. Can we try again to listen to each other and respect each other?"

- "What can I do to make you feel okay about turning the page on your anger and giving this a real go? How about trying it, with all the optimism and talent that you can bring? Then, after you give it a go, could we meet to talk over the changes you want to suggest? We could bring that to the others and see if together, we could come to something that we all can sign onto."

Learning from Resistant Teachers

It is important for a principal (and for any of us, as leaders) to be able to provide resistant staff members with some radical candor, stepping up to convey that rudeness is *not* okay. But it is also important for a leader to be willing to give credence to that resistant colleague, recognizing that if the relationship has gone bad, we may need to assume responsibility for our part.

Over the years, one of my biggest discoveries has been the fact that fairly often, the person who initially was the thorn in my side ended up becoming a true colleague, a leaderly partner. Decades ago, when the TCRWP was just embarking on research into the teaching of reading, we had a group of about twenty-five leaders who met often as a think tank. That group spent two weekends a year on intellectual retreats—burning the midnight oil as we talked and argued and role-played and invented and questioned. There was one very articulate, strong member of the group who was so critical of the group's every idea, so argumentative and testy, that I finally pulled her aside and suggested that the group was too fledgling in its thinking to withstand her critical stance—yet. Would she mind stepping away from the group, letting the group's thinking progress through early stages and gather strength so that in time, maybe, the group would be more ready to robustly defend its ideas?

Try talking one-to-one with a resistant teacher offering an encouraging request for collaboration.

That group member was stunned to hear of her effect on the group and asked to be able to stay in the group, promising to adjust her contributions so they didn't take the wind out of the think tank's brainstorming. She went on to become perhaps the single most important voice in that group and has continued, decades later, to be a leader of literacy work in the entire city of New York.

The lesson? It helps to realize that in the field of education, people have good reason to resist drinking the Kool-Aid. The entire field of education brims with snake-oil sellers who promote one "magic fix" after another. Many fixes amount to very little. Smart, thoughtful, independent thinkers have good reason to develop a healthy cynicism about the latest magic fix—including the reading and writing workshop.

Even though there is a gigantic well of knowledge and practice that sustains the community of thinkers who have worked together to develop Units of Study and the larger community of educators who have developed ideas about reading and writing workshop and balanced literacy, the truth is, this thinking is far from perfection. There are lots of problems with even the best iterations of these theories. The ways they've been implemented, often without much professional development, mean that there are even more limitations to many of the iterations of this curriculum. Critics have a right to be critical, and we need to be poised to listen to them.

Responding to Less Effective Teachers

You'll also have some teachers on staff who are less effective that they could be, and they'll pose different kinds of problems. Their students may not make the gains that students make in other classes. Perhaps parents come to you, asking that you not put their sons and daughters in those classes. Perhaps you find yourself feeling helpless and overwhelmed when you are expected to give these teachers tips—what to say that isn't just a bandage?

I want to suggest that some of the principles that can guide a school's efforts to help learners who struggle with reading or writing can also help these teachers. Start with this idea: when people struggle—whether they are youngsters learning to read or veteran teachers learning to teach effective workshops—they struggle because they are essentially sitting on a three-legged stool, with one leg missing. People struggle in very different ways, for very different reasons, and a one-size-fits-all response will never be ideal.

For example, some readers who struggle are missing fluency, while others struggle with vocabulary. Similarly, some teachers who struggle are too focused on management, some aren't focused enough on management. The result can be the same—chaos—but the *sources* of the problem will be different for different teachers. The first step, then, is to diagnose the problem, without any attempt to fix it. What is going wrong, why might that have gone wrong, and what next steps might be wise and accessible ones for this person?

The tendency is to get frantically busy trying to fix the problems without taking the time to understand them, or to send anyone and everyone into that classroom to fix things. Each person will bring a very different solution—and the result can be even more chaos than the initial problematic situation.

To assess the situation well enough to come to a next-step response, you'll need to let go of any fixed ideas you might have about the one way for all teachers to succeed. There are lots of possible pathways forward, and no one solution is bound to work for all. The initial job is to think tentatively, using language such as, "One possible next step might be . . ."

Meanwhile, to devise a possible solution, it can help to try to understand the logic that informs the teacher's struggles. Ask yourself whether that teacher might have a specific kind of mindset, and whether that mindset might be getting in his or her way. If this does not capture the logic of the teacher you have in mind, see if you can develop your own way to crystallize the dynamics that are in play.

Responding to Teachers Who Overscaffold to Create Illusions of Success

Might this teacher be so intent on showing that her students are achieving that she ends up overscaffolding and overcontrolling their work? This is equally common in high-need schools and in schools that regard themselves as ultra-elite. In both instances, the teacher seems to believe that her job is to show that the kids produce extremely high levels of work. To shortcut the process of reaching that goal, the teacher goes to great lengths to support the students. The result, however, is that the students become overly dependent on the teacher. This shows up, for example, when one contrasts students' on-demand writing assessments and their everyday classroom work (which are low level) with the writing that is displayed on the bulletin board (which seems beyond their reach). The displays of writing might suggest that these are very high-performing writers, but alas, their on-demand writing is at a far lower level.

When watching this teacher, these are some of the trouble signs you might see:

- Imagine the class you have in mind is a seventh-grade class. If there are students operating at a grade 3 level, do you sense that they are working at that level and aiming toward grade 4 level work soon (and then, toward grade 5 level work), or are they flailing away in an effort to produce grade 7 level work? Your hope would be that the kids are holding just-right books, working with mentor texts that are within their reach, getting next-step feedback that they can act on with independence—but this may not be the case.

- If you notice that many students' work seems very similar, one to the next, you may start to believe the teacher has actually done half that work. The kids may have been given worksheets that spell out the exact formulas for their work, complete with sentence starters and prefabricated transitions.

- When you listen to the teacher talking to a child, you may note she poses a question and then gives almost no wait time. Instead, the teacher produces a possible answer, leaving the learner to simply agree that the teacher's answer is correct.

- The classroom may show lots of finished work—often all neatly typed up—but there may be little evidence of work-in-progress. One wonders, for example, if the kids actually went through the entire process of writing and were given opportunities for repeated practice, or did the teacher carefully carry them along to make just one showcase piece? Are K–2 writers writing nearly a book a day, as one would hope to see, or do they take a week or two to write one teacher-controlled book, with kids all spending one full day to work on the opening to their book, then one full day to work on the next page, and so forth?

- Does the teacher seem intent on channeling you to watch, listen to, and work with only her more successful students? In a whole-class conversation, do you sense she gives more airtime to her bluebirds? Is there a sense that half the class is tuned out?

- Is the classroom a showcase of beautiful charts that the kids do not seem to use?

With these teachers, often you simply need to name the problem and to show the teacher example after example of the pattern, and to clarify that the teacher needs to teach the reader, the writer—and not the reading, the writing. If the learner can produce a successful product with the teacher at his or her elbow but can do nothing without that support, the teaching amounts to nothing. The only goal is to lift the level of what the learner can do with independence. The teacher needs to teach the learner to do work that is a few inches beyond what he or she can do alone, and then to show the learner that he or she has had success, and to push yet another few inches. In that inch-by-inch way, a vigilant teacher can support several years of growth within a year—and this time, the growth will be real.

You'll want to see an immediate turnaround, with an emphasis on learners working full-force with independence. The Up the Ladder series is especially designed to help students do the sort of learning that this teacher has yet to value, so if the teacher works in grades 4–6, suggest she work within that series for a bit.

Responding to Teachers Who Have Low Expectations, Who Don't Assume Accountability for Student Progress

Sometimes teachers are less effective than they could be because they have low expectations for their students. To think about the power of expectations, it can help to pause for a moment to recall a time in your life when you learned in leaps and bounds. Chances are good that was a time when someone saw more in you than you saw in yourself. I have found that when someone absolutely knows I can do work that is mighty and beautiful and when that person fully expects me to rise to the occasion, I tend to do just that. Children are no different.

It is easy to spot teachers who have low expectations for kids because those expectations just ooze out of them. You'll hear those teachers saying things like, "*These* kids don't/won't/can't . . ." These will be the teachers who take you by the elbow and steer you just out of earshot of a child and make side comments about the child's family or the labels that have been affixed to the child.

You see the low expectations in actions as well as words. The children are given paper with very few lines. Their book baggies contain just a few books and those books have been there for days or weeks. The teacher gives little time for kids to sustain reading and writing ("low attention spans") and asks many yes or no questions or ones in which the child is expected to produce known knowledge. ("What is the person in the book called? Is that the *character*?")

You see the low expectations when you ask the teacher about her students' progress, and her responses suggest that when students don't progress or don't understand something or don't succeed, she believes the issue is the child. She believes that the problem isn't a teaching problem, but a problem with the kids—"These kids hate to read" or "She's a resistant writer" or "None of them can spell worth beans." These comments all suggest that the teacher doesn't fret that the kids' lack of understanding or lack of progress is a reflection of her teaching—and that's a problem you'll want to address.

Naming this problem is easier than fixing it, because the teacher can guard against showing her expectations for kids—and if, in fact, she does have low expectations, telling her to change them probably won't make a difference. I can think of three big things that might help. First and above all, send someone else into that classroom to coteach and to show the teacher how much the kids *can* do, easily, when given high expectations and lots of positive regard all around. When the kids start succeeding, be sure the host teacher gets lots of praise for having worked that magic. This is a moment to glory over the success of that teacher's kids, making sure that the host teacher basks in their reflected glory and starts feeling thrilled with her kids and herself.

Second, it is not a bad idea to tell the teacher that even when she is not sure what a child can do, it'd be good for her to role-play her way into being a teacher who is totally, absolutely convinced her kids can move mountains. "For now, pretend to have total confidence in this learner, if you need to. Play the part." It turns out that there is a lot of wisdom to the song, "I Whistle a Happy Tune" from *The King and I*. "Whenever I feel afraid, I hold my head erect, and whistle a happy tone, so no one will suspect I'm afraid."

Finally, trust is contagious. Sometimes a teacher exudes a lack of confidence in kids, because others show a lack of confidence in her. You'd be wise to think carefully about ways you are conveying your expectations for this teacher. Could you do a better job of showing her that you are fully confident that she can work magic with her kids? Might you, inadvertently, be treating her in ways that resemble how she is treating her kids? Might you also have low expectations for her kids, and could it be that you have colluded with her?

Responding to Teachers Who Need More Professional Development

Sometimes teachers are less effective as workshop teachers because they simply do not have the knowledge of foundational teaching skills that workshop teaching requires. Perhaps these teachers have been steeped in a basal approach to ELA instruction or in a center-based approach, and they may not have had the conversations or the professional development necessary for them to build an understanding of effective workshop instruction. You might see such a teacher interpreting the minilesson as lasting for an entire class time, with the link of the minilesson coming at the end of the class. Alternatively, the teacher might expect that every student does the work of today's minilesson in sync with each other, and when done, sits with hands folded while the rest of the class finishes their assigned task. Both of these represent profound misunderstandings of workshop instruction—but the teacher holding these views may, simply, have not received the opportunities to learn otherwise. Such a teacher needs more professional development to build her foundational knowledge about workshop instruction and/or about units of study. Here are a few telltale signs that a teacher needs more professional development:

- The teacher thinks she is expected to correct (in red pen) the student writing and to leave little marginal comments on most of their drafts.

- The teacher thinks that it is his job to fix students' writing by almost doing it for them, so that the writing matches grade-level expectations—even if students on their own are nowhere close to those standards.

- A primary teacher thinks it is okay if most or all her kids work on one piece of writing for a week or two, with each day's teaching directing them to do one new little thing they each do on that piece of writing. The teacher has no idea that primary kids begin and end many pieces of writing within a week's writing workshop.

- A K–1 teacher has all her kids writing in spiral notebooks instead of writing in booklets. A slightly less alarming telltale sign is when all her kids are writing on booklets made from the same kind of paper, all year.

- A K–1 teacher thinks that phonics is the same as reading and teaches his phonics program in lieu of reading. He thinks the kids need just phonics until they have mastered it, and he doesn't understand that Unit 1 of reading is meant to be taught at the start of the year, alongside phonics.

- A K–1 teacher says to you, "My kids are still not reading," as if her job is to wait until the day when they *are* reading and to begin setting up reading time on that day. She doesn't know that reading workshop can flourish while kids are approximating reading, and that all kids can read at some level and can be taught the next steps.

- The teacher thinks that his role during reading time is to lead one ability-based reading group, each sometimes lasting twenty-plus minutes. He sees independent reading as a free-for-all, almost like recess time, and he gives little or no input into kids' reading during that time.

- The teacher thinks students need to read more complex texts, even if that means they simply hold those texts, not actually reading because the books are too hard for them, or struggling to do word-by-word work with the text.

- The teacher thinks that, during reading time, it is a good thing if everyone is writing and no one is reading. In her classroom, the ratio of time in which kids write about reading instead of reading is nothing close to 10 reading: 1 writing about reading.

- The teacher thinks that read-aloud is something you do for young kids who cannot read on their own, but that his kids are too mature for this. The teacher doesn't understand that through read-aloud, you teach kids to experience intellectual work that is a notch beyond what they are now doing with independence, and that reading aloud is an intensely instructional time.

The important thing about many of these indicators is that they are signs that the teacher is on a learning journey—and that she still has a way to go. The teacher who is glad when she looks around during reading time and sees that every student is writing about reading is demonstrating both her knowledge and the gaps in her knowledge. She is appreciating that students benefit by thinking in response to texts, and she shows her tendency to want to check and weigh and count everything students do by overemphasizing writing about reading.

For each of these indicators that more PD is necessary, you can also see indicators that the teacher is on a learning journey. Celebrate the journey, and go to the ends of the earth to give your teachers more time to study and more access to knowledge. Remember that creating a community of collaborative learners among teachers in your school will mean that whatever one teacher learns will end up lifting the level of teaching and learning for many teachers. Make time not only for professional learning but also for collaboration.

14 | Stay the Course while Integrating New Initiatives

I have spoken to thousands of teachers about school reform, and I can say unequivocally that there is one quotation I've shared that has resonated far more than any other. It is this quote from Michael Fullan:

One of the most critical problems in our schools is not resistance to innovation but the fragmentation, overload, and incoherence resulting from adapting too many innovations in ad hoc and superficial ways, uncoordinated with ongoing work and with each other. (2016)

Fullan goes on to suggest that schools are marked by so many innovations, people never have time to go from mandates to personal beliefs, from novice to expert.

This is the problem of our contemporary times, where everyone is rushing to ever-more new, new, new quick fixes. Consumers buy into the promise of magical diets—lose twenty pounds in just three easy weeks—and mystery potions that solve receding hairlines, saggy rear ends, declining mental acuity. The same penchant for instant solutions leads some schools to be swamped with a constant barrage of ever-new initiatives. How we all long for the day when a superintendent will rally all the people at the start of the new school year, then take the podium, wait for the room to grow still, and then announce with great fanfare, "This year, our new work will be . . . the same ol' thing."

IN THIS CHAPTER, YOU'LL FIND . . .

▶ A warning that for schools to thrive, they can't embrace every new trend and "fix"

▶ Lessons and examples in weathering the winds of change from a longstanding, successful educational organization

We laugh at the notion that such a thing would ever happen, yet in truth, that's often exactly what is called for. There is always new work to do that involves making the existing work stronger, more student-centered, more rigorous, more joyful, and often that is the most important work to be done. And no solution will ever work if it is introduced, done for just a year or two, then thrown out in search of a yet more perfect fix.

To develop communities of continual improvement, schools can't embrace every new fix.

The only thing that actually accelerates achievement is a system of continual improvement, where teachers and schools put something into action, then study the results, learn from them, and reflect on how to improve the work and make yet more improvements, studying the results once again, with this cycle continuing ad infinitum. The only thing that we know works for sure is for teachers and school leaders and students to be part of a community of practice that is engaged in that sort of continual study.

Jim Collins is a business leader, not an educator, but his book, *Great by Choice*, addresses the problem that is so rampant in American schools (Collins and Hansen 2011). He wrote this about business, but it applies just as well to schools:

> It is easy to feel, in the onslaught of new expectations, in the chaos of changes, in the acceleration of speed and the scale of it all, that we are dwarfed by a

tsunami of pressure. It's easy to lose our grounding, to become a stick washed in the tidal wave of ever-more mandates.

Collins's book addresses the question of why some companies thrive in uncertainty, chaos, and others do not:

> When buffeted by tumultuous events, when hit by fast-moving forces that we can neither predict nor control, what distinguishes those who perform exceptionally well from those who underperform or worse? . . . Some companies and leaders navigate this type of world exceptionally well. They don't merely react; they create. They don't merely survive; they prevail. They don't merely succeed; they thrive . . . We do not believe that chaos, uncertainty, and instability are good; companies, leaders, organizations, and societies do not thrive *on* chaos. But they can thrive *in* chaos. (2011)

So what distinguishes the companies—schools—that thrive in chaotic times? What Collins found was surprising: the companies that thrive are not *more* but *less* innovative. They don't change faster, but more slowly. His advice is relevant to schools:

> If you really want to become mediocre or get yourself killed in a turbulent environment, you want to be changing, morphing, leaping, and transforming yourself all the time and in reaction to everything that hits you. We've found in all our research studies that *the signature of mediocrity is not an unwillingness to change; the signature of mediocrity is chronic inconsistency.* (2011)

Doug Reeves, who has studied innovation, draws similar conclusions. He says that innovations that are adopted to low or medium degrees of implementation (or *intensity*, we prefer to say) rarely accelerate a school's achievement. I think of those innovations as rather like diets that I've gone on with low degrees of intensity. I'm on the diet until I see an éclair, then I'm off the diet, temporarily. Lips licked, I go back on the diet until I see a particularly tasty piece of cheesecake. That is, innovations (like diets) actually influence achievement when they are hard to implement, when they require real and lasting change. And that is most apt to happen when an innovation, like a diet, is done with fidelity.

How can schools handle the constant press for new, new, new?

So what does this mean for a school system or for a school? Our institutions exist in a world that is ever-changing. Around us swirls a Star Wars-like universe of fast-flying initiatives, mandates, flavors of the day.

These questions have been absolutely relevant to the trajectory of the Teachers College Reading and Writing Project's work in New York City schools.

If you think about it, there is probably no other organization that has had such a long-lasting, prominent role in one of America's largest cities. New York City has undergone one metamorphosis after another, as chancellors come and go, mayoral control comes and goes. It's not been an easy thing for TCRWP to remain as a constant throughout all of those comings and goings—and yet, the fact that we have done so is perhaps our crowning achievement. Well over half of our 200+ NYC schools have worked with our organization for decades.

You may be taken aback by that. Isn't the PD ever "done"? Don't schools ever "graduate"? The answer for scores of schools has been that no, this is not a fix that is applied. Instead, it's a fellowship, a think tank, a research group, a community of practice.

Much of the Project's work has involved studying new initiatives that come our way (and initiating initiatives and partnerships that *should* come our way), and then thinking carefully about how to rise to the challenge and the opportunity that the new partnership affords. In recent years, New York City has taken on accountable talk, backward planning, direct instruction, systematic phonics, Degrees of Knowledge, personalized learning, argument, close reading, several iterations of new standards (including of course the Common Core State Standards), data-based instruction, problems of practice, observational frameworks (especially Danielson), performance assessments, questioning, Universal Designs for Learning, measures of student learning, and the list goes on and on. If principals are told they need to focus on these initiatives, then our job has been to help them get to the heart of the innovation, often by partnering with the originator, so that we can help "our" school leaders understand how that new work can be implemented in ways that build upon their ongoing commitment to reading and writing workshop instruction. Of course, part of this has often meant that the reading/writing workshop itself needs to change. The question has been how to change—and how *not* to change.

Your job is to make sure that the one thing that really matters stays in place—that your school is an ongoing system of continual self-improvement.

This is work that school leaders need to do wherever you are, with or without TCRWP's help. If your district, for example, decides to take on a new commitment to Great Books or Personalized Learning or digital literacy or *anything*, you need to be an early adopter of that new initiative. Hop to it! Make sure that you (or one of your key people) get started studying the new initiative as quickly as possible. Study the new initiative with the lens of, "How can this be aligned to and deepen and add to the best of work we are already doing?"

You'll want to anticipate ways in which the new initiative might send your ongoing work into chaos and know that your job is to prevent that from happening. Trust that if it *could* happen, it *will* happen. School people are already braced for the school to hop from one initiative to another, and they'll be prone to interpret the new initiative as a message that the entire system is being jerked around. Your job has got to be to make sure that the one thing that really matters stays in place—and that is, that your school is an ongoing system of continual self-improvement. If it appears that the state or the district is sending the message for your teachers to forego everything they already know and become novices, poking at some brand-new initiative whether or not they agree with the tenets of that initiative, a great many of them will do just that. Or, with the best intentions in the world, some will invent their own hybrid that could well be worse than either the original or the new initiative (if it was done with coherence and fidelity). Your job will be to help your people hold tight to their beliefs while also being open, responsibe learners.

The TCRWP's Work with the Common Core as a Case in Point

Let's think about what TCRWP did when the CCSS emerged on our horizon; the way we handled that innovation illustrates our larger advice to you. First, because we keep our "ears to the ground" and listen for hints that an innovation is coming, we knew the new standards were on the horizon long before many other people knew. A team of us saw them coming, so we reached out to Sue Pimentel, one of the coauthors of the CCSS, and asked her if she could come to TCRWP and teach us the logic that informed the standards, giving us the backstory on them. We didn't know her and we aren't sure why she agreed to come, but surely one reason was that we were asking before the whole world began pounding on her door. We agreed to pay her any amount, but not surprisingly, she wasn't in a position to take funds from us. Before she arrived, we made sure we knew our stuff. We studied the documents that were available at that time and were ready with the sorts of questions that one arrives at only after close analytic study.

After that day with Sue, we set to work, figuring out how the CCSS could help our ideas on reading and writing to grow deeper, more rigorous, better. We had already been in a partnership with a few people from Educational Testing Service (ETS), and we knew that some of them were doing state-of-the-art work on argument. We created a think tank of brilliant teacher-leaders and organized a three-day retreat near the ETS campus. We convinced the ETS researchers to join us for the retreat to brainstorm how we could bring argument through the grades. We staffed the retreat with some of our most brilliant team members and talked one of them into writing her dissertation on the topic of argument. We connected to other argument experts, including Jonathan Osborne from Stanford University and Diana Kuhn from Teachers College Columbia

University, as well as Paul Deane, Mary Fowles, and Randy Bennett from CBAL (Cognitively Based Assessment *of*, *for*, and *as* Learning) at ETS.

Meanwhile, we plunged deep into a study of close reading, which of course wasn't new to us because of our own graduate studies in literary analysis. The new part was bringing that to very young children. We also needed to settle on and begin gathering language around ways that we disagreed with interpretations of the CCSS that started coming out, such as the cry to make sure readers "stay within the four corners of the text" when talking and writing about the text. We worked hard to think about the logic informing that push and to recognize there was wisdom to it. Yes, it is entirely reasonable to note that too often, in the name of a book talk, kids just gossip about life, and yes, they should be channeled to stay closer to the text. However, even after we acknowledged the rationale for that push, we solidified our commitment to the idea that it is neither possible

nor advisable for anyone to read without drawing on knowledge and experience beyond the text. That is, we pinpointed the relatively small but important parts of the CCSS that we were not going to embrace. And we tried to talk about those disagreements in ways that were convincing, and that still helped schools (and TCRWP) do the big work that the authors of the CCSS were calling for.

Although we handled disagreements carefully, in retrospect, it was very important that we were willing to say yes to many aspects of the CCSS and no to others. We said no to believing that readers could or should divorce all personal response from their reading. We howled in objection when Dave Coleman, author of the Common Core, said to large groups of educators, repeatedly, "Kids need to learn that no one gives a damn about their lives." And we were adamant that it was not a good idea for teachers to channel every reader to grade-level appropriate texts, whether or not they could read those texts. For a year or two, a small percentage of NYC schools stopped working with TCRWP because we weren't willing to forego our commitment to assessment-based instruction. After a year or two of working in some of the programs that were whipped up by the state and the city to support close reading of short passages from complex texts, almost all of those schools suffered large dips in their results, and they have since returned to our fold. Meanwhile, New York State developed Next Generation Standards that back away from the most troublesome aspects of the otherwise helpful CCSS.

It is always important to figure out your *no*s. Tim Calkins, my youngest brother and a marketing expert at Northwestern University's Kellogg School of Management, has said, "Your *no*'s define your brand. If you have no *no*'s, you have no brand." Linda Darling-Hammond once pointed out to the community at TCRWP that an association of physicians and anesthesiologists came together and agreed that they would not participate in the process of killing people as part of capital punishment. She asked us, as a group, "What will *we* as a profession *not* do?"

That first summer, when the CCSS were just being unrolled, Mary Ehrenworth, Chris Lehman, and I wrote a book, *Pathways to the Common Core*, which became a *New York Times* best seller. That book helped to "sell" the CCSS by showing people who were already teaching balanced literacy writ large how the standards could be a force for a good, helping us make reforms that would be good for kids.

Handling the Press of New Initiatives

So what can be learned from that journey?

Leaders, you'll need to keep your ears tuned and your eyes peeled for new initiatives that are en route to you. You'll want to try to remember the wisdom that any whitewater paddler knows (and handling the onslaught of ever-new initiatives is certainly like paddling in whitewater)—the only way to have control is for your boat to either go *faster* than the current, which means you gun it, or for your boat to hang back, going *slower* than the current. If you believe you might have the option to postpone getting aboard the new initiative for a time, you may decide to simply say, "My school is still working on other innovations, and we're going to wait until these are more solidified before thinking about how to bring that new work in." Otherwise, be an early adopter.

It is valuable to get yourself a seat at the table, so that you are part of thinking about how to bring the innovation into the school and the district. The best way to do that is to become as knowledgeable as possible, as quickly as possible. Frankly, it is also wise to find a way to get close to the originators of that innovation as that access gives you power and insight. If your district is adopting Personalized Learning, figure out where that initiative comes from. Research whether the originators are leading a conference on the topic, and move heaven and earth to get yourself to that conference. Before you go, study up so that you are primed to do the deeper learning and to ask the hard questions that you'll otherwise wish you'd posed. You'll be able to return to your district with special influence because you have firsthand knowledge of the innovation. Meanwhile, you'll be able to interpret the new ideas in ways that align to your ongoing work.

We want to go farther and suggest that for an initiative in your region, you might organize and host a conference on the topic, making sure to schedule it very early in the implementation process. If you become an important voice in the implementation of Personalized Learning or Danielson or Depths of Knowledge or Problems of Practice, interpreting that new initiative as we did the CCSS, you then get to help steer the implementation in ways that align with and improve upon your ongoing work. You become a spokesperson for the new initiative and do some showcase implementation, and meanwhile you have the chance to clarify, as we did with the CCSS, that as with anything, there will always be a few aspects that are problematic. You'll be ready to give people the data and the language to argue against those aspects of the innovation.

The TCRWP's Work with Teacher Effectiveness as Another Case in Point

A second case in point. When NYC schools first adopted Charlotte Danielson's Frameworks for Teaching as the tool to help with teacher effectiveness, principals' interpretations of that observational framework immediately threw a wrench into teachers' work with reading and writing workshops. Across the city, principals began watching minilessons, penalizing teachers whose minilessons didn't begin with a raft of questions—which would, of course, have undermined the minilessons altogether.

If your school is using a different framework for assessing teaching, know that there are relatively few differences between Marzano, Hess, Danielson, and another half-dozen similar frameworks. Regardless of which framework your district has adopted, know that if your region adopts a framework that throws your ongoing work totally out of kilter, it is important to spring into action right away.

We were fortunate because Charlotte Danielson's center is not far from New York. I immediately asked her if we could hire one of her best staff members to help us spend a few days thinking through some of the implementation challenges NYC schools were encountering. Charlotte sent us the person who was in charge of NYC's Danielson work, and she herself came along as well. We posed the challenges to Charlotte—the one pertaining to questions and some others—and she immediately explained that people were misinterpreting her work. Of course, there are times when questions help, and times when they don't help. No single fifteen-minute segment of teaching is necessarily going to illustrate every one of her principles! In no time, Charlotte and TCRWP had co-drafted a memo addressing misinterpretations of Danielson's framework, including the misunderstanding that questions were always advisable.

Meanwhile, Charlotte and TCRWP filmed distinguished reading and writing workshops, and Charlotte coded them, drawing on her framework. We put those out into the world, helping people to envision what workshop instruction looks like when done in ways that illustrate all of Danielson's elements. We also designed our own Danielson observation guide, helping principals to anticipate which of Danielson's elements they should be expecting to see at the very start of a reading or writing workshop, then during this or that part of the minilesson, during the start of the workshop, during small groups and conferring, and so on. That is, we helped principals to know if they are watching the start of a minilesson, which of Danielson's elements are they apt to see in those first few minutes in a workshop? What sorts of feedback can they anticipate giving teachers about, say, the start of a minilesson? What sort of feedback are they apt to give small-group work?

In the box is a snippet of our Danielson observation guide. The portion of the guide I'm providing you zooms in just on the central portion of a minilesson, when the teacher attempts to teach something to the kids. The full observational tool actually encompasses all parts of a reading or writing workshop, including small-group instruction and conferring. If you aren't familiar with Danielson's framework itself, you can still read this and imagine what Danielson's original documents are like. The important thing is that this tool reorders them, and adds examples that are drawn from reading and writing workshops, but otherwise stay true to Danielson. This is the sort of work that allows a school to stay the course, while still being deeply responsive to new initiatives.

These days, most schools and school systems face a barrage of new initiatives, and it can be a continual challenge to satisfy the requirements of those new initiatives while keeping the momentum going on your own literacy reforms. When faced with the pressure to take on even more initiatives, it is wise to learn everything you can about new initiatives on the horizon, determine how your existing literacy reform can fit into any newly mandated initiative, and do so as early as you can, so that when implementation of the new initiative begins, it won't derail your own reform. You may not be able to control the mandates that are imposed on your school, but you do have a measure of control over how you address them—how you ensure that you stay the course with your literacy reform, moving ever-forward toward continual improvement and real, long-lasting change.

Danielson Observation Guide for Workshop

MINILESSON

Connection

Teaching

3a. Communicating with Students

The teaching component of a minilesson is a time for you to especially notice if the teacher explains the content in a way that is clear enough that it develops students' conceptual knowledge or extends their repertoire of strategies. You are looking to see that the teacher is teaching in such a way that later, students will be able to explain this content to each other. Notice whether the teacher conveys strategies students might use, perhaps even modeling them. Does the teacher use grade-appropriate academic language? For example, does the fourth-grade teacher ask kids to "synthesize," rather than translating that into easier language and leaving it at that, perhaps referring to this as "hooking things together" without providing the synonym?

After the teacher demonstrates or explains, look for evidence that the teacher reflects on and debriefs the demonstration in ways that will help students hold onto what they have just been taught.

3c. Engaging Students in Learning

Continue to watch students for the signs of engagement described above. Look for eyes on the teacher and responses such as alert posture, laughter, gestures, and nods that suggest engagement. Also look to see if the teacher seems aware of the ebb and flow of student engagement and works to recruit that engagement, perhaps by picking up the pace of a lesson, by incorporating names of students into the teaching, by calling for "thumbs up" or choral refrains to show engagement.

If the teacher uses a text or another example during this component of the minilesson, are those materials selected to be engaging? If the teacher demonstrates during the teaching, as is common, you'll see that before the most effective demonstrations, teachers recruit kids to participate (not just to watch). Notice if the teacher sets students up to actively participate, rather than to simply watch, perhaps clarifying the students' role in the demonstration with a message such as, "I'm going to demonstrate. As you watch, will you list three things you see me doing? Later you'll have the chance to . . ." Better yet, does the teacher recruit kids to engage in the activity along with the teacher, perhaps by saying, "Let's all try this . . ." or "Will you help me . . . ?" and then recruiting kids to be thinking about what they would do while the teacher demonstrates that same strategy.

Perhaps the teacher tries to cognitively engage the students by slowing down her thinking in ways that scaffold kids to do the same thinking alongside her. ("What could we do to . . . ?" "How might we try that? Hmm, . . ." "How might that go . . . ?") Certainly the effective teacher will pace instruction, providing enough wait time so that students are actually starting to formulate answers or thoughts before the teacher proceeds to model his own thinking/work.

Students' participation may be evident in instances when it's all they can do to keep from blurting out what they would do, or in instances when they mouth along with the teacher, or nod in assent when the teacher does something, as if conveying, "Yes! That's how I would have done that too!" Ideally, students do not just hang on their teacher's words—there is a sense that they are mentally (or physically) involved in the work of the demonstration.

15 Advice on Using the TCRWP Assessment System

*I*n this chapter, I will first overview the assessment tools available to you and your teachers when you adopt the Units of Study in Reading and Writing. I'll then give advice about implementing them and about grading. Finally, I'll provide a detailed plan for one possible workshop that you might lead with your teachers to support them in using TCRWP's assessments.

Some of TCRWP's assessments are contained inside your teachers' Units of Study sets in Reading, Writing, and Phonics, whereas others are available (free) on our website. Someone in your school needs to review those in each place and make recommendations to teachers as guidance in making more informed choices among these assessments. My suggestion is that you decide on a leader who has responsibility for understanding K–2 assessments, another for 3–5, and a third for 6–8, and that each person read the overview pertaining to his or her grade levels. Then, with a knowledgeable teacher as a guide, he or she could study the actual assessments, the ways that data is collected on each, and then think about how to find patterns in the cross-classroom data. For example, you will want a leader in the school to be aware of whether children in your three kindergarten classrooms are roughly progressing similarly in their knowledge of high-frequency words, and you'll want to be able to provide extra support to a teacher whose students aren't making the progress that you see in the other classrooms. You'll also want a leader in the school to be aware of whether teachers are conducting informal running records frequently with their students who are reading below benchmark.

> **IN THIS CHAPTER, YOU'LL FIND . . .**
>
> ▶ An overview of assessment tools available in conjunction with Units of Study for Teaching Reading and Writing
>
> ▶ Advice about implementation of TCRWP assessments and grading
>
> ▶ A detailed plan for a "thin-slicing" workshop to support teachers in using TCRWP's assessments

An Overview of the TCRWP Assessment Tools

Letter/Sound Identification, Concepts about Print, High-Frequency Words, and Other Phonics Assessments

Free on our website, we offer assessments of:

- letter/sound correspondence

- concepts about print

- high-frequency words

These three assessments will be helpful to teachers who are teaching reading and writing units of study or any other literacy curriculum with emergent and beginning readers and writers. These assessments are similar to assessments that are embedded in any phonics curriculum teachers may be using, and it is not necessary for teachers who are working with Units of Study to use these particular versions of these assessments.

Assessing Letter/Sound Identification

This assessment helps teachers determine the extent to which students can identify the letter names of both upper- and lowercase letters, as well as the sound(s) associated with each letter. Determining the extent to which kids know their ABC's is especially critical at the beginning of the year in kindergarten, although this assessment can be useful as long as students have gaps in their letter/sound identification knowledge. Chapter 6 in *A Guide to the Reading Workshop, Primary Grades* and Chapter 5 in *A Guide to the Phonics Units of Study, Grades K–1* detail manageable ways teachers can collect this data on the run and use it to inform their whole-class and small-group phonics instruction.

A word of caution: you'll want to make sure that teachers don't hold off on launching their reading and writing workshops until students have mastered all their letters and sounds; instead, you'll want teachers to jump right in, encouraging kids to put the letters and sounds they *have* mastered to use, while they are still acquiring others.

In our Units of Study in Phonics, we offer some efficient ways to store and use this information. It is helpful for teachers to know they can collect and record information about a child's command of a letter/sound at any point: during a writing conference, while watching a child work, in a more formal interview. Teachers need not meet formally and privately on a one-to-one basis with each child to collect this information.

Assessing Concepts about Print

There are two versions available of the Concepts about Print assessment, one on the TCRWP website and another in the Units of Study for Teaching Phonics online resources. Both versions are designed to give kindergarten teachers a snapshot of students' knowledge about how print texts work, including their understanding of directionality, text orientation, spacing, letter versus word differentiation, and stop and go punctuation marks. We recommend kindergarten teachers wait until a few weeks into the school year to begin collecting this information. 👏

You'll want to help teachers determine whether they need to give the full version of the assessment, calling one child after another over for a one-to-one session in which each question is asked, or whether they can get the information they need by asking a few questions to the child in the midst of reading or writing time. For example, if the teacher asks, "Can you help me read this book? Where should I start?" and then, after reading a line, "Where should I read next?" and the child has no trouble doing this, it may not be necessary to ask the child, "Which is the front of this book?" And if the child enters kindergarten reading, it probably is not necessary to ask, "Can you show me a letter?"

Assessing High-Frequency Words

In grades K–2, it will be especially important for teachers to assess students' mastery of high-frequency words, ensuring they can read these words with automaticity. This will also be important for older readers working with A–J leveled texts. When kids can read high-frequency words with automaticity, their short-term memory is freed up to focus on comprehension. Chapter 5 in *A Guide to the Phonics Units of Study, Grades K–1* suggests ways these assessments could go in kindergarten and first-grade classrooms. A slightly different version of the assessment is also available for free on the TCRWP website.

It is easier for children to read high-frequency words than to write them, but progress in both is important, and you will want to clarify with teachers what your district's expectations are for the number of words children are expected to write with automaticity by the end of kindergarten, first grade, and second grade. If teachers note that the Units of Study in Phonics highlight a slightly different list of words than does the TCRWP website, know that both sources draw on Frye's research and that sometimes the high-frequency words a teacher chooses to highlight one month or another are selected because the words illustrate a phonics principle the teacher is teaching at that time. It doesn't really matter whether a particular word is taught in May of kindergarten or October of first grade. The important thing is that kids are building a bank of words they can read and write with automaticity.

You'll want to check that teachers have systems to track which words individual students have mastered and which words they are still working on. You'll also want to look across classrooms for this so you are ready to offer extra support to teachers whose kids may need extra help in this area. The best way for youngsters to become more facile with these words is to read and write a lot, and for the words to be prominently displayed on word walls that are referred to often.

Other Phonics Assessments

If your teachers are using the Units of Study in Phonics, you'll want to make sure they are aware of a few additional assessment tools, which are detailed in Chapter 5 in *A Guide to the Phonics Units of Study, Grades K–1*. "Robot Talk" is an assessment to determine whether students can orally blend parts of compound words, syllables, and individual phonemes into words and then can segment words into those same word parts. This is a one-on-one assessment, and Chapter 5 suggests ways teachers could make this assessment especially manageable, including simple tips such as skipping segmenting for students who struggle with blending.

The phonics units also contain several developmental spelling assessments. During these assessments, students are asked to label drawings or fill in the blanks in sentences with a set of words that were carefully selected to assess whether students have mastered the phonics features, rules, and elements teachers are teaching. The same assessment can be administered multiple times, and scoring tools are available to help teachers compare growth from one administration to the next. We recommend you set aside time for your teachers to analyze the results of their assessments, so they can determine which concepts to reinforce whole class, in small groups, or one-on-one with students.

You might meet with a team of literacy leaders from each grade level and study page 85 in *A Guide to the Phonics Units of Study, Grades K–1* to get ideas for how to create an assessment schedule that incorporates each of these.

Running Records and Reading Performance Assessments

Running Records

This book has referred to running records often, and you presumably already know that they are a critical way for teachers to gain insight into how kids are comprehending and processing texts at different levels of text complexity. Teachers use these to determine a child's just-right reading level—the level

of text that child can read independently with fluency, accuracy, and comprehension. Running records are used as soon as students are ready for leveled books, often around December of kindergarten, and they continue to be used throughout the K–5 years and for some readers who are not yet reading levels U/V/W.

As an organization, we publish suggested independent reading-level benchmarks on our website. We've found that students who meet the benchmark levels that we publish tend to also meet grade-level expectations on state standardized tests. These levels are similar to those that other standards espouse, although there are small differences over expectations such as different ideas about the end of kindergarten and a few other points. I recommend that you gather a team of literacy leaders at your school to study these benchmarks and see whether they reflect your community's expectations. I also suggest you develop assessment windows within which you'll ask teachers to turn in semi-formal running record data. You'll find suggestions for those windows on our website, although teachers will want to assess their students, especially beginning readers and students reading below grade level, far more frequently.

We've made a set of running records available on our website. While we don't think it's essential that you use our running records—Fountas & Pinnell, DRA, and QRI all offer alternatives—we think you and your teachers will like the fact that our running records are shorter (and free!). They span levels A through Z and include multiple sets so that teachers can assess a child repeatedly on the same level, if needed. You will need to purchase sets of A–L books to accompany the running records, available for order, as it's difficult to assess beginning readers on printed-out texts. You'll also need to think through a system to duplicate the assessments and keep them organized and accessible for teachers. If you opt to use the Fountas & Pinnell assessments instead, that will also work well.

We suggest you ask teachers to fully fill out each running record, including recording students' miscues and transcribing their retells and answers to comprehension questions. Complete record keeping gives teachers essential data related to children's fluency, accuracy, cueing systems for word solving, ability to retell and accumulate text, and ability to answer literal and inferential questions. We also suggest you ask teachers to assess beyond a student's independent reading level, the level they can read with 96% accuracy, along with adequate fluency and comprehension. Encourage teachers to assess until they find a student's instructional level; they'll gain more insights for instruction that way. Chapter 3 in *Reading Pathways*, as well as Chapter 6 in *A Guide to Reading Workshop, Primary Grades*, and Chapter 4 in *A Guide to the Reading Workshop, Middle School Grades*, provide more guidance on running records, including essential tips for keeping administration windows brief and for helping teachers get through these assessments efficiently.

Reading Performance Assessments

In addition to running records, we provide reading performance assessments for students in grades 3–5. These assessments bookend the four book-length units. Each unit includes a preassessment designed to be given at the start of the unit and a post-assessment, at the conclusion of the unit. As a new unit begins, students are usually given a text written at approximately grade-level expectations for that time of the year. Teachers across a grade level decide whether they want students to read the text or to listen as the teacher reads it (most teachers elect the second option). Then kids are asked to answer four questions that have been designed to assess a series of skills that are important in the upcoming unit, such as comparing and contrasting, analyzing how parts of the text fit with the whole, and inferring about characters. The assessments are designed to take just one day, so teachers limit the amount students can write in their responses. Fairly often, teachers decide to streamline the assessment by choosing only two or three of the skills (and the questions). In those instances, teachers need to make sure they give the pre- and the post- version of those questions, so they can track growth. Teachers can decide to score the assessments themselves—or they can devote a class period to helping students self-assess their work and set goals using student-facing rubrics. At the end of the unit, a similar performance assessment using the same skills with new texts allows students and teachers to measure growth.

For grades 3–5, performance assessments for each major unit are available for download from the online resources accessed with a code found inside your unit sets. An example of one is available in the online resources for this book. Additional information about administering and assessing performance assessments and using the results to teach can be found in Chapters 7 and 8 of *Reading Pathways*. The Units of Study in Reading for Middle School each contain suggestions for ways middle school teachers can develop their own performance assessments based on the goals they prioritize.

Writing On-Demand Assessments and Writing about Reading Performance Assessments

Writing On-Demand Assessments

We suggest teachers ask students to take a single period and produce a sample of their best writing in each of the three main categories of writing: narrative, opinion, and information writing. These on-demand samples give teachers a baseline sense of what kids can do totally independently prior to instruction. Teachers then teach a unit of study, and those units culminate with students producing published writing that benefits from teachers' feedback and input. After the unit is completed and the published writing is celebrated, students again have a period within which they produce another on-demand text, and this text is compared to the pre-unit on-demand for evidence of growth. This assessment helps teachers remember that they are not aiming to produce great published pieces of writing for bulletin boards but are instead aiming to produce great writers. The teacher's feedback and input on the writer's rough-draft writing is only valuable if that feedback can transfer to another day and another text. The ultimate goal of any instruction is to lift the level of what a writer can do on his or her own.

You'll want teachers to give this assessment right as the new school year begins. To give the narrative on-demand assessment, for instance, teachers might gather students together on Day One of school and say, "I can't wait until the end of our first writing unit to have your writing up on the wall. I thought you might write your first piece *today*, so that we can get them up in the room and celebrate your writing. Plus, I'm really eager to understand what you can do as writers of narratives, of stories, so today, will you please write the best personal narrative, the best Small Moment story, that you can write? Make this be the story of one time in your life. You might focus on just a scene or two. You'll have only forty-five minutes to write this true story, so you'll need to plan, draft, revise, and edit in one sitting. Write in a way that allows you to show off all you know about narrative writing."

The data teachers collect will be worlds more useful if teachers keep the on-demand assessment prompt language consistent from classroom to classroom. You'll find suggested language in *Writing Pathways*. That way, you can look across classes on a grade and across grades in a school to determine whether students are making significant growth. You can also notice times where one class is growing leaps and bounds and another class is more stagnant—key trends to follow up on. The data will also be more useful if teachers resist the temptation to jump in and coach during the on-demand. Encourage them not to interfere as kids write. This is a time for teachers to determine what kids can do 100% independently. Instead, you might suggest that teachers carry a clipboard and jot notes about students' volume of writing, whether they revise or not, and whether they appeal for help. This data can then inform later teaching.

It helps, also, if teachers are administering on-demand assessments around the same time. Many schools schedule dates for these assessments on their calendars as they pace out their year. That way, you can facilitate teacher teams as they come together to calibrate their scoring and to reflect on any trends they're noticing.

Chapters 2 and 3 of *Writing Pathways* will be an essential resource as you help teachers think through how to best administer and assess on-demand assessments. I often recommend that schools administer all three on-demand assessments—narrative, opinion/argument, and information—at the beginning of the year, so they have baseline data about where students are as writers. It isn't necessary, however, for teachers to score all that writing! But students' growth will be especially dramatic if their work is contrasted with the on-demand they produced at the start of the year, and giving students' evidence of growth is a way to celebrate and accelerate that growth. If students have a start-of-the-year on-demand and contrast that with an end-of-the-unit on-demand, that allows all stakeholders—teachers, parents, and of course, the writer himself, to notice tremendous growth. An added benefit is that giving these assessments at the very start of the year won't make teachers feel vulnerable, since they reflect what students learned in prior years. Of course, you and your teachers might also decide to start the school year with a single on-demand assessment, likely the narrative on-demand, and then to give the opinion on-demand assessment about a week before launching the essay unit, and so on.

On-demand assessments come with a host of scoring tools, including rubrics and learning progressions. The Reading and Writing Project website offers answers to a list of teachers' frequently asked questions about on-demand assessments, including advice about scoring student work when it falls below a 1 on the rubric.

Writing about Reading Performance Assessments

Writing Pathways also includes a few sample performance assessments that are designed to give grades 4–8 teachers a snapshot of students' abilities to write in response to their reading. These assessments were informed by work with Stanford Center for Assessment, Learning and Equity, the National Center for Restructuring Education, Schools & Teaching, the NYC Department of Education, and the United Federation of Teachers. Our goal was to create lean assessments that would assess students' abilities to write an argument about a text, drawing on evidence from a few readings, and to gear that writing toward a specific audience and purpose. For instance, fifth-graders are asked to imagine that the mayor is deciding whether or not to continue to fund the zoo, and they are told that she wants to base her decision on whether or not zoos are good for endangered animals. Assessments are not available for every genre, so Chapter 9, "Designing Reading-Writing Performance Assessments" of *Writing Pathways* includes tips for how teachers can develop their own performance assessments, using these as models.

Spelling Inventories

You'll want to make sure that your teachers have a tool in place to get a sense of students' current spelling levels. We've found that Donald Bear's spelling inventories are one of the best ways to get a quick snapshot into a class's mastery of different spelling features. To administer the assessment, teachers read aloud a list of words, first in isolation and then in context, and students write the words. Teachers then collect and analyze students' results using a spelling inventory feature guide.

Bear's spelling inventories can be found in *Words Their Way*, which he coauthored with Marcia Invernizzi, Shane Templeton, and Francine Johnston (2016). The book includes a primary spelling inventory designed for use by kindergarten through third-grade teachers; an elementary spelling inventory that can be used as low as first grade, especially if schools want to compare growth across the grades; and an upper-level spelling inventory, designed for use in upper-elementary classrooms and beyond.

Advice on Using the TCRWP Assessments

When you ask teachers who are *very familiar* with reading and writing workshops what they like *best* about the TCRWP curriculum, they're apt to name our assessment systems, explaining that the tools give them new clarity when they teach and give their students new agency—allowing them to be more deliberate and goal-driven. On the other hand, when you ask teachers who are *new* to the Units of Study what they like *least* about the curriculum, they're apt to name the very same assessments—describing them as overwhelming and disheartening.

Don't expect teachers to do all the TCRWP assessments in their first year of implementation.

My point: I encourage you to channel teachers to give serious attention to TCRWP assessments when the time is right and not necessarily at the very start of a schoolwide effort to implement reading and writing workshops. This method of teaching asks a lot of teachers, and it is important to do what you can to ease the load a bit during those first early months. The good news is that if you postpone deep work with the TCRWP assessment

system to bring them front and center when your teachers are plateauing, your focus on the assessments can be part of a larger focus on making teaching more responsive and accountable to data, and that can ignite a whole new cycle of learning.

Of course, "lightening up" assessments doesn't mean ignoring them altogether, because there certainly are some assessments that are foundational to all of your teachers' work. Your K–5 teachers will all need to give running records to ascertain the level of text complexity that readers can handle. Teachers in the K–2 grades will need to give other assessments, such as assessing kindergarten students' concepts of print, K–1 students' letter-sound knowledge, and their command of high-frequency words. And you will probably want all your teachers to give on-demand writing assessments at the start of the year and at least at some intervals during the year. But all of those on-demand writing pieces needn't be scored, and teachers may not use the TCRWP performance assessments in reading at the start of their work with reading units of study. When you start this work, the main focus needs to be on teaching. Plan to broaden your frame of reference during a second or third year.

Assessments can become toxic if they are the sole source of high-stakes evaluation.

Once you do turn your attention to the TCRWP assessment systems described in *Reading Pathways* and *Writing Pathways*, I have some guidance for you. Above all, keep in mind that assessments will always be powerful—which can mean they can be powerfully good, and it also means they can be powerfully damaging. There are ways to keep assessment positive.

The TCRWP progressions, checklists, and rubrics are purposefully very ambitious, so that they can be used as tools for accelerating growth. Research and common sense both suggest that goals and checklists only support growth if they are ambitious. If a person can fill in a checklist, saying "did it, did it, did it," then that checklist won't promote growth. The exemplar writing and the model answers on the reading performance assessments represent ambitious levels of achievement.

Use these to promote learning. Know, however, that if a leader is operating at level 2 on these assessments, the appropriate goal is for the learner to work to perform at level 3, independently and often. The goal might be for the learner to make that progress this month, even this week. But the important thing is that the learner could be any age at all—no matter the age, that learner can't jump from level 2 straight to level 7!

The power of the assessments is that they can be a way for students to set clear and manageable goals. If a reader's or writer's work is currently at one level, hopefully that learner can work with zeal to bring the level of work up a notch. The goal should be growth.

The question will remain, however: What if students don't achieve benchmark levels? What if they are producing work that is significantly below benchmark levels?

First, know that the TCRWP assessments are calibrated to match the achievement levels espoused by the Common Core State Standards and international standards. These standards were purposefully set at very high levels to galvanize teachers and students to hold higher aspirations and to make progress. Of course, since the rollout of the Common Core State Standards, many states across the United States have waffled on those expectations—a bit. However, expectations even in the states that *have* outright rejected the CCSS seem to be calibrated with an eye to those levels. But let's be clear: those levels were always high, and certainly the performance levels in the TCRWP assessments are high.

There is no harm in rallying teachers and learners to aspire toward high goals, as long as the goals for any particular learner are adjusted to be manageable and rigorous, and as long as there is no expectation that people will achieve mastery of every single thing. Even in very successful schools, many students do not end the school year producing work that matches every one of the grade-level descriptors in our progressions. The ambitiousness of these expectations can raise performance, but if teachers or students are labeled as failures when they don't meet every end-of-grade descriptor, and if, as a consequence, students feel deflated, that's not ideal.

> *The TCRWP progressions, checklists, and rubrics are purposefully very ambitious, so that they can be used as tools for accelerating growth.*

The conclusion: I hope you encourage teachers to tap into the teaching and learning power of the ambitious TCRWP checklists and progressions, and I hope you and your teachers also guard against using those high standards punitively. Instead, if mastery is the goal, encourage teachers to narrow the scope to a few elements within the whole progression (i.e., aim for mastery just in elaboration and craft, not in all of informational writing). In this way, ambitious goals can be part of the culture, but it will still be clear that it isn't held against a person if every target isn't met.

I definitely advise against turning results from checklists, rubrics, or performance assessments into report card grades. I recommend instead that report card grades reflect the full array of what you and your teachers decide you value. For example, in writing, perhaps you and your teachers decide to assess students' work with the writing process by assigning a 1–4 grade for the scale and ambitiousness of revisions that a student does within each unit. You might decide also that teachers value whether the student has tried whatever the teacher has emphasized in that unit, using the anchor chart as a sort of checklist and giving each student a score of 1–4 based on the extent to which the student has tried whatever has been taught. Perhaps you and the teachers decide to assess progress by using the difference between the pre- and post- on-demands and between the initial draft and final publication. Perhaps students receive yet another score based on the sheer volume of writing they have done. No doubt some attention will be paid to the sheer quality of the students' published and on-demand writing. Those scores then get added up into a cumulative score. Our point is that a report card grade should reflect more than just the score from the rubric. Grades should reflect whatever you and your teachers value.

Assessing Schoolwide Literacy Work: Thin-Slicing

The purpose of using all these assessment tools, of course, is to glean invaluable data about how students are learning. You'll want to carve out time for teachers to come together in grade-level meetings and in cross-grade teams to analyze this data—and use it! They'll need to make plans for responsive instruction. At times, you may need to hold norming meetings, where you gather teachers together to agree on what grade-level work looks like.

One of the most productive and exciting ways for a school team to use assessment quickly and efficiently is by gathering a quick sampling of representative data—what we have come to call "thin-slicing."

One of the most productive and exciting ways for a school team to use assessment quickly and efficiently is what we have come to call *thin-slicing*. By thin-slicing, we mean gathering a quick sampling of representative data—nearly always student writing or writing about reading—then extrapolating from that small sample to plan and to recalibrate teaching overall. This thin-slicing protocol has been wildly successful in our schools in bringing teachers together to learn from student writing and immediately go back to their classrooms with a tweak to their teaching that visibly improves student work. Principals often lead hour-long workshops in which teachers thin-slice and then quickly integrate their learning into future plans.

Following are the steps for a meeting in which teachers thin-slice their student writing and extrapolate what they learn from it to revise their planned instruction. Thin-slicing in this context involves four steps: pre-sorting, re-sorting, choosing exemplars, and then formulating action plans. Teachers will need to bring to the meeting a set of their on-demand student writing—all of it from the same genre.

Step One: Pre-sort.

First, you'll want to invite your teachers to pre-sort. They'll need to swiftly sort their pile of student writing into three piles: the middle pile will be most of the writing, the pile to the right will be the writing that seems higher level, and the pile to the left will seem lower level. This won't involve reading the pieces carefully, just skimming them. This pre-sort may mostly be determined by the length of the writing, though other obvious factors like paragraphing might also be apparent. Encourage teachers to not spend much time on this sort; it's quick, they'll be returning to these pieces.

Step Two: Re-sort.

Next, you'll invite your teachers to re-sort. To do this, name a few aspects of writing that could merit pieces moving into the high pile, or moving out of the high pile into the middle pile. When thin-slicing narrative writing with fifth-grade teachers, for instance, we often suggest that the presence of deeper meaning (showing *why* a moment was significant) or narrative craft moves (dialogue, precise detail, or inner thinking) would put even a short piece in the high pile, while less display of craft or meaning might move a long piece into the middle pile. You and your teachers would need to name these qualities according to what's appropriate for each grade level.

I suggest you move among your teachers as they re-sort, listening as they talk about *why* they might move a piece. Encourage them to skim, to trust their quick sense. They're getting a feel for the strengths and needs of the class overall, and of subgroups of kids, rather than preparing for individual conferences. Thin-slicing doesn't lead to teaching (or grading) for particular children; it's a way of gleaning what's generally going on and what might help to do next. You channel teachers to do similar work, separating the middle-level and lower-level pieces.

Step Three: Choose representative pieces.

Once teachers have re-sorted students' writing into the three piles, you'll want to ask them to choose one piece from each pile as a piece that represents all of the writing at that level. They can then move that piece to the top of the pile, describing what makes it representative. Even if you stop the meeting there, the process will have been valuable for teachers, since they've gotten an overall view of where their writers are, including the ways some writers are writing well and the ways some writers are struggling.

Step Four: Discuss implications and action plans.

Compare your students' representative work to grade-level expectations. Once teachers across a grade level have identified pieces of writing that they see as representative of middle-level writers from their classrooms, it'll be helpful for all teachers at that grade level to share those representative pieces, settling on one or two that they agree represent the norm.

It will be helpful if teachers are given a few minutes to compare their prototypical exemplars with the exemplars in *Writing Pathways*. You might ask, "If I had to assign a level to this piece, which level of text in *Pathways* does it come closest to matching? That is, if this piece is prototypical of the strongest writers in fifth grade, are our fifth-graders at the start of the year writing at the fourth-grade level (as we'd hope), or is it more accurate to say that the strongest writers at the start of fifth grade are writing at the third-grade level?"

It would be good to remind teachers that going into the year, you're hoping kids are at the end of the year standards for the grade level below. And expect that often, they'll begin two grade levels below and teachers will be able to catch them up quickly.

Study the sizes of each pile of student work.

As teachers are sorting and re-sorting their piles, you and your assistant principal or coach will want to notice the sizes of the piles. If teachers do this work using their on-demands going into the first unit of study, remember that you'll actually see how writing went *last* year. Imagine, for instance, that you see that your third-grade teachers have a lot of pieces in the "high" pile and a lot in the "medium" pile. That might mean that your second-grade team did a terrific job at teaching narrative writing. Now imagine that your fourth-grade team has many kids in the "low" pile and not many in "high." That suggests you may want to investigate what's happening in third-grade writing.

Study changes in writing over time as an indication of the effects of teaching.

At the end of the unit, students will write another on-demand piece, and you can engage your teachers in quickly thin-slicing again. Or, you and they study just the on-demands of three kids who represented groups of writers, asking, "How did our main group—most of our writers—grow across the unit? How did our higher-level writers respond to our instruction? How did our lower-level writers respond?" Because these pieces were chosen by a thin-slicing protocol, just by studying these three kids' pre- and post- on-demands, you get a rapid impression of how groups of writers grew or didn't grow across the unit. Tap those teachers who were particularly honest during norming and ask them what they're noticing. They'll be the first to say, "I feel like our higher-level writers haven't changed that much." You'll respond, "That's a great observation. Now you can plan more targeted small-group work in the next unit."

Study to learn which teachers can mentor others and in which areas.

If you and your assistant principal or coach study writing, you may notice that a lot of the writers in the high pile were taught by the same teacher in the prior year. That means you may want to invite that teacher to mentor the rest of the grade in that genre of writing. Thomas Guskey (2001) and Doug Reeves (2011), in their many articles on grading reform, suggest that often what looks like differences in achievement are really differences in educational experience. When you notice if certain teachers influence kids' writing growth in radical ways, that can help you spread that influence to other classrooms. You may quietly notice, as well, if a lot of the kids in the lower piles seem to have had the same teacher last year—or if none of her kids ended up in the high pile. That observation could lead to a quiet conversation with her about supporting her instruction of that genre of writing.

At the end of the meeting, you might collect and copy teachers' benchmark pieces so you can study them in more depth.

The most important message is that to improve our teaching and our schools, *we will always need to* collect, analyze, and act on data—whether it is data collected through high-stakes tests, through TCRWP assessments, through thin-slicing, or through other ways. Engage your teachers in learning from data of all sorts. Demonstrate your fascination with a student reading log that shows the number of pages a student read today, yesterday, the day before, both at school and at home. Treat that one page of one log as if it is a gold mine of information, as indeed it is. Ask questions, hypothesize, suggest potential teaching moves that might help this reader or questions the teacher might ask. Be a role model of the always curious, always learning person that you know every teacher—and every child—can become.

A final reminder: conclusions from assessments must be constantly revised.

As we end our discussion, keep in mind that we should all be appropriately tentative in drawing conclusions based on assessments that represent one moment in a child's life. Given that the goal of literacy assessment is to help us develop an understanding of what a student can do as a reader and a writer, it is important to rely on multiple pieces of evidence and to be sure that all conclusions are "written in pencil." Let's say a student does an on-demand piece of writing that is assessed at one level, then her subsequent work reflects that she can, in fact, do far more. That throws into question whether the on-demand was actually a good window to what the student can do, and it is important to give that student another opportunity to show what she can do.

When assessing reading, it's especially important for a teacher to consider all he knows about and can learn about a student. If a reader answers a question about a text in a way that seems out of sync with other information the teacher has on the student, it is important for the teacher to gather more information. Perhaps the teacher might suspect that the reader can *say* much more than she can write about the text. That insight might then lead the teacher to interview the reader about her response to the text, and the information gleaned from that might well change the teacher's original conclusion. That is, the relative formality and objectivity of an official performance assessment doesn't mean that the one assessment activity conveys more truth than all that the teacher knows from other indicators. Yes, the performance assessment/running record can be a wake-up call that helps a teacher notice that a student hasn't grasped something, but no single check-in point should lead a teacher to forget all that he or she knows about the learner.

It is helpful if more than one person looks over the data from a class, as a second reviewer may see different patterns. For example, if you notice that in a particular teacher's classroom, every child moved up one level of text complexity during each formal assessment window, this will presumably lead you to wonder if the teacher only conducts running records during the assessment windows, and perhaps also doesn't continue assessing until the child reaches his or her limit. This may suggest that the teacher believes that if children progress one level during each interval, that is sufficient growth even for readers who are functioning well below grade level.

16 A Few Words about Test Prep for High-Stakes Tests

We have colleagues across the nation—leaders of literacy reform—who take stands against high-stakes, standardized tests. We agree that there are many faults in the system of standardized testing that is in place in our country today. We agree that when kids have different access to preschools, to small class sizes, and to books, and when they have different interests, first languages, and goals, acting as if they should all reach the same end point and then crystallizing that end point into a test is problematic for a thousand reasons! Then, too, we know that the push to make tests easy to score means that many valuable skills do not have any weight on the tests. We know it is a problem that a child's performance on one or two days of the year, on these narrow tests, can outweigh everything else the learner has done.

Meanwhile, we also know that such tests are a reality for students today. Students' scores have very real consequences for them, for their teachers, for their principals. In New York City, for example, the scores that children receive on these tests channel them into their secondary schools. So, at the same time that we work to make the texts more fair and to find means of assessment that give information about teaching and learning, we must also focus on our current realities. For many children, achievement on these tests can open doors of opportunity.

IN THIS CHAPTER, YOU'LL FIND . . .

▶ A call to determine exactly the kind of work high-stakes tests require of students and the ways that work can be taught and practiced within a units of study curriculum

▶ Principles and practices for effective test prep, including dos and don'ts for classroom teachers

Our Units of Study are being adopted, in part, because this instruction yields results on high-stakes tests. Our experience has shown that when students are taught to read thoughtfully, to pay attention to the language and detail in texts, to cumulate as they read, to engage in evidence-based discussions about their reading, and to write with fluency and voice, structure and clarity, detail and ideas—their scores go up. Time and again, we have seen evidence that, given time, good teaching leads to stronger scores.

For several reasons, then, we believe it is worthwhile to work toward the goal of helping students do well on tests. We do not support test prep if that means that day after day, instruction mimics the standardized test, with children being asked to read prescribed passages and to complete multiple-choice questions. We are vehement that a yearlong curriculum of test prep should not replace authentic reading and writing, discussion, critical analysis, and collaborative work. The highest-performing districts around the nation do not give kids a yearlong regimen of test-prep instruction. But yes, we do support certain forms of test preparation.

At TCRWP, a small team of data analysts study our data and then use the results from the preceding year's tests to help a team of ten of us address any gaps between our curriculum and the expectations of the high-stakes test. We address those first in a first-draft test-prep curriculum we share with partner schools. After working with schools as they pilot those curricular plans, we eventually incorporate portions of the test prep into new units of study. Because of this cycle, the units as they are published absolutely reflect our deep knowledge of the expectations embedded in high-stakes assessments. We have been heartened to hear, in state after state, that districts using the Units of Study with rigor and intensity achieve especially high scores on high-stakes assessments. That data is available on TCRWP's website.

In many states, my colleagues and I meet with leaders of districts that are working with Units of Study to think about the crosswalks between this curriculum and their high-stakes test.

As this book goes to press, for example, leaders in some of Georgia's districts are thinking about ways in which Milestone aligns to Units of Study; the character and interpretation work that is taught in the fiction reading units set their students up well for major portions of that test. However, Georgia's test also asks for compare-and-contrast work between books, and so kids in Georgia need a bit of extra work on those skills. Georgia's students draw on their studies of narrative writing from the writing Units of Study, but we're finding that they also need a short burst of instruction to adapt their skills to the specific challenge of that test (which involves borrowing from a story they've read when writing a story).

In Texas, districts are finding that the *Up the Ladder Opinion Writing* unit in combination with the *Boxes and Bullets* unit, and the narrative units, sets fourth-graders up well for the writing portion of their test. Leaders in that state have come to realize that the "revision" portion of their test actually tests reading more than writing.

In yet another example, states that rely on SBAC have found that the Units align well with that test and have found particular alignment in the fifth-grade argument reading unit, *Argument and Advocacy*. However, if the state uses the *writing* portion of SBAC, for example, sixth-grade teachers have found it helpful to also teach an argument writing unit. They are borrowing and adapting the fifth-grade unit, bringing it into sixth grade.

We acknowledge that the high-stakes tests in each state pose slightly different challenges and encourage district leaders to collaborate to create crosswalks between TCRWP Units of Study and your state's test.

Overall, we have several recommendations for preparing students for high-stakes tests.

Test prep and test-taking are not the same.

Remind teachers that test-*taking* differs from test *prep*. In too many instances, test prep consists only of test-*taking*. Kids take old tests and then turn them in for correction. That work might simply reinforce bad habits and even undermine a learner's self-esteem. We suggest on the other hand that if your students are comfortable with a workshop structure, test prep should resemble a workshop, with a brief minilesson followed by work time where children practice what has been taught, especially the important skills that will pay off on test day.

For example, students need to keep in mind what they know about a genre when reading a passage. If this is a narrative nonfiction passage (perhaps a biography), readers should pay attention to the main person's motivation, traits, and life lessons learned. Kids can practice noticing the kind of genre they are reading in a variety of test passages and then reading with pen in hand to mark places that may end up being important.

Kids also need to learn to be ready for questions that ask, "How does paragraph 16 connect with paragraph 2?" To answer such questions, kids need to practice all they learn in the units about rereading with a specific lens, such as reading for information in a nonfiction text.

Effective test prep, then, means more than just taking and correcting tests. It means that teachers figure out key skills that kids will need and then use everything they know about good instruction to teach those skills, this time within the context of old tests or test-like documents.

> *We suggest that if your students are comfortable with a workshop structure, test prep should resemble a workshop, with a brief minilesson followed by work time where children practice what has been taught, especially the important skills that will pay off on test day.*

Match the time you take teaching each skill area to the payoff it is likely to have for students' scores.

In many states, teachers become fixated on a few kinds of questions and devote enormous chunks of the year to helping kids develop the skills they need for those questions. For example, there are questions on the State of Texas Assessment of Academic Readiness (STAAR) test that pertain to punctuation. A little instruction in editing and grammar can go a long way for Texas students, but we caution against overdoing this. Some teachers devote fifteen minutes out of every writing workshop—a third of the time allotted for all of writing instruction to working with punctuation. Time spent on one thing is time lost on other things.

This is particularly relevant to test questions that relate to vocabulary and to grammar. Research is clear that kids who are avid readers and writers receive higher scores on those questions than kids who are not. Therefore, neglecting reading and writing to teach grammar and vocabulary is likely to be counterproductive.

When students are *given* the correct answer, they don't learn as much as if they work toward that answer.

People all learn more effectively from the work they do rather than from simply listening to someone else talk. This applies to test-taking skills as well as all other kinds of learning. Instead of asking kids to take one practice test after another, then correcting their answers, we encourage you to set up the class so that students answer practice test questions on their own, then compare answers with a partner and talk together to settle on what they believe is the best answer, then share that with another set of readers, then argue again, if necessary. Only *then* ask them to check their answers against the answer sheet and try to understand instances when they've gotten it wrong. The talking and the interpersonal nature of the work will keep learning and engagement high.

Start within a child's zone of proximal development, then raise the level.

When learning to do something new and hard, the work should still feel within reach. This means that if you are teaching youngsters to work with a new kind of question, that new work will be best done with an easy, accessible text. That way, the question doesn't contain both new, hard work and also a new, challenging text. During test prep, teachers might start by asking test-like questions of a text they have read aloud to children. Once kids have worked with the questions enough so they're familiar with the tone and expectations in them, then they can try answering that kind of question with a harder or less familiar text. In this way, teachers can move kids along, so they eventually practice skills with test passages from previous years.

Kids need explicit teaching about the genre of tests: excerpts, questions, line numbers, etc.

If students in your school have been involved in a reading/writing workshop curriculum, they'll need to learn about how it is different to read an excerpt than to read an entire text. In any instance when an excerpt has been used, it is especially important for kids to read the italicized print that orients them to the passage. Those few lines function almost as a book introduction. For example, if the passage comes from the middle of Gary Paulsen's *Hatchet*, and readers don't recognize the book, the orienting sentences at the start of the excerpt will be critically important so the reader knows this is the story of a boy whose parents have just announced their divorce and now, on top of that, his plane has crashed in the Alaskan wilderness. In full books, readers do not need to read every sentence with the same intensity as they do with test passages that are out-of-context excerpts.

Kids also need lessons in *how* to take a test: how to look at the test question, select a letter answer, and find that letter on the answer grid. They need to be able to read the directions, expecting that the directions will clue them in to the genre of the passage and help them know how to read it. They need to know how many passages are on the exam and how many pages, so they can pace themselves accordingly.

Especially in the tests of today, kids often find the hardest reading work is the challenge of understanding the bizarre questions. For example, they are apt to struggle with questions like, "Which sentence from the story best shows how the character's actions develop the story?" Kids need to become familiar with the sorts of questions that will appear on their test and ways to answer them.

By grade 5, teachers probably want to find out what the kids have already been taught to do when taking their state's high-stakes test, so this is not taught over and over, as if it's new every year.

Some people wonder why our units are so rigorous, and part of the answer is that in writing the units, we have held ourselves to teaching kids in ways that will give them a good shot at doing well at high-stakes tests, which are aligned to rising national and international standards. But kids also do well on high-stakes tests because, as described previously, we acquaint them with the particular genre of high-stakes tests and teach a short burst of test practice that helps them consolidate skills they've worked on all year, so they have those skills at their fingertips when the test requires them.

Engaging Parents as Partners

W orking with parents can be a source of great energy and support. Yes, some parents are helicopter parents, and some fix the spelling on their first-graders' writing in ways that make us squirm. Some channel their child to books that are far too challenging, and some are so very quick to find fault in your schools, in you and your teachers. Still, in their hearts, parents are doing their best to help their children. Their energy can be a powerful, supportive force, and it's important to partner with them for the sake of kids, teachers, the school, and the community as a whole. You can be a source of information, helping parents have the fortitude to turn off the television, to unplug the computer, to put the phone in another room. You can be a source of inspiration, rallying parents to fall head over heels in love with the best of children's books and to move heaven and earth to be sure their children share that love. You can be a source of clarity, helping parents decipher all the conflicting information they get from media and neighbors about hot-button topics such as spelling, phonics, standards, and standardized tests. You can be a source of companionship, too, by creating a space in your school where parents can forge supportive communities for themselves.

It's helpful to teach parents as much as possible about literacy instruction and it is also helpful to give them ways they can be of help. In other words, think about what you'd like parents to *know*, and what you'd like parents to *do*.

IN THIS CHAPTER, YOU'LL FIND . . .

► Ways to teach parents about literacy instruction in your school, with examples

► Ways to enlist parents' support in children's literacy development, with examples

Teach parents about literacy instruction in your school.

If you bring parents in on the values that inform reading and writing instruction in your school, you'll find that almost always, parents become your biggest fans. Help them know that yours is a school that embraces explicit, clear instruction in writing. Teach them that just as published authors rehearse, draft, revise, and edit their writing, so too, children in your school participate in the essentials of the writing process. Explain that it used to be that kids were assigned writing and their writing was corrected, but they were not taught the strategies that proficient writers use. Let parents know that now, your school has embraced state-of-the-art writing instruction. Tell them that in your school, the skills and strategies of proficient reading are also demonstrated and coached. Teachers think about how students' work with any one skill will be different in second grade, third grade, fourth grade. Read-aloud becomes a time to mentor kids in the higher-level comprehension skills that they'll soon bring to their own books.

Bring parents in on your professional development as well. If your teachers study children's spelling so as to figure out a progression for teaching spelling to upper-elementary students who have gaps in their knowledge, take photographs of teachers at work and send those out via social media, complete with a small article celebrating the good work that teachers are doing. When parents know that you are partnering with Teachers College, Columbia University, in order to turn their children into more powerful readers and writers, they are more likely to be supportive when teachers are out of the classroom for lab sites or institutes. When they know that your goal for the year is for primary teachers to become experts on phonics instruction, they'll understand why you are asking for funding for study groups and curriculum.

Invite parents to end-of-unit celebrations.

One of the most valuable ways to give parents a sense of what literacy work looks like in your school is to show them. When you invite parents to reading or writing celebrations at the ends of units, you highlight the work in your building that you most want them to see. When children write inside the Units of Study, their writing is strong, full of voice and skill. When they read inside the units, their thinking and responses are sharp and caring and interesting. Celebrations help you to show parents the value of committed practice in literacy. Reading and writing celebrations, then, are not only celebrations of the work and learning accomplished in each unit. They are also public relations events, and you'll want to plan them that way. Early in the year, you may want to ask teachers to share their end-of-unit celebration dates, so you can put them on the school calendar and join teachers in alerting parents to those dates. (This also keeps units from running long. No one wants to let down parents who have put an event date on their calendars!)

This planning for public celebrations signals that the learning we undertake, the projects we create, are worthy of special attention. It also shows that sharing our writing and our reading lives is exciting and valuable both inside *and* outside school. We've seen children in the Bronx put on their first communion dresses for their writing celebrations. We've seen families in Portland, Oregon, meet at Powell's Bookstore for their fourth-graders to share recommendations of their favorite authors and series. We've seen girls in Amman, Jordan, meet in a classroom in the early hours before school starts, close the classroom door, and share their writing with their women teachers and their mothers, tears and laughter filling the room. These celebrations, when families are integral, bring communities together around literacy.

Planning for public celebrations signals that the learning we undertake, the projects we create, are worthy of special attention.

As you and your teachers plan the ways you can publicly celebrate literacy, be sure to consider the community's schedules. Most parents may find it hard to attend celebrations at 11 a.m. on a workday, and if they can't attend, that will be a loss for the children and their parents, as well as for the community. In some places, having a celebration right after drop-off or in the early evening in the school library or a local bookstore could work. At the very least, plan celebrations for different times of the day and week and in different locations, so that parents can attend at least some events. Consider ways to share parts of the celebration with parents who can't attend, perhaps by posting or texting videos or photos of the kids' work, or printing photos of the celebration and sending them home. (Just be sure teachers get permission to share any photos of kids, of course.) Invite comments and feedback to make sure the celebration engages the community, before, during, or after the event.

Even beyond the event of a celebration, some schools have innovated ways to get their children's writing out into the community. My colleague, Cornelius Minor, thought, "Where do people spend a lot of time? Where would they enjoy reading stories, articles, and book reviews created by young people?" That led him to ask the bookstores, coffee shops, bodegas, and laundromats around the Seattle schools in which we work to see if they would welcome displays of student work. The community came to treasure their young people's literacy work. Soon students were asking if they could have more time to polish their reading and writing work, as they knew it would be shared across their community.

Hold workshops and presentations for parent education.

It's very likely your school, like most, holds grade-specific curriculum nights. During those evenings, you'll want to teach parents about the writing and reading curricula for that grade. To show parents how reading and writing go, rather than simply tell them, you might encourage teachers to ask parents to take the role of students, for a portion of the evening. Teachers might rally parents to get started on a piece of writing or a bit of reading, choosing a minilesson that they could teach parents or a read-aloud they could give. Teachers might show parents some of the tools that they might channel their kids to use to lift the level of the work.

You'll want to support your teachers in the art of speaking to parents. Lots of your teachers who are perfectly confident when speaking with youngsters become less confident when facing parents. You may want to gather teachers at your faculty meeting before curriculum night and help them rehearse what they will say to parents, how they will run their presentation, what activities they might plan. If teachers are given the opportunity to watch a colleague, coach, or administrator demonstrate what they might say about their curriculum, they'll often be able to pull off their evening with more grace and power.

In addition to curriculum nights, you might hold regular workshops for parents to teach them about burning topics. To plan for these, you might anticipate what parents will need to know at particular times of the school year. For example, in December, right before kindergartners begin reading just-right books, you might hold a workshop for kindergarten parents titled something

like, "What to Expect as Your Child Becomes a Reader: What We'll Do at School, and How You Can Support at Home." Or, you might think about topics that are always on parents' minds, such as their questions about spelling and grammar, their surety that their child should be reading harder books. Planning workshops to address these issues can dampen anxiety, open up communication, and build closer relationships between parents and teachers. Another way to think about these topics is to think about the ones that you know will help children achieve. How valuable it will be if you or your teachers can help parents support kids' reading lives. Perhaps you can help parents channel students to do more reading at home. Perhaps you can help parents become sounding boards, encouraging children to rehearse their writing aloud.

For all parent workshops, plan ahead to consider the needs of your parent body. Provide an interpreter if a large portion of parents speak a language other than English, or an ASL interpreter for parents who are hearing impaired. For parents who work in the evenings or are unable to arrange for childcare, you might offer workshops twice, once in the evening and once in the morning. Or you might consider making a video of the workshops to share with parents who cannot attend.

Help teachers plan for parent-teacher conferences.

Parent-teacher conferences are another opportunity for parent education. These conferences are especially useful for showcasing students' growth in reading and writing, with student work on hand. As with curriculum nights, you might want to use a faculty meeting or teacher prep time to work with teachers on how to present children's work in ways that communicate where a child is on a pathway toward skill development.

Encourage teachers to show parents how to look at growth in writing through different lenses, such as growth in structure and organization, use of craft elements, or spelling of high-frequency words. Show parents tools that students use such as the student-facing checklist that goes with the genre. Help teachers plan for ways to share the gist of writing unit, perhaps pointing out a few classroom charts the children are using, and discussing next steps for the writer. A teacher might say, "The next steps for writers at this level are to . . . so in this case, we'll teach your child to . . ."

You'll also want to help teachers brainstorm how they might teach parents about reading development and about the expectations for reading that relate to a particular reader. Many parents, particularly of older students, have no idea how sophisticated the expectations are for upper-grade reading. To them, reading simply means a child sitting still with her eyes on a book, and becoming a better reader means holding harder and harder books. Because reading is such an invisible process, it is difficult to know how much a reader is understanding unless one knows how to assess this. Help teachers think about a child's artifacts they might show to parents to communicate about that reading progress, such as a child's Post-its or reading notebook.

No matter the topic, engage parents as partners. To do this, you and your faculty need to be able to talk about the work clearly, positively, persuasively. We suggest you try out your talks on a colleague and encourage your teachers to do the same. In addition to giving teachers some rehearsal time, and feedback if possible, before curriculum night or parent-teacher conferences, you might ask teachers for feedback on your own presentations to parents as well.

Plan displays in the school building for parent education.

Where do parents spend time in your school? A drop-off and pick-up corner in the cafeteria? The hall to the main office or the lobby? Do they congregate outside classroom doors to wait for students to be dismissed? Consider the places in your building that could be sites for setting up displays meant for reaching families and teaching them about the literacy work going on in your school.

The simplest of these kinds of displays, of course, are bulletin boards that showcase student work. Help your teachers consider how they might educate parents about students' work alongside the work itself. Along with a sampling of students' personal essays, for example, a teacher might post a brief summary of the unit of study, a checklist of some of the main goals of the unit, or a simple note from the teacher pointing out some of the great qualities of the writing. The note might say something like, "In classroom 4-203, students worked hard to craft lean, clear thesis statements. They took care to organize their information into supporting points and to include a lot of examples."

You can also use wall space to address parent concerns. If parents are worried when teachers don't correct every grammatical mistake on rough drafts, for example create a display titled something like "See how our writers grow across the writing process . . ." and display a few kids' notebook entries, early drafts, and final pieces, with annotations by the kids on what they were working on. Use strings to connect parts of a mentor text to parts in the students' writing influenced by it. Or, use strings to connect standards checklists to student writing to illustrate kids' growth as writers. Be sure to show the editing stage, when students learn strategies for self-correcting and peer editing for grammatical mistakes. That way, parents can see how their concerns are addressed.

That display will serve its purpose to educate families (and reinforce for your teaching staff) that skills develop over time, and different areas of focus receive support, instruction, and correction in each cycle of learning.

You might also think about how to use wall space to teach parents about a particular aspect of literacy, and to offer ideas for how they might support this at home. These kinds of displays, then, have the dual purpose of teaching parents and recruiting their help. For example, if you want to support families in reading aloud to their children, choose a highly visible, accessible spot in the building and use it toward that end. Create a lending library of picture books, chapter books, and magazines for families to borrow. If some families are anxious about reading aloud in a second or third language, try what a school in Barcelona has done. They filmed students reading aloud picture books, in multiple languages, then taped a QR code on the back of each of these books, putting them in a lending bookcase near the front entrance. Parents or children can borrow a book, and, if they have the technology, pull up a video to get a read-aloud in the language of their choice.

If, on the other hand, you are planning to ask your parent association for funding for books, then consider ways to communicate the importance of books through a display. We saw a school hallway titled "Join the Movement: Turning Every Child into a Reader!" The length of it was plastered with photographs of kids reading, each photo paired to a list of books that child would love to be able to read next, if they had the books. On an iPad set out on a desk, parents could watch a partner book talk or club discussion. Articles about reading were also set out on tables for the taking, such as "The Impact of Independent Reading on Lifetime Achievement" and "Books Matter Most for Learning to Read Well." What better way than this display to make the case for more books?

The main thing is to remember that there are some places in your building that can be *your* sites for communicating vital information about your school's literacy work with families.

Consider using other formats of communication for parent education about literacy.

There are many other formats and forums to consider for parent education. Newsletters, either hard copy or digital, are a common way for schools to communicate with parents. Certainly, much of the real estate is often used for communicating schedules and logistics, times for PTA meetings and parent coffee mornings. There might be sections that highlight one teacher or one student or one subject area. But you and your teachers can also use this common communiqué to teach parents about the reading and writing work going on in your school in ways that not only showcase student work, but that also let parents in on your school's core values regarding literacy instruction. For example, rather than including a group of finished essays in your newsletter, you might spotlight process and revision by showing a few students' essay work all the way through the writing process, including any note-taking and brainstorming they did in their notebooks, and their earliest and final drafts.

Even if a newsletter is too much, consider what you or your teachers can send home to teach parents about how reading and writing goes in your school. Might you share a list of recommended read-aloud-at-home books? Might you share books that might inspire budding student writers? Recommended websites related to classwork? Podcasts with great stories? Share the wealth of knowledge you and your teachers have with parents.

Then again, perhaps you suggest to teachers that they establish quick and informal ways to update parents more frequently, including sending home miniature versions of the anchor chart that the teachers have been teaching that week. When parents see a chart—say, one titled "Readers Find the Main Idea in Nonfiction Texts"—and see all the tips for doing this work, this gives parents ways to talk with their children about the work they are doing in school and builds a bridge between home and school.

Many principals and teachers send quick little videos home in which they talk to parents about a topic they know will be on parents' minds. I've included a few examples of such videos in the online resources that accompany this book. These are included in a toolkit of resources that my colleagues and I have made for principals of the schools with which we partner, but your teachers can easily make similar videos.

Support family literacy growth.

Many of you are leading schools full of recent immigrants. Some of these are educated families working in tech industries. Other have fled violence and danger, seeking asylum and a safe place to raise their families. Others come seeking work. Some children and their family members may not have had the opportunity to learn English. You can make a difference in your students' growth, by supporting family growth in literacy.

You might, for instance, offer a lending library of simple picture books (including some of the beautiful books written in two languages), that parents can borrow to read to their children or which their children might read to their parents. You might videotape older students reading aloud, so that at home, families can watch these videos and participate in a read-aloud together. You might open your school to adult literacy nights, where primary teachers teach writing and reading lessons, or bring in your second-language specialists to run programs for adults. And of course, parents should be encouraged to support their children's literacy development in their home language. An invaluable way to do this is for parents to read aloud books to their children in their home languages.

You'll also want to find out more about your families' home literacies and cultures. In her watershed article "Toward a Theory of Culturally Relevant Pedagogy," Gloria Ladson Billings clearly shows how important it is to always work toward more culturally relevant pedagogy (1995). Teach your teachers to find out how to say good morning in all their students' home languages. Make sure they find out if their students read and write in those home languages, and encourage them to talk to parents about seeking books and reading in those languages. Literacy growth is literacy growth, in any language. And the more you and your teachers learn about your families—their histories and stories, their beliefs and values, their traditions and gifts, the more enriched the teaching and learning will be in your building.

Enlist parents' support in children's literacy development.

Parents are often not only eager for information about their child's education, but also eager to find out how they can help. It's a team effort to raise a lifelong learner, after all, and parents are an integral part of this team.

Invite parents to share information about their children.

First, parents will be infinitely more open to offering their support if they feel they have a relationship with their child's teachers and with the school as a whole. In many schools, principals help to establish this relationship by encouraging teachers to reach out to parents (especially parents of young children) early in the school year to ask them how their child's first day, week, or month of school is going. How I remember my youngest son's second day of school, getting a phone call from his teacher, Suzanne Robertson, saying, "Lucy, I just wanted to tell you how much I have enjoyed having Evan in my class." Suzanne went on to describe the tiniest of moments. As I recall her comments now, thirty years later, I remember her saying something like, "I watched him during reading time. There was a shaft of sunlight coming into the room, and he moved himself over, so he was sitting in the sunlight and Lucy, I swear he even patted the warm rug. He knows how to take care of himself."

I do not remember the rest of the conversation, but I do remember hanging up the phone and thinking, "She likes him, she likes him. She likes my son!" And of course, at that moment I decided she was a very discerning and insightful teacher indeed—I was ready to go to the ends of the earth to support the school from then on!

One of the simplest ways to recruit parents' help in their child's literacy development is to ask parents to tell their child's teachers about their son or daughter. Anyone who has ever been a parent, who has ever zipped up a son's or daughter's jacket and watched as that child heads off with lunchbox in hand, ready (or not) for the first day of school, knows how much it would mean for a teacher to write, "Will you teach me about your child, so that I can make your child feel at home in our classroom, and so that I can offer her the very best instruction?" When parents write back, their letters are full of information about their children, but they also convey an overwhelming sense of the infinite preciousness of each child that can give your teachers new energy and commitment right at the start of their year. For example, one parent's letter about her son began like this:

> As I begin to think and write about my one and only child, my first thought is to thank you for wanting to receive my insights on Joshua. I've just watched my son and his two cousins setting up a lemonade stand on a warm Saturday afternoon. I love the excitement, gleam, and joy he's experiencing as he sets out to do business and makes a sale. . . . I have to tell you that the joy and love I receive every morning when I see my son's face gives me the understanding of what life is about. . . .

As a principal, you want your teachers to learn these details. Once Joshua's teacher has received a letter like this one, it won't be hard for that teacher to teach Joshua to write. If you are a principal in a school where you worry that kids are living in conditions of chaos, or if you worry about reaching out through language and cultural differences to the families of your students, then it's all the more important that you encourage your teachers to ask families to tell them about their children, however they can.

If kids are living in conditions of chaos, or you worry about reaching out through language and cultural differences to your students' families, then it's all the more important to encourage your teachers to ask families to tell them about their children, however they can.

Further, many of the letters will help you and your teachers begin to understand each child's history as a reader and writer. Sarah loves to make detailed, map-like drawings with roads, tunnels, and bridges, and she uses Legos, blocks, and road sets to create similar empires. Scott's mother drilled him every day all summer long on initial consonants and sounds, and he doesn't like to read.

In journalism there is a rule of thumb that says, "The more you know, the more you can learn." If her teacher knows about the intricate worlds Sarah creates with Legos, then that teacher will be especially surprised when her writing shows hurry and impatience. Once teachers build up mental portraits of each child as a learner and a person, then it's almost impossible to avoid constantly learning and needing to learn more.

Know too, that when you encourage your teachers to ask parents to write to them, what you are really doing is opening a communication channel. You are coaching your teachers to find out more about their students, and you are creating an avenue for parents to communicate with the school. These letters are not surveys to get data—they are intended to begin a relationship, and they need to communicate care, respect, and curiosity.

As principal, you likely can't personally write and receive letters from each family, but you can support your teachers in doing so. This will deepen and strengthen your own relationships with teachers, parents, and the students themselves.

Recruit parents to support reading and writing at home.

How parents love hearing about ways in which they can make reading and writing an integral part of kids' lives! Teach parents how much it matters that they read aloud to kids at home. Share favorite read-aloud books, help parents know that these are times for snuggling and giggling and rich, intimate conversations. Help them to know the value of pausing in the midst of a read-aloud to ask, "Whoa! Why did he do that? I'm so surprised because I thought he'd . . ."

In some schools, teachers or literacy coaches put together more detailed information for parents to help support reading aloud at home. They send home descriptions of the big reading work kids are expected to do at particular levels, along with prompts parents could use to help kids get at that big work. For example, for kids reading levels K–M, the handout might explain that the big work for readers is to track a problem all the way through a longer story. When parents read aloud books such as those in the Magic Treehouse series, they might then pause to help kids think about the big problem in the book, and about the steps the characters are taking to solve it.

So, too, can you recruit parents' support with writing. You'll want to encourage parents to help children notice all the little things that happen in a day that make for great stories. Help them say to their child, "Are you going to write about that in writing workshop tomorrow?" At bedtime, a parent might say, "Wow, look at all the writing ideas you have just from today! Let's say them on our fingers so you can choose which you want to write about tomorrow."

You can tell parents to anticipate that their children will collect papers they find around the house to use as writing paper—and that this is worth encouraging. Urge parents to have writing tools—pencils, crayons, paper that kids can fold and staple to make booklets—in a special place at home. And let parents know that perhaps the best job they can have is to be their child's cheerleader.

"Oh, I love that story. Can we read it together?" Or, "You learned so much about flying a kite today, and you were smart to put it all down in writing. Let's tape it to the kite so next time we fly kites we can remember all you learned." Of course, teachers of upper-grade students will need to alter these examples to fit the kinds of writing that those students do.

Then, too, you might consider how parents can support their children's literacy development in ways that support academic success in content areas, not just in reading and writing. It turns out that kids who are doing very well in science or social studies are often watching the History Channel, going to science museums, and reading books on black holes and dinosaurs.

If you can help your parents understand that kids who, for example, already know a bit about the solar system or who have watched films about historical events do very well in content classes, you'll find that parents will become thoughtful partners on how to engage kids in loving science and social studies.

You may want to alert parents of young children to consider the nonfiction books they assume kids want to read. Those choices can become inadvertently gendered. Dinosaur books, often marketed to boys, and pony books, often marketed to girls, are not the same. The former are full of archeological explanations, taxonomies, and nuanced classifications. The latter often are not. When you look at current statistics on women in the sciences and technology in this country, you'll find that women are still not well represented in the hard science and engineering majors in college or careers. It's sobering. Alert your parents so they make a special effort to get their daughters to science, math, and technology museums, and to read books on insects, planets, and engineering feats.

Once you and the teachers say clearly to parents that every science class, every history class, every high-stakes exam is built on reading and writing skills, those parents will become partners in making both a priority. The main thing is that many parents, across the income spectrum, don't know or haven't thoughtfully considered how crucial reading and writing is for academic success.

Elicit parents' support in getting kids to read and write all year, including summer.

You'll want to support reading and writing at home year-round, not just during the school year. In their book *Summer Reading*, Allington and McGill-Franzen discuss the achievement gap that is created when some kids read in the summer and some kids don't (2013). Gladwell looks at this research as well, in a chapter in *Outliers*, "Marita's Problem: All My Friends Now Are from KIPP" (2011). To broadly summarize, kids who read a lot over the summer go up levels, maintain or improve their reading rate, and learn from books. Kids who don't read much over the summer may drop a reading level every five weeks. That means

it takes until about February of the following year for kids who haven't read over the summer to catch up to where they had been the previous June. Meanwhile, kids who have been reading all along forge ahead, so every year the gap widens.

One way you can help your families understand this research is with this metaphor: reading and writing are a lot like running. Imagine that the school trains a group of runners, asking them to run every day. In September, they can run about one mile and are exhausted after ten minutes. By June, the runners can run for miles and miles, for hours, without flagging. But if they don't run over the summer, they can't start in September where they left off in June. Their muscles will have softened, and they'd have to start all over again to build up their strength and stamina. So, too, with reading and writing.

There is a misconception that only families with low incomes or low-achieving children need to spend time on summer reading and reading outside of school. This is not true! Research shows us that to become strong readers, *all* kids need to spend lots of time reading. In *The Smartest Kids in the World*, Amanda Ripley looks at how American parents spend a greater proportion of their time, money, and emotional support on athletics than on academics (2014). Yet when you talk to parents about the implications of these choices, they don't say, "I'm planning on my child becoming a professional athlete, so academics don't matter to us." They simply haven't thought about making reading a priority. You can be the one who helps them think about this.

Sometimes recruiting parents' help in supporting children's reading and writing at home can lead to new initiatives that pay off in unexpected ways. At PS 6 in Manhattan, after the principal put together a parent workshop on the significance of summer reading, parents formed a committee to call their summer sleepaway camps to ask for thirty minutes of quiet reading before bed. The camp counselors were thrilled! In Gwinnett, Georgia, teachers and parents started bookmobiles and summer book-fair days where kids could talk to each other about their books, get new books, and trade in old ones all summer long. At Avenues: The World School in New York City, athletic coaches set kids up to read on the bus to and from away games. At East Side Community High School (6–12), principal Mark Federman held mandatory sessions for parents of incoming sixth-graders to explain the school's promise to turn every kid into a reader and writer and the family's role in supporting them. Parents welcomed the information!

Consider ways parents can contribute to the entire school community.

We think often of what parents can do to support their children, but sometimes we don't think enough of how parents can also support *us*. Parents can help with fundraising, organizing classroom libraries, running celebrations. They can clear lots, shift furniture, build shelves. They can co-plan parent workshops. They can truly be our colleagues in the challenging and amazing work of creating a community culture of literacy. Brainstorm a list of all the ways you'd *love* to have more voices and support from parents toward building a culture of lifelong literacy learning. Here is our list:

- Invite parents to read aloud a child's favorite book on that child's birthday, rather than sending cupcakes.

- Ask parents to write letters to the class describing their best reading moments from when they were the students' age, or moments of kindness they've experienced, or some of their favorite opening lines of books, or a favorite memory from school.

- Tell parents you are looking for certain kinds of books or books on a particular topic. Ask if they have recommendations and if they have copies to send to school.

- Ask parents to host discussions to help kids think about hot topics, such as current events (role of the Supreme Court) or popular television shows (*13 Reasons Why*) or online games (*Fortnite*).

- Invite parents to help with bookshelves and furniture for meeting areas.

- Invite parents to find and send in examples of grammar mistakes in the world (menus, signs, publications, etc.) for kids to correct or to enjoy their effect.

- Recruit parents to stock rooms with nonstandard materials, such as furniture or lighting, making classrooms more inviting for readers and writers.

- Ask parents to help find and prepare a venue for a celebration or display of published writing, such as bookstores, laundromats, restaurants, community centers, or other public spaces.

- Ask parents to send in names of their personal heroes, helping build diverse visions of leadership from all walks of life.

In your role as your parents' teacher, confidant, chief information officer, and enthusiastic supporter, remember that raising children is an enormously difficult job. Help parents know that you stand with them.

18 Build Your Own Support Group

This book won't be complete without at least some mention of the importance of you, cultivating your own learning. The best way to do this is for you and other principals in your district to come together as a learning community to support each other's leadership. I know, I know: you don't have time. I totally get that because like you, I wear twenty hats and am chronically overstretched. Yet the single most important decision I have made is that I devote every Thursday to studying with my colleagues. The decision that we will meet together as a learning community for a full day a week, twenty-five weeks a year, is the defining decision that has allowed each of us to provide shoulders for others to stand upon. You won't be able to devote a full day a week to learning with your colleagues, but I can't stress enough how important it is that you do make it a priority to take care of your own learning. None of us can give and give and give without in the end, being depleted. Renew your resources.

My colleagues and I have been honored to learn from some unbelievably brilliant and effective school leaders—and always, when we pause to figure out how that person became so very talented and wise and energetic, we find that he or she lives and learns within a network of colleagues. Take the school principals in New York City's famous District 2. What is their secret? It's that they have each other. They have each other and frankly, they have those of us at the Teachers College Reading and Writing Project.

IN THIS CHAPTER, YOU'LL FIND . . .

► A discussion on the importance of finding and building a professional community for yourself, with some advice for making that community stronger

► An invitation to join the TCRWP Professional Learning Community

You may be thinking, "I wish." You may be mourning the fact that you don't have like-minded school leaders working to your right and to your left. My suggestion is to realize that these learning communities often start with just two people. If that twosome is open and welcoming, the group snowballs. Others join. The group may not consist of leaders from within your district—in many parts of the country, district leaders from neighboring districts have formed support groups. In my hometown, our group contains coaches, directors of literacy, a school principal, an AP.

Try to plan on meeting at least once a month. Chances are, one of those meetings will get jettisoned by a snow day or a special event, or you'll need to be absent from one of them, and if the dates are farther than one month apart, it will be hard to build or maintain momentum.

First things first: Be real, be honest.

If you do set aside time to learn together, make a commitment to avoid the one-upmanship, the posturing, that can make any of these groups so tedious. It usually just takes one person to change that useless dynamic—someone who is willing to ask for help, to be vulnerable, to regale others with tales of recent troubles. That one person can break the ice and turn the group into what it needs to be—a positive, action-oriented support group. To be that one person, you might get started by saying things like:

■ I'm really struggling with how I can turn things around. Can I tell you a bit about what's going on and get your ideas for next steps? So far nothing I have done has worked at all!

■ I've made a list of things that are keeping me up at night, and I wonder if any of you have your own lists. What I'd really love is for us to get help from each other with these things. Can I tell you my biggest challenge?

When talking with each other, remember that details matter. They matter to a good story, but they also matter in a think tank. Interestingly enough, the more specific you are, the more universal you are. People can recognize themselves in the details!

Certainly, my colleagues and I invite you to consider the TCRWP part of your professional learning community as well. Whether staff developers visit your school, or you attend one of our institutes, or you tap into the resources on our website, or you join our Facebook group—we welcome you! We hope we can make your job less lonely, more heartening. We hope we can make your school's approach to reading and writing instruction richer.

And I, personally, thank you for spending time with me as you read this book. I know your time is precious. You carry the world on your shoulders. Thank you for your time and your trust. Happy trails.

REFERENCES

Allington, Richard. 2002. "You Can't Learn Much from Books You Can't Read." *Educational Leadership* 60 (3): 16–19.

Allington, Richard, and Anne McGill-Franzen. 2013. *Summer Reading*. New York: Teachers College Press.

Barth, Roland S. 1991. *Improving Schools from Within: Teachers, Parents, and Principals Can Make the Difference*. San Francisco: John Wiley & Sons.

———. 2004. *Learning by Heart*. San Francisco: John Wiley & Sons.

———. 2006. "Improving Relationships in the Schoolhouse." *Educational Leadership* (March 2006): 8–13.

———. 2007. Address given at Principals as Curricular Leaders Conference, 7 November, Teachers College: New York.

Bear, Donald R., Marcia Invernizzi, Shane Templeton, and Francine R. Johnston. 2015. *Words Their Way: Word Study for Phonics, Vocabulary, and Spelling Instruction*. New York: Pearson.

Bernhardt, E. B. 2011. *Understanding Advanced Second-Language Reading*. New York: Taylor & Francis.

Billings, Gloria Ladson. 1995. "Toward a Theory of Culturally Relevant Pedagogy." *American Educational Research Journal* 32 (3).

Brown, Brené. 2015. *Daring Greatly*. New York: Penguin Random House.

Bryk, Antony S., Louis M. Gomez, Alicia Grunow, and Paul G. LeMahieu. 2015. *Learning to Improve: How America's Schools Can Get Better at Getting Better*. Cambridge MA: Harvard Education Publishing Group.

Calkins, Lucy. 1983. *Lessons from a Child*. Portsmouth, NH: Heinemann.

———. 1994. *The Art of Teaching Writing*. Portsmouth, NH: Heinemann.

———. 2001. *The Art of Teaching Reading*. New York: Pearson.

———, et al. 2014. *Writing Pathways: Performance Assessments and Learning Progressions, Grades K–8*. Portsmouth, NH: Heinemann.

———, et al. 2016. Units of Study in Opinion/Argument, Information, and Narrative Writing, K–8. Portsmouth, NH: Heinemann.

———, et al. 2017. Units of Study for Teaching Reading, K–8. Portsmouth, NH: Heinemann.

Calkins, Lucy, Mary Ehrenworth, and Christopher Lehman. 2012. *Pathways to the Common Core: Accelerating Achievement*. Portsmouth, NH: Heinemann.

Clark, Roy Peter. 2006. *Writing Tools*. New York: Hachette.

Collins, James. 2001. *Good to Great: Why Some Companies Make the Leap . . . And Others Don't*. New York: HarperCollins.

———. 2011. "How to Manage Through Chaos." *Fortune*. October 17, 2011.

Collins, James, and Morten T. Hansen. 2011. *Great by Choice*. New York: HarperCollins.

Covey, Stephen. 2004. *The 7 Habits of Highly Effective People*. New York: Simon & Schuster.

Cummins, J. 1991. "Interdependence of First- and Second-Language Proficiency in Bilingual Children." In *Language Processing in Bilingual Children*, edited by E. Bialystok, 70–89. Cambridge: University Press.

Darling-Hammond, Linda, and Nikole Richardson. 2009. "Research Review/ Teacher Learning: What Matters?" *Educational Leadership* (February 2009): 46–53.

Duhigg, Charles. 2014. *The Power of Habit*. New York: Random House.

Elbow, Peter. 2005. "Bringing the Rhetoric of Assent and the Believing Game Together—and into the Classroom." *College English* 67 (4): 388–99.

———. 2008. "The Believing Game—Methodical Believing." (January). University of Massachusetts–Amherst.

Felps, Will, Terence Mitchell, and Eliza Byington. 2006. "How, When, and Why Bad Apples Spoil the Barrel: Negative Group Members and Dysfunctional Groups." *Research in Organizational Behavior* 27 (December 2006): 175–22. New York: Elsevier.

Fullan, Michael. 2007. Address given at Principals as Curricular Leaders Conference, 24 January, Teachers College: New York.

———. 2014. *The Principal: Three Keys to Maximizing Impact*. San Francisco: John Wiley & Sons.

———. 2016. *The New Meaning of Educational Change*. New York: Teachers College Press.

———. 2017. *Indelible Leadership*. Thousand Oaks, CA: Corwin Press.

Gay, Geneva. 2018. *Culturally Responsive Teaching*. New York: Teachers College Press.

Gladwell, Malcolm. 2007. *Blink*. New York: Hachette Book Group.

———. 2011. *Outliers*. New York: Hachette Book Group.

Glass, Ira. 2008. "Ruining It for the Rest of Us." *This American Life*. Minneapolis: Public Radio International.

Guskey, Thomas. 2001. "High Percentages Are Not the Same as High Standards." *Phi Delta Kappan* 82 (7): 534–36.

Hakuta, K., and M. Santos, eds. 2012. *Understanding Language: Commissioned Papers on Language and Literacy Issues in the Common Core State Standards and Next Generation Science Standards*. Palo Alto, CA: Stanford University.

Harste, Jerome, Carolyn Burke, and Kathy Short. 1996. *Creating Classrooms for Authors and Inquirers*. Portsmouth, NH: Heinemann.

Harste, Jerome, Virginia Woodward, and Carolyn Burke. 1985. *Language Stories and Literacy Lessons*. Portsmouth, NH: Heinemann.

Hattie, John. 2009. *Visible Learning*. New York: Routledge/Taylor & Francis Group.

Kirtman, Lyle. 2013. *Leadership and Teams: The Missing Piece of the Educational Reform Puzzle*. New York: Pearson.

Kotter, John P. 2007. "Leading Change." *Harvard Business Review* (January 2007).

Lortie, Dan. 2002. *Schoolteacher*. Chicago: University of Chicago Press.

Mandela, Nelson. 1995. *Long Walk to Freedom*. New York: Hachette.

Murray, Donald. 1982. *Learning by Teaching: Selected Articles on Writing and Teaching.* Portsmouth, NH: Heinemann.

———. 1989. *Expecting the Unexpected: Teaching Myself—and Others—to Read and Write*. Portsmouth, NH: Heinemann.

———. 2004. *A Writer Teaches Writing.* Boston: Heinle, Cengage Learning.

Nieto, Sonia, and Patty Bode. 2018. *Affirming Diversity*. Hoboken, NJ: Pearson.

Peters, Thomas J., and Robert H. Waterman Jr. 2015. *In Search of Excellence: Lessons from America's Best-Run Companies*. London: Profile Books.

Reeves, Douglas. 2006. *The Learning Leader: How to Focus School Improvement for Better Results*. Alexandria, VA: ASCD.

———. 2011. *Elements of Grading*. Bloomington, IN: Solution Tree.

———. 2015. *Inspiring Creativity and Innovation*. Bloomington, IN: Solution Tree.

Ripley, Amanda. 2014. *The Smartest Kids in the World*. New York: Simon & Schuster.

Rock, David. 2007. *Quiet Leadership: Six Steps to Transforming Performance at Work*. New York: HarperCollins.

Rolstad, Kellie, Kate Mahone, and Gene Glass. 2005. "The Big Picture: A Meta-Analysis of Program Effectiveness Research on English Language Learners." *Sage Journals* 19 (4): 572–94.

Sahlberg, Pasi. 2015. *Finnish Lessons*. New York: Teachers College, Columbia University.

Scott, Kim. 2018. *Radical Candor*. New York: Macmillan.

Sergiovanni, Tom. 2004. Address given at Principals as Curricular Leaders Conference, 20 October, Teachers College: New York.

Stone, Douglas, and Sheila Heen. 2014. *Thanks for the Feedback: The Science and Art of Receiving Feedback Well*. London: Penguin.

Stone, Douglas, Bruce Patton, and Sheila Heen. 2010. *Difficult Conversations: How to Discuss What Matters Most*. New York: Penguin Random House.

Ury, William. 1993. *Getting Past No*. New York: Bantam Books/Penguin Random House.

Wagner, Tony. 2015. *Creating Innovators*. New York: Simon & Schuster.

INDEX